To

Elaine:
x

A LIFE
NOT WORTH TAKING

JEREMIAH DOUGLAS
(Douglas Gauld)

MAY THE DOG NEVER BITE
your toe's, BUT BARK AT
your BEHIND.

TRAFFORD
• Canada • UK • Ireland • USA •

Note for Librarians: A cataloguing record for this book is available from Library and Archives Canada at www.collectionscanada.ca/amicus/index-e.html
ISBN 1-4120-9243-4

Printed in Victoria, BC, Canada. Printed on paper with minimum 30% recycled fibre. Trafford's print shop runs on "green energy" from solar, wind and other environmentally-friendly power sources.

TRAFFORD
PUBLISHING™
Offices in Canada, USA, Ireland and UK

Book sales for North America and international:
Trafford Publishing, 6E–2333 Government St.,
Victoria, BC V8T 4P4 CANADA
phone 250 383 6864 (toll-free 1 888 232 4444)
fax 250 383 6804; email to orders@trafford.com
Book sales in Europe:
Trafford Publishing (UK) Limited, 9 Park End Street, 2nd Floor
Oxford, UK OX1 1HH UNITED KINGDOM
phone +44 (0)1865 722 113 (local rate 0845 230 9601)
facsimile +44 (0)1865 722 868; info.uk@trafford.com
Order online at:
trafford.com/06-0997

10 9 8 7 6 5 4 3 2

ACKNOWLEDGMENTS

Well, it's hard to acknowledge people in my life, as it always leads to something, so what I will do instead is say something about the people who mean something to me in my life.

I will only use their first names as they will know.

Foremost my mother, Kay: Who for her own reasons that I will never question, kept interested in finishing this story and has stuck by my side since I've come home and told her I was dying. She has witnessed the transition in my life. I hope she is proud.

Mike: Again for his own reasons never once turned his back on me about anything I did or wrote. For that matter his input was sensational and for most who even attempted to work on this, other than my mother, well, let's just say, they, even in marriage, went their own way and have since lost touch.

Gina: Who showed me, or should I say "taught" me controlled passion.

Erin: Showed me what it's like to (to respect) want.

I also want to say this story is for my daughter Brittney-Lynn whom I have not seen since I got sick. This is to let her know her father is a good man and would one day like to see her, and even though I only mention her in this book I think of her everyday.

And lastly let me not forget my Grandmother who has seen and been through more than I can describe. She gave me a punch in the arm one day and said "Get it together". And I have. I love you Grams.

I work with three organizations in the fight against AID/HIV/HEP C. They are:

Kimamow Atoskanow Foundation (KAF)
Canadian Aboriginal Aids Network (C.A.A. N.)
Pauktuutit Innuit Women of Canada
I would like to thank the Kimammow Atoskanow Foundation for giv-

ing me the strength to go forward and become a public speaker for the HIV/AIDS fight and the opportunity to help those infected.

… Canadian Aboriginal Aids Network for developing my abilities in the fight against those dreaded diseases, and meeting thousands of people in the same field. Thanks CAAN!

… And last of all Pauktuutit Inuit Women of Canada. I have done extensive traveling and work in the AIDS fight with Pauktuutit. I have come full circle in the fight and could not have achieved this without their efforts. And for sending me on some of the best adventures of my life!

Thank you for purchasing this book. Part of the proceeds will start a youth/retreat camp for all needs. (Special needs a must.)

INDEX

A LIFE NOT WORTH TAKING

Damn. This is going to be the hardest thing that I have ever had to do. It won't be easy to discuss some of the events of my life, but I was always told: the demons in your closet will one day come back to haunt you. I find this to be true some thirty years later as my world is starting to crumble.

I never thought that I would lead the life I have, but I guess that no one ever really knows what they will do in life until a time comes along when one has to pick which side of the road to walk on. I walked on both sides, reveling in the dangers on one side and the safety on the other. I was never one to be denied, as in my eyes the world was my playground and I was going to take advantage of it.

This is a story of my life. It deals with some very touchy, even disturbing subjects. At an early age my wanderlust took me places that a child should never have had the chance to see, let alone exist in. Writing this book helped me realize one thing. I had to grow up alone, fast. The wisdom I found, the hard way, is a gift I have to share with you.

IT IS NOT WHAT YOU DO IN LIFE, IT IS HOW AND BY WHAT METHODS YOU DO IT...

The language and subjects will be offensive to some and even hard to understand for others. It will be hard to believe, but I plan on changing nothing except names. I do no want to hinder anyone's life...

THIS IS A TRUE STORY

CHAPTER ONE

DESTRUCTIVE FOUNDATIONS

Things started for me around the age of 7 or 8. We lived in the west end of Toronto, an area not known for it's wealth or fancy houses. As a kid you did what ever there was to do or you went and made something happen.

My family. Let me tell you about them.

There is my mother, her name is Elaine, then there is my brother George, then my sister, her name is Pat, then there is me, Jeremiah.

We were not a well off family. As a matter of fact, at certain times we were close to the poverty level. My father, whose name is Bill, had left the family when I was about 1 year old (for reasons unknown to me until twenty years later).

I remember going over to my dad's house. I would sit on his lap and he would pat me on the bum and we would hug and talk of Easter and silver dollars. If I behaved, my dad would reward me, sometimes with a dollar, other times with a treat from the chocolate factory where he worked. But I had to sit still. I loved my dad's smell. He wore this musky cologne, and I remember the stubble on his chin when he'd kiss my cheek. To this day I turn my head when I catch the scent. I never thought it was wrong that I should sit on his lap, so I did it every time that we went over to his place.

Our house was on Dupont Street, in a not-too-bad neighborhood. It was an old three-storey, with the landlord and his family living on the first and third floors, and us on the second. I remember the landlord's oldest daugh-

1

ter had a small room or suite on the top floor. She was slightly older than me, and her father positioned her with letting me play with her breasts, as long as I sat on his lap. For a short time, he could play with me. It was the summer of '67. I was a young kid who wanted too much too soon. School was easy, but I daydreamed of what I'd rather be doing, somewhere else.

At school, the boys always tried to impress the girls in one way or another. I knew this girl that lived down the street from us, and as little boys do, so do little girls. One thing led to another, and after we became good friends, we would play the kissing and touching game. My friend would keep time, making sure he got his fair share.

Everyone goes through a phase of sexual awakening, so did I! I came to the cold conclusion, if you let someone do something to you, you'd be in a position to ask for something in return.

There was a trade thing with the landlord, but it only lasted till my mother was offered a new place, close to work. Once we moved, I found myself wanting to visit the other landlord, because he smelled like my father, I did not want to lose that again. My father now lived far away from us. Mom and Dad had decided it was unsafe for me to make the trip alone. The disappointment was intense. Sometimes, my older brother George would walk over to dad's place, only to be heartbroken when it was time to leave.

Once my family and I were settled in our new place, things really started to go bad. I started to smoke, not the easiest thing for a kid. Too young to buy smokes, I had to steal them, from my mother or from any store where I could get away with it. I would get caught by my sister, and as an added bonus, I would have to smoke a big stinking cigar, getting violently ill in the process. This did not stop me.

Soon, problems at school started happening. I started playing hooky, wandering all over the city. Small thefts were becoming boring. I'd run away from home, returning whenever the hell I chose, and then the war would be on. My mother tried her best, but I was not the type of kid that was going to be the goody two shoes. To me, it was not important what anyone wanted. It was what I wanted that started to overrule my life.

I was surrounded by things that would remind me of my father. There was this barber across the street from our house. He would let the kids from the area hang around his shop. He would leave "Playboy" magazines out, and we would read them. Every once in awhile when I was there alone he would take me in the back room, leaving the door ajar so that he would be able to tell if anyone came in the shop. I would look at the mags and he would rub my pants - never going any further, I guess he was afraid of being caught. This did not last long but again I found someone that smelled like my dad. I was on a downward spiral, never thinking ahead, nor did I give any thought to what I was doing with my own life. I was only seven years old. Something must be said about the fact that I was always searching for a father figure, but never finding it. But men took advantage of it.

In the summer of '68, another warped father figure arrived. My family had moved once again and my new school, Davenport Public, offered Mr. Richards. Mr. Richards seemed like the type of teacher that every kid should have. The school had all the regular public school facilities. Mr. Richards was in charge of the gym, as well as the pool. When it was time to go swimming, Mr. Richards would look after the boys and some other teacher would look after the girls.

Mr. Richards told us we were forbidden to use the pool unless we were naked. My outlook towards Mr. Richards darkened. This bizarre power trip signaled a turning point for me. My friends and I would spend time playing hooky, and exploring the area where we lived. When the swimming thing started, I did not want to go to school any more. I would skip so much school that they would call my mother, leading to me getting the belt across my ass. I was now also becoming a very belligerent little boy.

I was stealing, running away, not going to school. I went from bad to really bad. My mother was getting very tired of dealing with the police. Social Services decided I was well suited for a big brother, through their service. I could not stand the thought that this guy was to be the replacement for the father I was lacking, and that this was supposed to have a positive effect on me. He allowed me to smoke, to say anything I wanted and basically do whatever I wanted. As soon as this guy realized there was not going to be this incredible bonding he was looking for, it was over. I was not going to trust another guy with any of my emotions, as I had already built a wall around me. I felt unable to talk to my mother about any of what had happened to me. We were at the point, where any conversation, would lead to the next world war.

FEBRUARY 12, 1970
Jeremiah was made a ward of the Ontario Government.

I've included some of what was said in court.

COMMENTS:
Mrs. Elaine Douglas, the subject's mother, states that Jeremiah was unmanageable at the age of nine and that he was placed in the care of The Ontario Government at that age. As far as can be ascertained, truancy from school and running away from home were the prime problems at that time.

In Toronto the city police department is split up into zones, or divisions. In one particular division, the police got to know me very well; we lived close to the station. This one cop took a liking to me. He asked my mother if he might spend some time with me. She thought this would be the best thing for me. We got along at first, but soon started to argue. This guy was trying to be my dad and acted like it whenever we did things together. I could not accept this. This cop would never replace my father no matter what kind of image he tried to portray. This relationship was doomed. I was often caught stealing and being truant. It seemed like nothing I did was acceptable to the people in my life. I was already at the point where I was not out in this world for other people. I was out for myself and my family. This would be the hardest problem I was to face.

COMMENTS:
Prepared on July 6, 1976
In response to your request for information with regard to the above noted ward, and in confirmation of our telephone discussion of July 5, 1976, the following summary is provided:
Jeremiah was admitted into the care of The Children's Aid Society in September of 1969. At that time his mother indicated that he had been a problem for about two years. He had been involved in running away, truancy and minor thefts.

The judge handling my case was not impressed with so many run-ins with the law at my early age. Judge Little (I'll always remember him as the judge that took my life away)...

I had just turned nine years old. I was told I was going to a place called The Children's Aid Society. I hated the idea of being away from my family. I had no say in the matter. I lost my grip on my feelings as I was taken from court straight to Three Eleven Jarvis Street. (This was also the court

4

house for kids.) I was taken to an area that housed fifteen boys and was immediately scrutinized, as I was a very small boy. Each boy had a cell; we ate together in the main dining room. It was worse than boot camp for a kid of my age. The stay at this place lasted only a couple days, and man was I glad to get out of there! The set up was for adults.

They sent me to the Children's Aid which was, of all places, in downtown Toronto! The Aid tried to do as much as they could for me, but there was no way I was staying. Every time I escaped, my mother would call the Aid, they would send the cops, and the cops would take me back. I hated the place, wishing to return home, only to be denied again and again. My family did not want me. The place felt like jail. The attention was endless and smothering, while my words fell on deaf ears.

There was just no fucking way I was going to conform to the Aid's idea of who I was and how I should act. For example, if you were caught smoking, all the privileges that were given you were taken away. They (The Aid) would give us kids an allowance if we behaved.

On the rare occasion that I got an allowance, I would spend it on smokes. To my surprise, my brother George was sent to the Aid as well. I guess my mother was having more trouble than she could handle. Together again, my brother and I quickly found all kinds of ways to get in trouble. Finally, after a month or three, The Aid could no longer deal with my behavior, and felt that I would benefit from a different setting. Now the **GOVERNMENT** was in total control of my life.

I was sent to this place called **CHILDREN'S VILLAGE, NOTRE DAME OF ST. AGATHA.** This was too much!!! It was close to Christmas and all that I wanted to do was be with my family.

Once there, I found that I was not well liked by the other kids, as I would not eat the food they made! I had never seen it before, or smelled anything like it either. Also, the staff at this place consisted of "house parent" types that never left. Kids had to call them **MOTHER and FATHER,** or lose privileges. This shit did not fly with me. I would not call someone else my mother or father, no matter what. I'm not a rotten little brat, just to curious.

I had other things on my mind besides school: getting home, chasing girls at school, smoking, and doing what I wanted to, rather than listening to the rules. I was getting into fights at school and this carried over into the village. This time I was told that, if my behavior did not improve, I was going back to the courts. My life was already a shamble. I'd been molested, in trouble with the law, and to court more than once. I wanted a normal life, with a father figure, mother, you know, the whole kit and caboodle, but this was not going to happen.

COMMENTS:
Mr. Douglas, age 51, was born in Scotland and worked as a truck driver in Toronto at the time Jeremiah was born. He left the family home in 1961 when Jeremiah was an infant. According to Mrs. Douglas, he was caught molesting and propositioning her two small sisters. She states that charges resulted, and the couple eventually divorced in 1971. There has been no contact between Mr. and Mrs. Douglas since approximately 1968 or 1969.

There was a great amount of hostility building in me. Not allowed to go home when I ran away, I would sleep where ever I could as long as it was close to my family. I would spy on my family sometimes, and if I was caught, I was sent back, as if my presence was too much for them. It hurt like hell. Alone I would sit and cry, as it felt like no one wanted me!!! It seemed like the only people with any interest in me were those who would pick me up hitchhiking, as a run away. The only gratification that I got from anyone was when I did something for them and then asked for something in return. I never once was told that anything I did was good.

When I was about five years old, I found a bottle of pills in the garbage and started to eat them. Then my brother wanted some as well, and before you knew it, my sister was right on us, saying that if she did not get some she would tell mom. She told anyway, and then all hell broke loose. Mom came running outside and found the bottle was now empty and read the label, only to find out that the pills were not smarties (as I thought), but sleeping pills. Man, getting your stomach pumped is no fun. I almost died.

As a little kid, I thought about suicide… in St. Agatha's. Thinking, if only I could find a bottle of **SMARTIES…**

Fighting (and not doing what I was told) was what landed me back in the court system. To my serious disadvantage, I was put before Judge Little again. The judge thought my best interests would be served in this place called **WHITE OAKS VILLAGE FOR BOYS,** after I failed to respond to the care of Three Eleven Jarvis Street. Three Eleven Jarvis Street was what I would call Kingston Penitentiary for kids. One guard there demanded to be called MR. SHULTZ. He reminded us kids of SHULTZ from Hogans Hero's, only that he went from a klutz to one mean son-of-a-bitch that had no time or concern for kids.

Being taken from my mother, first when Judge Little sent me to The Children's Aid, and then to St. Agatha was too much for me to understand. I couldn't even tell *what* I was feeling, let alone identify it. No longer was I in control of my life... nor was I in control of my emotions...

I was in control when I was by myself. I would explore the city that I lived in and would take advantage of the T. T. C. (**Toronto Transit Commission**). The subway was phenomenal for a kid. I could sneak on and go downtown and mess around. Mostly I would go to City Hall. There was a rink out front, and I would panhandle for smokes and money for food. Christmas had come and gone with only vague memories of the ones that I had with my family. It was now the first month of 1970 and things were not looking good.

COMMENTS:
Jeremiah was committed to White Oaks Village, a Training School for Younger boys, on February 12, 1970, when he was nine years old.

Several attempts were made to have Jeremiah returned to the care of his mother, but in each case the placement broke down.

I did not start hitch-hiking till I ran away from White Oaks Village and had more first hand knowledge of it. If I let someone (man or woman) do something to me, then I could ask for something/cash and get it. When I ran from these places, it did not necessarily mean that I would let just anyone that picked me up hitch-hiking play with me. This only happened once, but the reward was what I said. I was only nine years old.

My experience with sex, and the manipulative connotations that go with it was the **Conditioning** that would start me on the road to porno, prostitution, drugs, murder robbery... the list goes on.

CHAPTER TWO

WHITE OAKS VILLAGE FOR YOUNG BOYS

Well, I got transferred to this place, and it was quite the experience to go there from Three Eleven Jarvis. It was like going from the frying pan to the freezer. The first thing I did was carefully watch my surrounding, so I would have no trouble finding my way home. It was traumatic for me to leave Toronto once again, and I cried for sometime on the drive to White Oaks.

Going through Hamilton was an experience in itself. ALL of a sudden I was surrounded by this other city that offered something new, but I could not identify the feelings. I knew inside I was going to have to see this city for what it was. The further we got from Toronto the smaller the towns got. This was scary, as I thought it would only make it harder for me to escape.

As we drove into the gates of White Oaks, all I could do was think of how I was going to get out. I was not into meeting anyone, but that soon changed. The staff would take the new kids to what was called Stores. This is the place where they would give you clothes and shoes. I was to later find out that this place was once an old Army Barracks that was turned into a school for boys. The way that this place was situated was that the big building and hangers were on the other side of this village. I guess it was at one time the heart of the whole complex. The main buildings were to house the bigger kids. The younger kids had to stay in the village.

I was put in this house labeled number 16. Being put through the basic introduction was not anything new to me, as I been there on more than one occasion already. It took a little while for me to get acquainted with my new environment. I soon realized that I could get away with a lot more here than in Three Eleven Jarvis, St Agatha, or The Aid.

By now, my world was full of deceit and frustrations. I wanted nothing to do with this place, but then I started to make friends, and there were little perks if you were a good kid. I was not even ten years old, but not afraid of very much, the way my life was going. All that was on my mind was to make my way home, any way possible.

There where a few staff there that I remember. First and foremost was Ed. We became friends. Still, I was astounded when he asked if I would like to spend the weekend with his family. Here was a guy who looked after at least 10 kids at a time, then went home to look after his own. Permission was granted, and I went to Ed's family home for the weekend. The first night there, I pissed the bed. I could hear the argument that Ed had with his wife, as he tried to cover for me in some sort of way. (Shit, I thought I was only marking my territory, just kidding). Later that same day Ed took me out in the field with his gun and taught me how to shoot. I swear I could see one shot as the bullet just went over a gopher's head. I was going to spend only this one time with Ed and his family. I felt that his wife did not want me there. Ed was an all around decent type of person. I wished I could be his son; anybody's fucking SON for that matter.

I never saw my own dad when I was out. The only person I trusted was Ed, although I did not tell him what was going on in my life. I felt good around him, but was still not able to open up to him (or anyone for that matter).

There was another staff member there that I kind of took a liking to, his name was Lee. He was there for me when I needed him. I believe he was a supervisor of some sort or another. I was going to have a long relationship with Lee.

I was going to spend my tenth birthday locked away from my family. When they came to visit I chased the car as it drove away. I could see my sister's face in the rear window of the Volkswagen, and this tore me apart.

I was not even eleven years old, looking for a father figure in all the wrong places. No one can take the place of a father, especially if the only memories of him were filled with rejection, loneliness and pain.

One time our family walked all the way across town. We had no money at all and Dad was to give Mom some money and us kids some silver dollars. We were hungry, and Mom had to deal with 3 kids, a very long walk and the wait when we got there. We were told my father had moved, and we could not believe this. We cried and argued all the way home. My sister and brother where not to taken back by this, but they have their own stories. My mother was very upset and took it out in her own frustrating way.

Lee would chase me when I ran away. Sometimes he would find me, sometimes not. I developed a true rapport with Lee. He would offer the best he could. We remained in contact for fifteen years, as my troubles mounted.

This one time, I ran away from White Oaks. Lee was chasing me, and I climbed a tree, refusing come down. I was crying because I wanted my family, my whole family. It took three hours for Lee to talk me down.

I had already been exposed to abuse, and this always got me what I wanted. There was another staff member named Rob Cedar. Upon first impression one could see there was a feminine character to this man. He tried to hide it, but the kids still made fun of him.

Rob was the one who controlled the tuck (a canteen for kids). Rob worked in the house as well. He would retrieve me when I ran away from the Village. On one occasion Rob Cedar took me back to the Village, put me in a room and told me to strip. He said I was going to stay there, naked and humiliated, for however long it took for me to learn my lesson. Rob Cedar sexually harassed me many times while I lived at White Oaks. He used his authority to coerce children. Countless times, this scumbag would feel your bum; touch your cock (all the while justifying his behavior by doling out favors in return).

I never said anything to anyone. I was a frightened kid who believed this was the way to get what I wanted. One time I ran away and some guy picked me up and offered me money to masturbate him. I agreed, as I was starving, and I needed the money. We went to this guy's apartment (somewhere near Sheppard and Keele St. in Toronto), which happened to be close to my family's home.

He gave me a drink and then started to play with himself. He asked me to do it. I grabbed this guy's cock and he started to come all over the place. This degradation was the price of survival. Time and time again, with Rob Cedar or whoever, I was manipulated, coerced or abused, but was always given something in return. I was a sexual politician at the age of 10 years….

Rob would make me feel so uncomfortable. He would hug me and kiss the top of my head. When I was a bad boy, he would be there to restrain me. His behavior was contradictory and erratic. There were times when kids would have to go to the Village Hospital for a check up, or whatever. One time I was in the Hospital for something. The nurse said I was going to get a needle. This freaked me out, as I was very scared of needles. Rob Cedar and three or four other staff members had to hold me down, hurting me more than the needle. The pain lasted for days. I was getting conflicting messages from Rob, and I could not tell what to believe from anyone there.

I realized you could get what you wanted, if you let someone touch you. It never occurred to me that I was prostituting myself till years later. My relationship with Rob Cedar lasted for three years or so. There was few other staff that I trusted there. It seemed to me I was the only kid to sit on any of the staff members' lap, being felt up, or whatever.

Many years (and drugs) later, I also remembered sitting on the lap of this older staff member and smoking his pipe. Always, when I'd sit on his lap, he would hold me in such a fashion that he would have his hands close to my behind. Again I was letting someone do something, so that I could get what I wanted, and did not say anything to anyone as it was working for me. The only reason I remember this guy was that he had the biggest feet I ever saw in my life. I remember as he would always call me "son". I was told one day I was being transferred, as my behavior was not improving, and it was felt I would be better off in a more secure setting.

> **COMMENTS:**
> Mrs. Agnes Samler, a social worker in Ontario who is familiar with Jeremiah, states that Jeremiah has been in three training schools in that province. Jeremiah was initially placed in White Oakes as a youngster and then progressed to Glendale training school, a secure facility, from which he graduated.
>
> **COMMENTS:**
> Submitted by Roberta Roberts, M. S. W. ACSW
> **Chief Social Worker**
> **Oakville Reception & Assessment Center**
> **Oakville, Ontario**
> **Previously-Chief Social Worker**
> **White Oaks Village**

Hagersville, Ontario.

Jeremiah was committed to White Oaks Village, Hagersville, Ontario on February 12, 1970.

He was returned home in July 1971, but because of truancy in the spring of 1972 following a move and subsequent removal from the special education classroom, he returned to White Oaks in May 1972. Because of continued running, he was placed in Glendale School for three months.

I was told I was going to a place that housed young men, not kids. When I got there, I was earmarked for trouble by all the people that worked there. I suppose they received reports that I was a runner. I was told by some of the staff that I would never be able to run from this place. They did not have the foggiest idea of who they were threatening. I was determined to escape this place. Surrounded by teenagers, I was eleven years old, and an easy target for harassment.

This place was more like a prison than a facility for kids. There was a sixteen foot fence around the yard (that we were allowed to use) and the top four feet was made of a type of mesh you could not stick your fingers through. All the doors were alarmed, as were the cells. If you were lucky you got your own cell. It was obvious this place was not equipped to handle children, and the staff was incapable of controlling what went on there. Another boy from White Oaks arrived soon after I did. The intention was to provide me with a friend, and the staff assumed, for some reason, that schooling would be easier for two than one. It was absolutely ridiculous for us to be there. The format at Glendale was established for teenagers, not 11-year-old kids.

This new kid's name was Collin. We had been friends back at White Oaks, and played together while we were there. Collin and I would become good friends.

A councilor was specially chosen to work with us, because we were so young. They tried to keep us separated from the general population, but this did not work. I don't know what it was about me, but I was always the one in trouble with the other guys. Maybe it was because I wasn't going to take any shit from them. They were no better than me. I got into a fight with this one guy. The staff thought that it was funny that a little kid would take on a guy that was twice his size. Collin and I were put in the dorms with the other guys and some days, mostly on weekends, you got to do your chores, then what ever you wanted.

One day I was tired after playing in the gym. I went to my bed in the dorm to take a nap. Well, this was when my troubles really started at Glendale. I was sound asleep when the same guy that I'd fought with out in yard thought it would be a good idea to masturbate in my face. Suddenly I woke up, and he was just finishing what he started. I freaked out, and went after this guy with whatever I could get my hands on, all the while the rest of the guys were laughing at me as I tried to beat this big guy up.

The staff locked me up for fighting, and did nothing to this guy, as all the rest of them told the staff I was fighting because of what had happened out in yard that day. I thought, you mother fuckers can all go to hell. I was being punished for something I did not do and the guy who jerked off in my face was laughing at me. I felt that everyone at Glendale was laughing at me. I swore I would break out of there and show these fuckers what I could do-and they could not.

This whole bullshit situation infuriated me. Jerk-off boy got off scot-free, I got punished. I confided in Collin, as he was the only one that I could talk to. I had a plan. We had this rather good looking tutor. One day I got her to take Collin and I to the gym. I was going over the fence one way or another, and he was coming with me. We distracted the tutor by telling her we had to go to the washroom, and then made a break for it. We got to the last door, difficult to see, at the end of a twisting hallway. Once at the door, I wedged my comb into the alarm to stop it from going off, and made it to the fence. At the fence I used the wall and the fence as a wedge for myself and worked myself to the top and over. Collin did the same but it took him longer, as he was having foot problems. I thought that we were going to get caught for sure. Time seemed to go by in a rush. Once over the fence we bolted to the tobacco fields that surrounded the whole back side of Glendale. It was easy for us to hide. I knew where the road was, so we headed in that direction. We had to cross a golf course. As we were running, I saw the school van heading in our direction. I took cover, but Collin was not fast enough. He was caught, but I was AWOL (absent without leave). I was gone from there for at least three or four days. I wandered around Toronto, stealing what I needed for food. I slept in the subways, where the trains would run almost all night. The security force, such as it was, would make the rounds every two hours, but I never got caught.

I didn't last at Glendale. They tired of my behavior, and after only three months, it was established that I had completed whatever it was that Glendale was suppose to offer. I broke out three times. I stole the van (crashing it once). Not one other person, other that Collin, ever broke out.

To this day, I believe my experience at Glendale was of no benefit, what so ever. I was abused with impunity. The system was becoming easier for me to manipulate. Supposedly anyone sent to these places was to receive some sort of schooling and understanding. What a farcical concept.

I developed a friendship at Glendale that was to end in tragedy. His name was Mark and his family lived in Wawa, Ontario. We would chum around while I was in Glendale. After I was caught, he promised to stay in touch, to hook up after we were finished with these places. Soon after meeting Mark, I was transferred back to White Oaks.

> **COMMENTS:**
> **By Roberta Roberts;**
> **Jeremiah was returned to White Oaks and placed in a group**
> **home in November of 1972. This lasted about four weeks, before**
> **Jeremiah ran back to his home.**

Once back at White Oaks Village I fell into the old routines of trouble and punishment. I was told if I behaved, I would be sent to a group home close to my family. I would only have to stay there for a short time, until I had proven to the system that I could play ball. By now I had grown into a master manipulator of the system. I was far ahead of my age, with the ability to manipulate anyone I came in contact with.

They enrolled me in a school in St. James Town, a community within the big city. I had missed so much school. Much of my education was from the street, which taught me to get whatever I wanted by using my body and mind to my advantage. I received private tutorials at the group home, with mixed results. One day I found out my Uncle was critically ill in the hospital, so off I was again. A.W.O.L. I did not give a damn how I was to be punished. The person in the hospital bed did not look like my Uncle; rather, someone totally black and blue and yellow with a great big wire sticking out of his head, and the side of his face totally smashed. Though it was repulsive, I was compelled with sick fascination to look closer. Suddenly, he moved, and I almost lost it. He looked at me, telling me that it was wrong for me to be there, and that I had better go back to the group home before I got myself in trouble. I told him it was too late for that, I was on my own again and I was going home soon. We visited for awhile and then I left, wandered around Toronto for a day or so, and then went home.

My mother told the system she was planning to marry and move to British Columbia which enabled me to leave the group home.

My mother worked for her fiancé. His name was Ric German. At first he seemed like a good man. Later, I learned that he did not like kids.

While I bounced between White Oaks and all the other places, my mother had developed a relationship with Ric. One time he came over to our house, when there was no food. We had a pet rabbit and Ric killed it right in front of us, and made my mother cook it for dinner. He sat there and made us kids eat it. As you can imagine, I lost all respect for Ric. This was going to have lasting effects on my family.

One day, while I was out, I got in touch with Mark. He introduced me to pot. Soon I was smoking on a regular basis. Whenever I could, I would score from Mark and take it home. I liked Mark. We would talk about whatever was on our minds. I started to really trust him, and our growing friendship was a comfort zone. When I told him my family was moving, and that I would not see him again, we both cried. After all the shit I had been through, finally finding a friend and then losing him was too much. We made plans for a going away party.

I started drinking and doing other drugs. Whenever I went to Mark's house, we would get a six pack of beer and catch a buzz. One time Mark came over and told me he had scored some California Orange Acid. I'd heard of acid but never done it. Now would be the first time, so we included my sister and her girlfriend. We all got set for the party at Valerie's place. She was a knock out black haired beauty, and I was trying to start something with her. We never became intimate, just friends.

Everyone started to show up around seven, our parents were out doing one thing or another, and this left Val's place the best choice for the party. Things were going really good. There was cold beer and there was hard alcohol and we all had a glass of something.

Mark showed up around eight with more booze. He said that he wanted me to go to the wash room with him and I did. He showed me a tin foil ball, this was the Acid. He opened it. Inside were all these little round pieces, not balls, but thick flat yellow things. I took one and a half, then went out and got my brother. Soon there was a minor line up to the washroom. Mark was selling the acid for five bucks a hit, and he made some money that night. Later that same night everyone was having a good time, till someone

15

got rowdy and the cops were called. This created a frenzy, people started to run all over just to get to the stairs. Pat and George and I were ripped on acid, all the while hoping mom was not back yet, as she surely would have caught on that we were more than drunk. I went to my bedroom and tripped out on the ceiling, as it was that spray texture stuff, and it would look as if it was molding into itself, and moving around. I thought this was cool and did not think of anything other than the party and the acid. I do not recall what happened to Mark that night, but found out later he had the time of his life. We all laughed about it the next time we got together.

Moving was right around the corner. The family was doing the goodbye thing, but I was still "in the zone". This was not really going to happen-there was too much to give up in T.O. I went over to Mark's place one day, and we drank a few rum and cokes and talked. Then to my utter surprise, Mark made a move on me. I was a twelve years old, crying into my drink. Mark was consoling me. Suddenly he kissed me and tried to fondle me. I told him to stop, as this was not the way I wanted things to be between us. I thought we had a real friendship, not one where we did anything like this. Mark apologized, saying he was going to miss me more then anything and he wanted to be as close as possible before I left. I told Mark that no matter where I was, he would be with me, even in British Columbia. I did not want to have sex with the same sex, and when we talked this over it seemed to make our friendship stronger. But when I was picked up hitch-hiking, I would turn off my emotions and play the game.

Moving day was upon us, and there was no avoiding it. We were all packed up and the next stop was going to be Kamloops, B.C. Everyone was a mess at the train station. I was all fucked up. I could not believe this was really happening; I was crying out of fear and sadness and hate. I could not even think straight. Mark had promised he would come and see me off and time was running out. I was crying even harder, as I wanted desperately to see him before we left. He arrived in the nick of time. We embraced with the knowledge that we would not see each other for some time, and my feelings were running rampant. Just before I got on the train, Mark slipped me two packs of smokes and a little bottle (the type you get on planes) of rum. He told me to have a drink for him once we were well on our way.

I will never forget Mark. He was capable of achieving something great in his life. I was attracted to Mark, but I was too young to fully understand my feelings, whether I was getting them all fucked up. No one ever told

16

me about these kinds of feelings. I knew one thing. I was going to miss the big city and this was not going to sink in till it was too late.

For me, traveling across the country was an experience in itself. Our family had bunks and during the day we would concentrate on our family cat, in the baggage car all drugged up. I would go back there, wishing I was drugged up as well. I felt lost and out of control. I was very impressed by the Rocky Mountains, as I had only seen pictures of them. The sight of them helped ease my pain. I was a long haired kid with an attitude. I would go through the bar car on the train and get everyone's empty little bottle and go back to our section and put them on top of each other so that anything left in them would go into one bottle, and thereby I would have myself a drink as we traveled.

Once in Kamloops, we were met by Ric German, who told us we had about a two and a half to three hours drive till we got to our new home. It was beautiful!! It was situated just six miles from Vernon, B.C., and the little community that was closest to our house was called Lavington. Lavington had a corner store, and a school (where I was going). I never realized my past history would follow me here. I was determined to do well at school, however difficult it would be. I got to be known as the kid from the big city, the type of kid that was going places.

Starting school was hard but we adapted. Fuck did we adapt. Going from these big fucking schools, to one that probably only held one hundred kids, I was immediately aware that I was not going to get away with much. The teachers got to know you very well in such an intimate setting. Our house was big, on a five acre lot that had a barn and a few out buildings that we turned into dry storage and a chicken coop.

I was finally happy. I was given chores to do and the fact that we lived on a farm (sort of) was great. It seemed to me that even my mother was happy, and that we would finally start a real family life. In the back of my thoughts was this picture of Ric chopping at our pet rabbit and the way he acted when it was dinner time. You could say that I did not completely trust this man, and this ugly feeling was going to stay with me. We got cows and pigs and chickens and all this responsibility. I started to get frustrated, as I was having a hard time trying to explore the new digs, so I started to skip school just so that I could go to town and check it out. This behavior got me known at school as the kid who did not listen to the rules. I went after the best looking girl in school, and my behavior must have been the lure. This school was not ready for me.

17

There were these two guys I started to hang around with. We would drink this one guy's dad's gin, and go to town and trip around. One thing led to another and, before long, I was up to my old tricks, and this was unacceptable to Ric. I started to drink with my friends. I hooked up with the kid down the street and would score dope from him (pot at that stage). No one really knew of acid, or anything, really. The guys I hung around with were Frank and Dale. It was the spring of 1973, and we were the talk of the school by this time. But with little to do other than tripping into town and stealing the odd thing, we started to break into farmer's barns, taking their guns and whatever else we could sell, for more gin, money and smokes.

I was now starting to have problems with Ric. One day, after I told him to go fuck himself, he went berserk. Ric chased me into my room and said he was going to cut off all my hair. The fuck did it too, but it was how he did it that made me really hate him. He sat on my chest and took these hedge trimmers to my head with no regard for my safety. He cut me once that day, and made me go to school, wearing a hat and the brand new hair cut. Not good at all. I was going to get revenge one way or another. Ric had this collection of firearms, and one day, while I was still fuming, I went to school as usual, but returned home when no one was there. I loaded up this old duffle bag and took the 30-30 rifle that belonged to Ric. I thought that I would go to the top of the mountain, right behind our house, and wait for him to come home from work and shoot the fucking asshole.

All this hate was building inside me, and I did not know what to do about it. All that I wanted was to hurt him as much as he hurt me. One day while I was going through some stuff in the basement, I found a bunch of Christmas presents for some other family. I knew that Ric did not like us kids, and this was one of the reasons for me sitting on top of the mountain with a gun. I did not know what I was going to do, but the thought of killing Ric was going through my mind. I sat there all afternoon, crying, thinking of all I had done, and the problems that I was going through. I went down the mountain and put all the stuff back. Then I told my mother that I was going to start smoking, and that I did not care what Ric thought. I started to get home sick, and this was going to cause me great difficulty, as I was going to have run in's with the law out here. My spring in the new house was just that, a spring, as I was in front of the courts once again.

COMMENTS:
Prepared by Mr. W. G. Heinrichs

Probation Officer, Probation Services
Provincial Court of British Columbia
June 13, 1973
Vernon Family Division Court:
  Jeremiah appeared in court this date charged with being
unmanageable and beyond the control of his mother.

I wanted to be left alone, and most of all, I wanted to be back in Toronto and close to my real Dad. Ric did try, but deep down inside, he knew that he was not going to be able to work this out. I was running away again. One time I got a ride from a guy who worked on the Highways, as a maintenance worker. He gave me a ride from Armstrong to Revelstoke, B.C. We arrived late. He thought it would be best if I was to spend the night in his place. He would put me on the highway first thing in the morning.

Once at his place he offered me beer and tokes, then some speed, and said he would make sure nothing happened to me. I was stoned, and this guy really wanted to suck my cock. I told him I needed some money for my trip; he said he would give me some in the morning. I waited till he was asleep, then went through his pants pockets and took his wallet and his car keys. I was through with the little shit I was given, like Onion soup, or more candy like what I got from Rob back at White Oaks. I rolled the car down the driveway, started it and drove away. At first I thought I would hit the highway straight to Toronto but I was scared and uncertain I'd be able to pull it off. So I turned the car around and headed to Vancouver, B.C.

I picked up a hitch-hiker and drove him to Vancouver. On the way we stopped and got some pot, paying for it with the money I stole. I would still be able to make it to Toronto. I assume this guy was a drug dealer. I found a big stash of speed in the stolen car. I started to do some with my hitch-hiker. When we got to Vancouver, the hitch-hiker said he knew of a party, and we should attend. I was ready for anything now. I was not going to miss a party full of girls. I don't even remember the party to this day, as I did so much speed, beers and pot. I remember finding my way to the road, then heading east on the Trans Canada Highway.

I started to get scared of the highway, as I took a wrong turn at Kamloops. I found myself on the Yellowhead Route heading through the Columbia Ice Fields. I stuck close to a Greyhound Bus. It stopped, and the driver came back to my car and said I was scaring his passengers. I told him I was low on gas, so I was following close. Shit, I was just plain

19

scared. I picked up some hitch-hikers, letting them drive as I was tired and had been going for two days on speed. My sleep was interrupted by a cop standing by the back doors, yelling at me to get out of the car. I thought for sure I was going to jail, as I had driven from Revelstoke to Dryden, Ontario. I was put in jail there for two days, till the cops arranged for me to be flown back to Vernon, B.C. I was never charged for car theft. I assume the guy did not want it known he was into little kids sexually. It was another experience to remember.

The law kept notes on my moves. I pushed too hard, and ended back in court for being truant and unmanageable. I was placed in a school for alternative kids. I was going to be in the first program, with some of the valleys kids. For an alternative school, it was starting out right. The first day we had to meet in the back of the church. Once the formalities were over, the guy running the school made us all take seats, telling us this was not your average school, and that we would be doing quite a lot of things, but first and foremost, who can roll the best joint. I thought I'd lost my mind, and asked if he was serious. Then, to my utter amazement, he pulled this bag of pot out and asked if we had any papers. This was going to be good!!!

My family had moved out of Ric's house into a trailer court in town. I was not involved with the move. It happened when I was on the run somewhere. Mom seemed happy, as far as I could tell but then, I understood how close she held her feelings. My mother thought I was doing well, as she never once got a call from the school regarding my misbehavior. I WONDER WHY THAT WAS. The dope was good; we traveled all over the Okanagan basin. I would come home, just ruined, from a full day of smoking pot and doing everything from sailing to planting dope for this guy in the hills of Vernon. I was twelve years old.

CHAPTER THREE

SCHOOL ON THE RUN

School was going good except for one big problem: smoking pot around the church was getting more and more difficult. We were wards of the state, thus the responsibility of the Government. All us kids and two of the teachers, (if you could call them teachers), after a smoking session, came up with the name School on The Run. It seemed fitting; the kids were running from one thing or another and the teachers were probably doing the same. Our Government funding was spent on dope, gas and beers once in awhile. Some paid for the school's new location on Bernard Street, right in downtown Vernon, British Columbia.

The place was once a bank. Upstairs was a printing company (long haired hippies worked there) and by some fluke coincidence the other side of the second floor was going to be our school. In this new place, we had an old vault, and the teachers said we could smoke up there as long as the doors were closed. It was the cats ass, as far as us kids were concerned. Coming home from school one day, my mother asked me why I looked so tired and had bloodshot eyes and the lies started all over. I was becoming a lot less responsive to my mother. I found out one of the reasons my mom and Ric had split up was because he hit my mom and was apparently still recovering from trying to kill himself (back in Toronto before he moved west), over this other lady that only had one kid. There were three kids this time and the pressure must have gotten to him.

I was attending school (on a regular basis) and would even bring my school work home with me, and then smoke up the neighborhood and not do what I was told. This would lead to continuous arguments with my family. I was told I had no respect for the law or other people's property. Things went from good to bad real quick. My attitude was affecting my school. There was no school work to show mom when she asked, as there was no school at all, just a bunch of kids following this guy that was paid by the Government of B.C. to look after us. Shit, sometimes he was not there at all. To this day I still think he looked like Jerry Garcia of the Great-full Dead...

I got to know this one kid from "school". After some beers one day, he told me we could score any kind of dope from this other guy he knew. I went with him to this guy's place and found out why it was so easy for kids to score dope from this guy. He liked little boys the best. He would offer free dope if he could suck our cocks. This guy lived right behind Safeway in downtown Vernon, and worked at the Husky gas station. His name was Mike. One day, I was with my mother and she had to get gas. Mike served us, and it was hard to tell her how we met, so I lied. I let Mike suck my cock on the odd occasion, as it was hard to find money and my friend and I would go to Mike's house sometimes just to get fucked up on something.

My life was a real mess. I was not able to tell anyone of the things that I was doing or had gone through. I did not trust anyone. I was only thinking of what I could get away with, where I could go. I wanted desperately to return to Toronto for school. What school??? At this stage I was only going with the flow, and if I could not go with the flow I was told by the court I would have to go back to this place for kids. I really wanted to go back and get the fuck away from this school, these people and the law. Then I started to think of leaving my family. Fuck, I was only 13 going on twenty.

The following are excerpts from the court documents:

COMMENTS:
Prepared by Mr. W. G. Heinrichs
Probation Office, Kelowna, B.C.

SOCIAL HISTORY
ON
JEREMIAH DOUGLAS
    In examining Jeremiah's record in B.C. it is at once apparent that Jeremiah was never placed in a secure facility and it is clear that the dispositions made were largely ineffective. Ontario

authorities on the other hand provided four successive secure
treatment type facilities from which Jeremiah graduated
in succession, and yet the record demonstrates that these
programs had little or no effect in changing Jeremiah's long term
behavior...

April 20, 1974 - Vernon-theft auto
April 29, 1974 - Rogers Pass, theft auto and theft under $200.00
May 7-19 1974 - Placed under supervision of Garth McGuire,
    Child Worker Vernon, B.C.
May 20, 1974 - Placed at Camp Kopeji at Winfield, B.C.
May 24, 1974 - AWOL: apprehended in White River, Ontario

Ahh, the spring of '74. It was not looking so good for me. I had stolen
one too many cars, and this brought up the stolen car I was caught with in
Dryden, Ontario. I thought about turning the owner in for the sex act, but
there were too many things I had done and was in trouble for. I thought it
pointless to rat him out. In any case, I was soon sent to a new facility. All
the schooling I got from Jerry Garcia and troop was going to have some
effect on this place. And I thought I hadn't learned anything there! This
new place was called Camp Kopeji.

It was like a summer camp but had been turned into a sort of Juvenile
co-ed center for kids. It was not bad. We all had our own rooms, if there
was more than 7 to 10 kids you would share a room. Once there, I found
the staff to be okay. We all got our own space or as much as we were allowed. One time the camp organized this outdoor adventure. I got picked,
much to my amazement. This trip was going to be on the west side of
Okanagan Lake, since the camp was located just west of Winfield, B.C.

It was going to be great. We were going on horse back. Back when we
lived with Ric, I had a job cleaning barns and helping to tend the orchards.
In return, I was told I would receive a pony for the summers work. It never
panned out, but my interest in horses remained. This new trip seemed like
a second chance. It was beautiful up on top of the mountains, riding a horse
and tripping to the sounds of nature, and I was finally happy. I noticed this
girl watching me once in awhile, so I went over to her and started a conversation. Her name was Debbie. Well, we talked for sometime, then we
rode together, and man, was I on top of the world!!! Here was a beautiful
girl, who seemed genuinely interested in me. The country was breathtak-

23

ing; I had never had the pleasure of sleeping with a girl, and was looking forward to it that night.

After all the camp fire stuff, I went over to the horses and grabbed my bed roll. I went and made this area to sleep in, and then some of the other kids did the same and this girl Debbie got her sleeping roll close to mine and we talked of everything under the stars, literally. Then we kidded and started to fondle each other. Then she asked me to climb into her bed roll. Just as I was getting in, I got busted by the staff, and the woody I had was going to never be satisfied by this beautiful girl.

Back at the main camp, I got the lecture of my life. This left me angry and wanting to get the fuck out of there, so I'd never have to ask permission to have sex or smoke or drink. It was building. I was smoking dope with this guy I met there when he told me he knew where the staff payroll was kept. That was all that I needed to hear. I broke into the room, took the money and headed for town.

Once in town, I got some beers and a bag of pot and went to Polson Park and started to drink, and before long some of the old gang showed up and things started to get good. We were right in the middle of scoring some more dope when the cops showed up. I got busted and sent back to camp. They got most of the money, but because I was never searched the crew back at the main camp could enjoy my dope. I was charged, but they kept me at the camp anyway, so nothing really happened to me.

One night, as I was going to smoke a joint, I was called over to Debbie's cottage. Around back, there was my brother George. I was in a state of shock. He never came to places I was in, other than White Oaks, and there he stood. I asked him what he was doing. He told me he came to get me, as he was heading back to Toronto. That was all I needed to hear. I went back to my cottage and grabbed some stuff. I went over to Debbie's cottage, and by this time George was talking to her. I said if she wanted to come, she could. George had his buddy waiting down the road and we all took off. It turned out to be quite the trip, the three of us going across the country. George's buddy drove us to the main highway, dropped us off, and the games began.

George started to make advances towards Debbie. I told him to back off, but she was the one that was persistent. By the time that we got to Winnipeg, it was suggested we split up and meet at dad's place in Toronto. I was not at all happy when Debbie wanted to go with George, but there was nothing I could do about it. So I went on, ahead of them I thought, but they got ahead of me. I was riding with this guy headed to Thunder Bay. Suddenly, near Dryden, we passed George and Debbie. I told the guy, he stopped, and they got to ride in the back of the pickup. I was wondering why the guy was always looking at the rear view mirror. I turned around and there was Debbie, fucking George while he lay on his back. We were doing eighty miles per hour and I thought, "You fuck's." I left them in Thunder Bay and told them we would meet at dads. I was on my own again and this time my heart was broken.

As I walked up my dad's walkway, he appeared in the doorway. "What the fuck are you doing here?" I told him that I came to be with him after all the shit I had been through. My dad told me I had just missed George and his little girlfriend. I was about three days longer than them getting to T.O. He would not put up with them so he told them to go elsewhere. Then he looked me in the eye, told me "I do not have time for you, my cab will be here any moment, I'm leaving." I could not go with him and he did not want me. I was absolutely crushed. He went into the house and got his bags. After saying those words I will never forget, he walked by me and did not look at me. Then the cab showed up, I was crying and screaming at him to take me with him, I had traveled all the way across Canada just to be with him! He said that he did not have time for me.

Crushed!!! Fuck, I was devastated. I was only 13, soon to be 14, and had traveled all the way across the country to be with MY DAD. He got in the cab, without even so much as a "good - bye son", or even a last look. I was completely lost in this world. I did not know what to do or where to go. I sat there and watched my whole world drive away and not look back. I cried and screamed till I could not anymore, and then came the task of deciding what to do or where to go. My father had crushed the dreams I had held for so long, worked my life around, for a moment that lasted ten fucking minutes.

I thought I would go back to my mother, and then find dad, as I remembered him saying he was headed to Jasper, AB. Well, I hit the highway. I was never afraid of hitch-hiking, having had no bad experiences since I first did it back in 69. I was going home, the whole time pondering how I could improve myself, work out the problems, go to school and be good. Around Sault Ste. Marie, Ontario I got picked up by this couple. They suggested I spend the night, eat dinner with them and start out at first light. I accepted the offer. That night, while they lay sleeping, I stole their car and hit the road north. I went to Wawa, knowing Mark's family lived there. I had not seen him since the train station when my family was going west.

I was fucking up big, and not caring, as nothing seemed like it was worth doing. My reunion with Mark was priceless. We got some beers and went driving this stolen car through the bush, scratching and denting it like hell. I guess our reunion only lasted a six pack and a bus ride. As soon as we got back to town, Mark drove like a mad man straight to the cop shop. He ran in and told them I was a runaway in a stolen car. I sat in the seat for a minute, laughing and thought, "you fuck", as the cops put the cuffs on me. What could I do? It was over before it started. I never blamed Mark for what he did. I was placed with this family till the courts decided my future. He sent word that he was doing this for the best, that he loved me and wanted me to get on with my life and not do this shit anymore. He wanted me to be with my family and that hit home. Later I found out that Mark committed suicide in downtown Toronto, having suffered from sever depression over me and his new life at home. I was placed in Cecil Facer School. Going back to my family was out of the question, I was now back in Government hands.

COMMENTS:
Prepared by Mrs. Roberta Roberts:
Chief Social Worker
Oakville Reception & Assessment Center, Oakville, Ontario.
Apart from an inquiry from the Department Of Human Resources, Victoria, B.C. (File # 11896) in May of 1973, little is known of his behavior until June of 1974, when he was committed to Cecil Facer School in Sudbury, Ontario following car theft. He was frequently absent without leave. His overall behavior was not considered satisfactory, although he was able to maintain acceptable behavior for brief periods. From August to November, 1975, Jeremiah was at the outward bound program at D.A.R.E. Camp, Wendigo Lake, and here Jeremiah responded well with excellent behavior. He graduated to his mother's home in Calgary, AB with supervision to be provided by the Probation Services.

On December 24, 1975 it was learned that Jeremiah was charged with break and enter and auto theft in British Columbia and was held in custody until his return to the Oakville Reception and Assessment Center, Ontario on January 1 1976 as Mrs. Douglas refused to have him return to her home. On January 9,

1976 he was transferred to a Ministry of Correctional Services group home in Sudbury, Ontario, but he ran away on February 27, 1976 and was apprehended on April 5, 1976. He was again held at the Oakville Reception and Assessment Center until April 14, 1976, when he was recommended to transfer back to the group home. While traveling back to Sudbury, Jeremiah ran away and there was no further contact until June 1976, in reference to the present charge.

FAMILY SITUATION:
Reports indicate this has been a very unhappy family situation. Jeremiah's parents were married on July 15, 1955 when his mother was almost 18 years of age and his father was 29 years of age. They separated in August of 1961, reconciled in August 1962 until September 1962.

FATHER:
Mr. Douglas was born September 2, 1925 in Scotland. He came to Canada in 1950 and worked as a truck driver and a warehouse man. He had five or six brothers and one sister. None are living in Canada. He was reported to have had an alcoholic problem and was irregularly employed and that he physically abused his wife.

MOTHER:
Presently living in Calgary was born on September 23, 1937. She is the second oldest of a family of seven. She is of the Mohawk Indian Reservation in Oka, Que.

SIBLINGS:
Brother George born April 26, 1957 has had some trouble with the law and was placed in a residential treatment center and training school. Sister Pat born July 24, 1958 has never been involved with the law and was never a problem to her mother.

DEVELOPMENT:
Jeremiah was seen as a healthy boy with normal developmental milestones. He was a very active child and the usual childhood diseases. At 8 months he contracted Tuberculosis, (no wonder I was afraid of needles) and he was treated on an out-patient basis and there was no recurrence. His mother had Tuberculosis for six years.

27

After awhile at the group home I ran. Once I got to the Ontario/Manitoba border, I knew I was going to make it to B.C. I thought of going to my family's place, then I thought of all the other times I went there and they turned me in. I was not going to take the chance this time. I spied on my family for the first day or so, then got hooked up with this group of people that lived out near Mabel Lake (about twenty miles from Vernon and my family). These people all lived in houses they had built themselves. The funny thing about that was the houses were all round, and in town they were called Round House People.

These were the people that started the Habitat festivals. They lived off the land. I didn't see what I was getting into, and before long I was living with them. I got to know the leader (so to speak), John. One day he asked me if I wanted to go with him to Vancouver to deliver a bunch of bee hives that the Round House people built for money and drugs. I agreed to go with him for a ride. This was going to be one hell of a bad experience for me, and there was nothing I could do about it. John had total control of all that was happening to me, as I had become dependent on these people for everything. I didn't know if this new family that accepted me and let me do anything I wanted was a cult or not; in those days who could tell. The drive to the coast was good. John bought me all the stuff that he thought a kid my age should have. New jeans, runners and a shirt. Then we went to the place to drop off the bee hives Once we got there, these people accepted me as if I had always' been one of their own. It felt good. I was able to voice my opinion about certain things, and that made me feel wanted and accepted.

John and I were going to spend the night with my new friends. Little did I know this was going to change my life. That night, we sat around English Bay (in Vancouver) and drank an awful lot of booze. Suddenly, this guy came to me and asked if I wanted to do some drugs. We smoked some weed and before long, I was so stoned I could not think straight. I told them I was going to go upstairs to lie down for a while. When I came to, John was in the same bed and had been playing with me while I was passed out. I was too stoned to fight him. He was too strong. He flipped me over on my stomach, pulled off my shorts, and stuck his cock in me. I started to scream. He put his hand over my mouth and told me to be quiet or else he would beat me and leave me here all fucked up. I was only 13 years old. After it was over, he told me to go to the washroom and clean myself up. There was blood all over my legs. I was so scared, and didn't know what to do. John pushed me out of the bed.

The next day, John spoke very harshly to me. I was under his influence, unable to break free. I had some good friends back at the Round Houses, in particular one girl who lived alone and played the flute. I did not want to lose them, and if John abandoned me, I would not be allowed back in the same circle. I ended up going back and living with John. He kept trying to have sex with me. He would entice me with these other girls that lived there, always swimming in the little stream that ran through the property, asking me to go swimming with them. I wanted to escape this nightmare. I had finally found somewhere I could feel good about myself, only to be raped and abused. John left for Kamloops, so I decided to escape. I ran all the way to Lumby, then headed south hitch-hiking, never telling anyone of what had happened.

After watching my family for another day, I decided to go to the United States. It seemed that all anyone wanted from me was sex. I was starting to understand the bartering power of sex. I could trade it for food, money and drugs. Drugs were my escape from cold reality.

I was able to get across the border without any trouble. I found hitching much easier in the U.S. It was very easy for me to get what I wanted from anyone I traveled with. I would play on whatever it took to get money for the road. I decided to go to California to check out the beaches I'd seen on TV so often.

The first ride was from this old man. I told him that I was going to go to California, maybe find a job and live there for awhile. All I had for gear was an old army duffle bag. It held the things I got from John, and the things I thought they wouldn't miss. No sleeping bag or anything, as I thought I could get there in one day. This old man asked if I wanted to sleep in his trailer. His wife would fix me some food and there was a sleeping bag in the trailer. I accepted his kindness. This old couple was so genuine. It felt strange. After they said their good-nights, I was left alone in their trailer. I laid there for the longest time, thinking that one of them would come out and try something, but I fell asleep. I awoke sometime around two or three in the morning, and just compulsively rolled up their sleeping bag and was gone in minutes.

I was off to a beaming start after one night in the U.S., bag, bed roll, decent clothes and some money: I had panhandled enough for food and a few beers.

29

I was standing on the side of the highway, thumb in the air, when a station wagon pulled over and asked me if I could drive. Jumping into this car I noticed a woman so beautiful that I still think of her. Her name was April. She was traveling with this guy named Brian; they were sharing the costs to San Francisco. Bonus, I thought. They took me in as the third. April and I talked of everything. Brian would get a word in every once in awhile, but he seemed more like the quiet type. Fine with me: I would score more points with her that way.

At the end of the first night on the road with them, Brian pulled over and said he was going to put his sleeping bag out side and call it a night. I started to do the same, but he seemed adamant that I sleep in the car with April. Shit, I thought, who was I to say no to be sleeping with a beautiful woman. We curled up beside each other and talked till we drifted off to sleep. In the morning, April said she was very pleased that I did not try anything during the night. She kissed me. I was in love!!!

After a day and a half in the same car, I had gotten to know them pretty well. Brian was even quieter the next day, as if something was on his mind and he was brooding about it. April was in the front seat, Brian was driving, and I was in the back seat. I saw April's purse was open, and that was all it took. I was never going to see them again anyway. I took a hundred dollar bill out of her purse as we talked, getting closer to San Francisco. She did not even notice the missing bill when we stopped for gas and munchies.

San Francisco was just as I'd seen on T.V. I was overpowered with the size of the city. Brian drove April and me to the city center. He said he was glad the trip was over and that we could get out.

I had no idea of what to do, but I offered to carry April's bags to the nearest hotel, on Regent Street. April went in and got a room. It hurt to say goodbye. We had become friends, and it was over just like that?. Not likely. I walked around town for awhile, then went back to her hotel and rented a room with the hundred that I took from her purse. I picked up the phone and called her room. She told me to come up. I thought I was going to get together with her but that was not the plan in her mind.

She came right out and said, "she wanted to be friends" and I thought, what the hell. I asked if she wanted to grab some food, but she said she would rather relax from the road trip, that maybe we could do something later. I asked the front desk for a T.V. I was told that it would cost more. Walking back to my room, a guy introduced himself, asking if I was from this town. I told him I had just arrived and didn't know anyone. He asked if I wanted to go for a beer. I thought, this is great, even in the hotels people try to pick you up. It turned out this guy was just lonely and wanted to talk to someone. I was that someone.

After a few beers, I told him I wanted to go back to the hotel to get an early start the next day. As we passed the front desk I asked if the TV was ready. It wasn't. I said good night to this guy, went to my room and called April. She did not feel like doing anything, so we made plans to go for breakfast and I turned in.

At six the next morning, the phone rang. It was the manager, asking about the guy that I was seen with the evening before. I told him I knew he was from Tennessee, but I barely knew him otherwise. The manager told me the guy had jumped off the top of the hotel this morning. He asked if I knew the next of kin. I was freaking out. I did not know this guy from anyone. The manager started talking about police statements and all that shit. What the fuck was I supposed to tell them? I was just a 13 year old runaway from Cecil Facer. I called April. After telling her what was happening I said goodbye. I was out of the hotel by 7 a.m. Outside, cops were crawling all over the place. I wanted nothing more to do with San Francisco. The scene was horrific.

On the south highway, I was picked up by a guy who offered to suck my cock for twenty five dollars. He made me a belt for my bed roll (so I could carry it over my shoulder) and I jumped out of his car one hundred dollars richer. I was still in a state of shock over that shit at the hotel. I wanted to find the beach, to chill out and not worry about anything. The further south I went the warmer it got. I felt out of place at the beach. Everyone was dressed in beach gear and I was looking like road dirt. I was near one of the biggest army or navy stations in the south. After the one hundredth weird look, I just moved on.

Just about everyone that picked me up was willing to give me money if I let them suck my cock. It was unbelievable. I decided to hitch to San Diego, work my way over to Florida, then head back to Canada. I got a ride from a young guy who made me feel comfortable enough to tell him I was from Canada, just tripping around the country, in no hurry. He said I could make some bucks helping him get all the stuff he needed for his big beach bash. I was in. This guy did not make me feel like he wanted anything but help. I was also told that I could crash at his house, right by the beach.

This was going to be my introduction to the California beach party

31

scene. I was accepted without trouble, and it was great. That night, I did so many drugs I was walking on air, and the party had the best women all over the place. They were friendly and willing and the fire on the beach could be seen for miles. Every time the waves crashed on the shore, it would light up almost florescent. Just as I was running to the water, my new friend grabbed me, saying I could get real sick if I swam. It was Red Tide. No one swims or eats seafood when this occurs. I was saved on one wild night. The next day was brutal. We were all suffering from drugs, booze, and to clean the beach as well as his house. His house was a mess. Drugs in big bowls all over the place, beer cans everywhere. It was a real party house, if the cops had shown up some people would've gone to jail.

After cleaning up, this guy gave me a bag of pot and twenty bucks, and drove me to the highway. That night was unusual for the fact that no one had attempted to coerce, abuse, molest or rape me in any way. I was thirteen years old.

CHAPTER FOUR

MANIPULATIVE TRAVELS

I was in Southern California and was free as a bird! I was happy, no one could tell me what to do. Once I got near L. A. I could see how different things became. There was spray painting all over, and the crowd was an unruly looking type. It was not hard for me to steer clear of that-as I did not want to go to jail down here. A lot of things had happened already and I was not sure about staying in this area.

I got off the highway at the Hawthorne Blvd. exit. I was in awe as I walked. The city just got bigger, and I felt smaller. I felt almost as if I was suffocating. I walked up to this taco stand and ordered a burrito. I started to talk to the manager and I could already sense that this guy was interested in more than just tacos. Bill was his name, and as I worked on the burrito, I also worked on him. I could sense that he would offer a place to stay, once I laid the ground work. There was a sign in the window that said "Help Wanted", an added bonus. I applied and scored the job and a place to stay, as long as I let this Bill guy suck my cock.

Bill had a big apartment in Hollywood and this kind of went to my head. I was in Hollywood, until now a T. V. dreamland. I worked with a beautiful girl. We would talk of everything. One day she invited me to her parent's house, where she lived, because she wanted me to meet her parents. I was in love with this girl. At night when I was alone, I would masturbate and think of her. Bill hated the fact I was s spending time with her, so he gave me an alternative. Either I drop her or lose my job. I'd done a lot with this girl and met her family. We had watched the Concorde land, holding hands together. In the back of my head was the thought that Bill would tell her what he and I had been doing together since I had shown up. I told her I was having a problem where I was staying, and I was moving to San Diego to find work. I hated the thought of never seeing her again. But I was afraid to share the horrors of my young life with her, afraid to scare her away. It looked like I would be running free from love again.

I thought fuck it, I'll stay in Hollywood and do something to make money. So I hustled. I worked tricks on the Hollywood streets. Some would spend money just to talk. One time, I hooked with a trick at his place and did a bunch of drugs. I don't know what they were, but the effect was to be rendered totally useless. After a short time, the trick and his friend started to have sex while I was more or less paralyzed in the sofa chair.

In my haze, it seemed as if I was watching a film, not seeing reality. Suddenly the trick started to tie up his friend, slapping him rather violently. It freaked me out. The thought suddenly entered my head that I was going to become the toy for later. Being beaten and raped was not part of my $100 deal with this trick. Adrenalin kicked in, the drugs seemed to just disappear, and I was getting ready to fight like hell. The trick sensed something was up. He came over and talked to me about what was going on, asking if it bothered me. I told him it did, and they stopped, which surprised me. Then we all sat there and talked until dawn.

After all was said and done, the trick gave me a job! His name was Dennis, he worked for a rich Hollywood dude, named Abby Mann. His house was located in the hills off Hollywood and Vine, otherwise known as Beverly Hills.

Dennis was basically Abby Mann's minder; he kept Abby's house in order. I was now going to be Dennis's helper, and sex partner, at his place-part of the offer. We drove around in Abby Mann's Cadillac, shopping for dinner, and then cooking for him and his guest. He had beautiful guests, a new one everyday. We would clean up after them. This meant we could keep some of the smaller amounts of drugs that were left out or in the ashtray. A bizarre situation: I came from Canada, with nothing and now I was living large in Hollywood. I had money, and food and a place to stay.

Then one day it hit me: I was homesick, it was time to move on. I was restless, I had had my fun in California. I stepped where they had stepped and put my hands where they had put their hands (the stars), and it was time to go. I had some money saved so I hit the road. I thought what the fuck, let's go to Disneyland.

I walked through the gates, proud as shit. I made it here all by myself, using the skills I had I learned at White Oaks, and from all the others that had wanted something from me. It was time for me to do the dealing. I was no longer a kid that was willing because of need. They needed sex and I wanted something in return. I spent almost every cent that I had in Disneyland, without a worry. I was capable now to never go hungry, or without the things I wanted.. Almost broke, with a fat belly, I was ready to go to San Diego.

It seemed to me that one adventure would lead to another again. I was walking toward the highway, through the Disneyland parking lots, when I spotted a bundle of papers rolling in the wind. I ran over and picked them up. One hundred and eighty dollars in unsigned travelers checks! I stashed them in my pack and hit the store for beer and smokes for the road. I hooked up with another guy. I told him about the checks. This would prove to be one of the strangest encounters in my life. I can't recall the names concerned so it will be Him/Her, He/She.

He told me he had just been dropped off by this chick, the key to cashing the checks. The hitcher tracked down the girl. We went to a restaurant and ordered. We acted like we were a real family. Dinner was great, and the change from the checks was even better: we could buy all the shit we needed.

Fat from dinner, we rented a hotel room and went looking for some dope and a party. We drove around in her car looking to score. After finding drugs we were almost out of travelers checks. We hit this natural hot springs to party. It was there I enjoyed my first experience with oral sex with a women. Amazing! We were in the springs, and then dude went to the car for booze. Suddenly the chick grabbed my cock, playing with me. I went under the water, and started to suck on her. This went on for sometime, till we both were out of breath.

We talked about getting a room, and the plan was, that they would rent the room and I would sneak in. That way we would still have enough for booze and food. We would worry about tomorrow when it came. This chick had an old Renault, the one with the trunk in the front. I hid in there while they booked the room. We started drinking. I really wanted to fuck this chick proper, not in the water, but the alcohol was getting the better of me. We were talking about ways of making money. The table turned when we started to talk about a robbery. In the morning, when there was nothing left of the checks and booze, we woke and drank what little was left. I was still drunk and a little bit just set me off again. Before I was aware of what was going on, this chick showed me a towel wrapped around a forty-five caliber hand gun. The plan was set. I was unaware of a plan, but they had made one while I slept. I was chosen to be the front player, as I was the smallest and would look good as a girl. I said no way, but soon caved under pressure...

The plan was to rob the hotel where we stayed. The entrance was on the other side of the building . I was dressed as a girl with long red hair and a hat and purse. I walked around the front. I walked into the lobby and asked to rent a room. The manager turned around to get the register book, so I pulled out the gun and put it on the counter. I told the manager to put one hand behind his back and tuck it into his pants. With his thumb and index finger on his other hand he was to open the till and put the money in the purse. The rush that I was getting was the best I'd ever had. I was not afraid of doing it, I was afraid that it might not work as planned. The manager did what I told him, and the door to his room slowly started to open, and his wife saw what was going on. I yelled at the manager to lay on the floor and count to one hundred. I bolted out the door and ran behind the hotel. I jumped into the open trunk of waiting car. The guy shut it and then went back in the room. I laid there for an hour.

I could hear all the cop sirens, and people were all over the place asking what happened. I could even hear the fire department. I was shaking so badly that I thought the car was rocking. Then the guy and the girl came out. I heard them talking to the cops. I thought for sure I would be caught, but the guy and the girl got in the car and drove out the front entrance. The last cop to stop them asked if they saw anyone that looked like a long red haired girl. I was in the trunk, not five feet from this cop, and they pulled it off by saying that they were just going for a bite to eat and that they would keep their eyes open when they got back to the hotel. We drove away, and, after a few blocks, the guy started yelling "we did it." We drove straight to Long Island and stopped in front of the amusement park, where I got out. We counted the money, and I told them I was out and I did not want to do that ever again. This chick started to come on to me again. I guess it was because I did what I said I was going to do. The booze started to flow, and then the search for drugs, and before long we were all almost broke. I stole $345- only $115 each..

We all acted like high rollers for the day, but soon reality set in. I was coerced by this chick sexually to pull off another job. I was so drunk and uncaring, about what was going on in my life, I caved again for sex. Sex was the big player-not me. I dressed as a girl again for two more jobs. After the last job I told them both I was out, and if I ever saw them again it would be too soon. I left and never saw them again. I was done with those people, not only because they did not trust me for the robberies, but mostly for the reason that if I stayed with them I was bound to end up in jail or dead. I hung around the San Diego area for awhile. One day I was walking toward the highway from the beach, and saw this chick hitchhiking. When I got close I recognized the same chick with that I had done those robberies with. She said the guy had dumped her, and she was going to go to the Bay area to do something. All that I could think of was thank goodness she was going in the opposite direction and said my byes and never saw her or that guy ever again.

It was beautiful out here, and I felt free do go anywhere I wanted, so I thought I would head over to Florida and see what that side of the world was like. As I sat there, waiting for a ride, I was over whelmed with the beauty of my surroundings. The highway stretched out in front of me, and it suddenly occurred to me: I was a Rolling Stone, and that was fine by me. My first ride east was a friendly, long haired dude. We talked of all kinds of things, and he even offered me a job for two or three days. I was more than willing to work, as it was better than having to let someone do something to you, so I eagerly accepted his offer. The best thing was, it was on the way to San Diego. His name was Hans, and he had a wife Sue. They lived off the highway about a mile from Mexico. Hans and Sue were down to earth people, with no desire for material gain or fame. They had all that they needed for money. They grew pot for a living, and would go to town once every three or four months to cash in. I stayed with them for about three days, leaving with a lot of pot for the road. The money in my pocket was worth every cent, as I had worked honestly for it. I did not have to lay down on some bed for it...

All I wanted was to travel, to see different places and everything that went with it. Hitch-hiking was fun, I did not have any trouble getting a ride. The next stop was going to be somewhere in Arizona, but I was not sure where. So out went the thumb and the games began again. Some people just want company, some want all they can get. My first ride going east, after Hans dropped me off at the highway, was from a biker. He stopped and said that he was going about fifty miles down the road. I did not immediately clue in, but that fifty miles led to a hotel and more money in my pocket.

I was also wondering if there were any people that would pick me up to talk, rather than suck my cock, or get me to fuck them, or the other way around. There seemed to be a lot of gay men in America. Suddenly a van pulled up, and out popped this chick who made my head spin. She asked where I was headed. I looked in the van and her old man was driving I thought, fuck, oh well, at least she was worth the trip. So I said to the east coast. Off to a great start. They did not have enough money to get past Texas. I was with them for two days, watching them fuck at night. I would pound the pudding as I watched. Their names were Sandy and Pat and they were *different*. They *had* to know that anyone would get excited if a couple was rocking the van, and they were up front as I was. This was going to be a fun trip. We all were just about broke and Sandy was told by her old man that she was going to have to turn tricks for gas, as I had the drugs and Pat had the van. He told her it was only fair (I don't know where the fuck his head was with a statement like that, fucking guy was turning out his own girl. No sense, no sense, but I was in for the ride).

My trip with them was going to take us across five states, and Sandy was going to hook all the way. Pat would not let me drive his van and Sandy did not like to drive, so we slept or tried to sleep along the highway. Sandy and Pat knew some people in San Antonio, Texas and that was going to be our first stop (other than truck stops) so Sandy could work. Pat told me his chick had been turning tricks for years, and that now they wanted to travel at the same time. Close to San Antonio the van started to fuck up, and we just made it to their friends place. Once there, we found out it would take about three days to repair the damage. Sitting around in the hot sun, drinking beer and looking at women, seemed like a great thing to do, but for Pat and Sandy it was too much. They argued, and threw things at each other, and all that shit, but I sat and kept my mouth shut. I was hardly there, other than when they wanted to smoke some dope.

Once on the road again, all was well with them, and the time passed quickly. Before long we where on the outskirts of New Orleans. For the last few days you could hear Pat yell whenever he took a piss, and the same for Sandy. She would curse and blame Pat for getting her sick. By the time we got into the city, we went right to the French Quarter to find a free clinic. We all walked into the clinic. Sandy went one way, Pat and I went another. This nurse came and asked me some questions, then told me to wait out in the lobby for Pat. Sitting there was nice - the highway gets to you if you don't get off once in awhile. Suddenly I heard an inhuman scream. Pat came out of the exam room, holding his crotch, swearing like mad. The doctor made him get a hard-on looking at books, then grabbed his crotch and stuffed a q-tip up his dick. I could almost *feel* the pain, the way he described it. We waited for Sandy, then we went back to the van. Pat asked me to look after this little puppy Sandy found a day or two back, so I thought nothing of it. I took the little fucker for a walk and when I came back the van was gone. Right off, I knew that they had fucked off and I was stuck with this dog from hell. I went back to the clinic. I was told they had just been in, and that they both had VD. They had left arguing at each other. They had my bed roll, all my extra clothing and nick knacks, and they were gone. I walked all over the French Quarter and could not find them.

I got to talking to this big woman, who was sitting on the front stairs of a house, drinking tequila. She offered me some and I ended up telling her my story. She gave me some hints as to where to go and what to avoid. I never knew her name, so I'll call her Angel. I was fucked up, in a city that was not to nice to transients, with no money. I walked for hours hoping to find the van and then punch the fuck out of Pat, but nothing. I tied the dog up out front of this store and went inside. There were games where you could win stuffed toys, sunglasses and other things.

I was playing one machine when I noticed this older looking guy watching me, so I played on it a little. I went right up to him and asked if he could break a dollar for the machine. We chatted for a bit, then went outside to check the dog. He was yapping away to me about all kinds of things. Then I let him have it with both barrels. Before long, as I expected, it turned out he was feeding, me and buying me beers and then he asking if I wanted to go to his place. I told him I would go if he paid me $100 first, and that I was not going to stay long, as I wanted to get more gear and hit the highway.

Josh was his name, and after we had sex he wanted to take me out for dinner and then anything. I said take me shopping for some new gear, and son-of -a-bitch, he did and then some. That very first night with Josh, we spent about $1000 dollars. It was as if Josh wanted to help me, not just fuck me or suck my cock. He really wanted to help. His house was perfect, the pictures on the walls must have been worth thousands, like everything else in his house. The next day when I woke up and saw this guy in the same bed, I thought, what the fuck are you doing? All your life you crave the company of women, and there is a guy in bed with you. That was it. I looked at the situation and told myself that I would not let anyone do that again. I told Josh how I felt and he was very understanding. We went all over Southern Louisiana.

I stayed with Josh for about a month, then one day, out of the blue, Josh came home with an airplane ticket for me to Toronto. He told me it was time I went home and if I ever needed anything, to just call. I was totally distraught, as I felt that I was safe with Josh and did not want to go back to Canada. I knew what was in store for me if I went back, and that to me was not a pretty picture. Once again I had this sinking feeling that I was not wanted for anything but sex. I cried for three days and tried in earnest to talk Josh out of sending me back, but he felt that it was for the best and that I could get my life in order. The last few days in New Orleans were great. We went all over the country and saw some of the old cotton plantations. It was beautiful.

One day, we were sitting in the house talking, when a tremendous blast of thunder sounded, though it was totally sunny outside. We thought it was a bomb, so we both ran outside. We saw nothing out of the ordinary, only people milling around. Josh turned on the TV and got a news bulletin-one of the local refinery's big, big, tanks had exploded. This was the loudest noise I ever heard. It settled down quick and the next day we went for a drive to see if we could find the tank, but could not get close enough to the site, as there was still too many people around.

I was going back to Toronto. It was useless trying to talk to Josh out of it. He really wanted me to go home. Josh bought me luggage and gave me a couple hundred for a room once I got back. In a twisted way, Josh had become something of a Father Figure. Fuck, I was sick and tired of not being wanted, and this feeling was going to be my down fall. At the airport I gave Josh a big hug and told him I would stay in touch with him.

I was scared and anxious to be back, and did not know where I was going or what I was going to do. I had family here, but they were not my blood, and I felt that I could not trust them as they would phone my mother and then the cops. I went to my Dad's old house and asked if there was any knowledge of his were abouts, but no one remembered him. I went to the Y.M.C.A. in downtown Toronto and rented myself a room. This room was going to be what turned me out on the street.

40

Once I was downtown, it seemed like there was always something to do. I walked around until I met some people that offered to smoke a joint. I figured it couldn't hurt. While we smoked, the people told me they had just come from a bar called The Saint Charles. They offered me a beer, and I thought, what the fuck. I had never been in a gay bar before. When I walked through the doors and saw all these guys sitting close to one another, I was speechless and awkward. There was this chick, at least I thought it was a woman, and her name was Michelle. I was sitting close to her as I did not want anyone thinking that I was gay. I only whored myself so that I could travel, so I told myself.

I watched all kinds of things go down. Far from being shocked, I was rather impressed, as there was money to be had here. The Saint Charles was shaped like a horse shoe, and the place was full, with people that looked my age, and this was comforting. At least I was not the only chicken. I was later to find out that is what the young stuff was called. I sat there drinking beer with Michelle and her friends the rest of the night, and they all asked where I was staying, and I told them at the Y until I can find a place, and that I would see them later. I went back to my room. I was fairly drunk. On the way to my room, this guy came up to me and asked if I wanted to go to his room. I lost it on him. I was yelling and caused a scene. The staff came and walked me to my room, they told me to be careful, as there were a lot of gay men staying at the Y, and I should just watch myself. When I woke up in the morning I went out for breakfast and took note of where I was.

The Y.M.C.A. was located on Collage Street, just around the corner from Yonge St. Little did I know that this was almost gay central. There seemed to be someone looking at me everywhere, and this was something new. The Saint Charles was on the corner of Yonge St and Groverner, only a block from the Y.M.C.A. I walked around the area and found the old Children's Aid where my brother and I had lived. I was only 9 when I went there, and here I was, looking at it from a totally different prospective at the age of 14.

I had just traveled about 7 or 8 thousand miles around the continent, done some wild shit and now, as I stood there, I wondered what was in store for me next. Walking around the downtown area, I saw guys kissing, and girls kissing, and was not sure what to think. I kept to myself. I needed to get high somehow, and was asked by this guy if I wanted to buy tops. I told him I did not know what he meant. He pulled out this joint that was at least five inches long. I said there was nothing in this world that would hold me back. We went for a walk and smoked this joint. His name was Doug, but he told me everyone around called him Blue. I said they call me Jeremiah. We talked for some time, and then talked of the bars around, and where you could pull a trick if you got low on money. Blue made me feel comfortable, so we exchanged numbers. The rest of the day I walked around town stoned.. Blue seemed to treat me the way Josh had, and not the way it was in the beginning, with porno books from the Barber, or extra tuck from Rob, or the landlord who willingly gave his own daughter.

So many degrading memories! So many sick people! I just wanted to find someone that was not going to use me. I wanted to make some serious money, and sex was by far the best way to make it, besides drugs. It was a part of my life now, as it had been from the start. I could not shake the fact that this was all I had to work for me, and not against me. That night I called Blue, and my life was going to change.

I met Blue at this night club called The Manatee. When I got to the door, I was made aware, it was a gay club, and that I had to know someone to get inside. I told them I was meeting a guy named Blue, and they let me in. I do not know how I got into bars and clubs at that age, but, if I looked that old back then, I must look *ancient* now.

Once inside, I found Blue. The club was like something out of a movie. There were guys dancing around on platforms (that were six feet off the ground) wearing G-Strings. The place was full, and what can I say, I was looking for women. Much later I spotted Michelle, the chick I smoked a joint with when I just got into town. The people were dressed up, and there was a definite theme to certain parts of the club. There were guys that liked to wear leather and chains, and little top hats with spikes, wrist bands and boots. Some were all tanned up, with rolled up short sleeve shirts, hair in place, looking in the mirror every five minutes. Some had long hair and blue jeans. Some sat and drank and did drugs. Others sold drugs and hung out with chicks like Michelle. There was Tony, who I was convinced was tranny. I did some MDA with Blue at the table, which made me feel warm and cozy and wanted. The room was filled with people that wanted to talk and dance and have fun.

I could see how easy it would be to make money in this club, as long as I watched what was going on. I could hustle here, I thought. I asked Blue if he agreed, and he said no. I got fucked up that night, and when I woke up, I had about ten different phone numbers. I called Blue and we went out for lunch. It was past noon and I felt like shit. We talked for awhile, went back to his place, did some more dope and then had sex. I did not see Blue for a few days; by that time I was caught up selling acid for this guy named Mark, a real prick. He would sooner punch someone out than sell them acid, but sell he did, and he was good at it. After three days, I was sick of his shit. He was physical and rude.

One night Mark and I went to the Carriage House and sat there and sold acid all night. We had a fight back at his place. When he finally went to bed I stole all the money and drugs and took off. I went to the Y.M.C.A. grabbed my shit and went to Blue's house. I had never stolen drugs from anyone. With no where to live, I was taking a big risk. But, Blue was nice enough to put me up, even though I was in trouble. It was not long before Mark found out were I was. I was scared shitless. I was sitting on the couch, when all of a sudden there was banging on the door. It was Mark, saying if I did not return his shit that I would be killed. I ran to the kitchen, grabbed a knife and waited for him to kick open the apartment door. It didn't happen. Mark made so much noise, that some other tenant screamed they were going to call the cops if buddy (Mark) did not leave. That was all that it took; Marks last words were that he would "see me around."

All day I sat there, frozen to the chair, waiting for a knock on the door. I was a fucking bag of nerves. I did not know that Blue was living with someone till he got home that night. I told him about what had happened. He got kind of mad at me, but we talked it out and that night I met Merv. Merv was the same height as Blue, but only way more heavy set, weighing around two-seventy on a five foot seven frame. Blue was about one-eighty on a five foot seven frame. In other words, they looked like Fat and Skinny, as I told Blue later. That same night, Blue and I decided to eat a good dinner and stay at home. Shit, I did not care if I went out for a week. The three of us ate, played cards and drank. Blue and I did two hits of acid each and then Blue told me that he had spiked Merv's drink, and Merv was in for a good trip. Blue said Merv always did acid. Still, I thought it was wrong to spike anyone's drink and told him so. No matter, as we were all having fun playing cards. Later that night I would have a hallucination that would be with me for life.

As the night wore on and the acid kicked in, Merv went to bed and Blue and I partied in the living room. Sometime later I went to check on Merv. When I opened the door to his room, I saw a body on the bed in dirty white underwear, only this body looked like a pig with his hands bound and his face in a gas mask and eyes that only stared into emptiness. Sweat was running off it and it tried to move but couldn't, I slammed the door shut and told Blue what I had seen. He was skeptical. I told him to go look. When he got back he told me I was hallucinating, and that it would go away. Acid is a very potent drug. It hit me hard that night. Blue talked me down, explaining what was going on. I appreciated the fact that he hadn't tried anything funny to fuck me up on drugs.

For the next week I hung out with Blue, meeting all types of players, hustlers and tricks in the St. Charles area. There was a strip that was only for boys and young men. The cops would check out all the hustlers to see if they were clean and not wanted. In order to satisfy my needs like clothes, food, drugs and booze I had to turn tricks. I thought, I did it in the U.S., why not here? I was not blind to what we did to survive. We all carried knifes, and by all, I mean about two to three dozen boys and about the same number of young men hustling, turning tricks, getting drunk and high night after night.

I was always stoned on one thing or another whenever I went out on the street. It was impossible to turn tricks otherwise. It was a job, but also a self-imposed prison. I was a 14-year old drug-addicted prostitute. Most kids my age were playing sports, meeting girls and going to school. My world was drugs, guns and solicitation.

Then one day Blue came home and told me he'd met a connection for a modeling agency, with an opportunity for us to make serious jack. I told him I was in. I knew we had to look right when we went to the office. My mind was on the money, where it could take me, and how I would get there.

Blue and I became regulars at The Manatee. I got to know all the drug dealers and hookers, and earned a reputation for always having good drugs. I was soon introduced to Weasel, who'd been dealing out of the club for sometime, and was not happy when I showed up. We managed to work out a deal were we would share the customers. Blue and I celebrated our new prospects as models by doing drugs, hanging out with street people and partying all the time. No one could tell us what to do, and I was growing quite comfortable moving in my new circles.

CHAPTER FIVE

DAYS WITH NO NIGHTS

Blue and I went to this place called MALE CALL MODELING. All over the office were pictures of boys and young men, dressed in good looking clothes, just looking like they were worth something more than just models. We met with the manager, Stan. He was quite openly gay, and also quite a flirt during the interview. Stan told us we would be sent out to various locations to do modeling work. At first I thought I was going to get my break after all, because fucking guys (and their wives) was getting to be a real drag. Some days you would not make any money, and some days you could get a bad trick. This was *not* what I was in this game for. Then there was the constant fear of VD.

During the interview, Stan told us the firm would put out about two hundred dollars to each of us, for good clothes and a picture portfolio. Potential clients could chose whomever they wanted, just by perusing the photos. I was again excited, thinking of the money, the travel, the drugs and the women.

Blue and I were at the point where we pretty well hung out all the time, frequenting one particular night club. It was for gay men only. At the door they would stop you and check I.D., asking if you were gay or not. Access would be denied if they or any of the door staff thought you were uncool. We got to be well known there, as we always had good drugs. Blue and I were in competition with one drug dealer named Weasel (and his little boyfriend) for drug income.

The days wore on, and Blue and I were waiting for the agency to call. Our photos were ready, and we wanted to start making some money. Once I was hooked up with Blue, I stopped turning tricks. I continued to deal drugs to support our habit, and pay for nights out. Don't get the wrong idea. I was not the only one to work in this relationship.

We both did as much as we could. I thought that I was going to be gay for life. This was not going to be the case. The street has a way of swallowing you up along with the people who live and work the street. It will spit you out in the gutter when you are either too drugged or too used up. It is relentless in it's search for new blood. I wanted nothing more than to get ahead and get out, no easy feat. I no longer worried about Mark, (the one that I ripped off for the acid). By going to this club (The Manatee), I got to know most of the tough gay guys who liked little boys like me and would do whatever I asked, if they thought it would give them a shot at fucking me. In the movies, these types are portrayed all dressed in leather and little black caps with silver all over them.

One such guy was Harry. He knew Weasel and his boyfriend Gary. Harry had a crush on Gary and me, because we were young and we hung out with older men. My recreational drug of choice was acid, but the drug I liked to have sex on was MDA. It was readily available through Weasel and Harry. Although Harry was not the dealer, he was able to supply Weasel through contacts. My downward spiral started here. It would be years before I woke up and told myself, "enough."

In the early 70s downtown Toronto gay scene, it was hip to cheat on the one you called your lover. The promiscuity of the scene was rampant. It seemed almost every week that we went to the club there was someone different with someone that we knew. The old saying "As the cock crows, so does the relationship crumble," summed the scene up concisely.

Blue and I finally got the call from the agency to start work. We went to the office, got all the info on the client and went out on the shoot, or so I thought.

My first job was with a judge living in east Scarborough. At the end of the transit line there was this limo waiting for me. I thought this was good. We drove to a really posh area. The judge's place was very extravagant, and well maintained. This judge was very worried that I would feel uncomfortable.

He offered me a drink, and then another, and before long I was buzzed. Suddenly he blurted out "Why don't you take all your clothes off so that I can suck on your cock before we go any further". I was stunned, and then it clicked: this was the shoot. I asked what he meant by "go any further". He told me he wanted to suck my cock before I fucked him. This judge, who will remain nameless, kept offering me a big tip if I did a good job. Back in the limo, on the way to the transit station, I counted the money-$700. I was walking away from my first trick from the Male Call Modeling Agency. I understood why the guys in the pictures looked so good.

I went back to the office. Stan asked me for the paperwork, for the work I did. Fuck, it was only glorified prostitution. Stan explained that $450 of the money was mine, and the rest was going to pay for the office and health care and anything that came up. The more I "worked" the more the money I'd make. I asked him to explain. Stan told me there were three levels of models. I was only a one star; there were two star and three star levels. The money changed at each level as work changed.. My only focus was more money.

With my $450.00 I went out and bought all kinds of cloths and shoes, including a pair of mens platforms. I met up with Blue, who had done his first one (trick) as well that night. This modeling job was good for the money, but once in a while you got a weird trick. The money was there, but the act itself was crude, for lack of a better word. One guy would spend an the average of about $1000 a week. He wanted you to drink as much beer as you could. He would put porno movies on, and lay out a plastic sheet. He wanted you to piss on him, and sometimes he would drink the piss right from my cock. I would walk away with $1000, but in order for me to deal with what I had become, I did drugs and drank as much as possible. I was moving nowhere fast... Some tricks wanted even stranger, sicker things. Nothing violent, but some fucked up trips.

Despite the depravity I had surrounded myself with, I wanted a girl-friend, and this was killing me. I did not have any family that I felt that I could trust. Blue would console me, in exchange for sex. It was cold and empty. What about my needs? What I liked, needed, wanted, searched for and never got was driving me mad. I started to flirt with the manager one night and ended up at a steam bath with one of his buddies. I remember sitting in this little cubical which held a bed, chair, me and this guy mixing up the dope. I thought I had done drugs before, then this shit hit me. I shot up in both arms at once. The feeling was out of this world. At first it started like a warm sensation at the top of my head. Then it moved, almost con-trolled, to the center of my body and right to my groin. I came, right then and there. After a few hours, I did some more. This time I got very sick and the guy fucked off on me because I was throwing up blood. I thought for sure I was going to die. I called out for help, and the manager of the club (with someone other than his lover,) saw me. He took me to his doctor, then back to his place. I was told to stay there till I was well, which took two weeks. I ended up having an affair with Dave, which gave me free access to the club and extra protection from the cops and other dealers.

I was tired of feeling like I belonged nowhere. Empty relationships were draining me. I went to the club and talked to Weasel. I told him my situation, and he said that I would have to explain to Gary, Weasel's boyfriend. Gary was my age, or a year or two older. We hit it off, doing drugs and laughing all the time. The job at the modeling agency was going good. I was making money and spending it on everyone and everything I wanted. I never thought of anyone but myself.

Things started to go from good to bad. Blue and I had worked for the agency for sometime. Rumors started to fly that the cops were going to bust a downtown prostitution ring. Upon hearing these rumors, Blue and I went to the office-there was no one there. So we walked in, and took the Rolodex, and our portfolios, (as well as a few others) and split. As we were going out the door, the cops were rushing up the stairs. Both Blue and I started to run as soon as we hit the street, then into the first cab that came along. I was scared but excited by this little world I made for myself. Well, so much for the modeling career.

Back at Blue's place, things were very hectic for the first few moments. Blue and I were not seeing each other, but still looking out for one another, which saved us in the end. We could have been busted.

We conspired to take over the prostitution ring. We would not have to go out with tricks ourselves, we could control what we did. Blue set everything up, and I started to fade into the background, only working if I needed the money. We would see each other at the club, and dance. We would discuss details and paperwork, and I'd get my share of the money other people made for us. I was only fourteen years old, and in control of a lot of money. Blue and I were in control of at least one hundred and fifty people through grabbing that Rolodex.

My life was in such a shambles, I was incapable of understanding what I was doing to myself with all the drugs and alcohol. I trusted no one. I was devoid of self respect. I felt disconnected from life and those around me. The tricks I used became things, not human beings. They were just vessels to deliver money to me, money I had almost already spent. The act was over in my head before it ever started.

Things were rocky for the downtown people for awhile. I was caught right up in all the hustling and drug dealing. Nothing that was ever done was done for any reason. Still, I had somehow, at the club, met some good people. One such person was Weasel. I got to know him real well. I ended up living at his place, with Gary, and sharing all the drugs and money from dealing . Living with Weasel and Gary was one long drug trip that did not stop for years. The first place we had was on a street that later became very well known in the downtown core. Maitland Avenue, #51 to be exact, apartment #102. This is were I had my first run in with the cops over drugs. I was never busted for drugs till the late seventies.

Because I was now a partner in the drug trade with Weasel, I went to the dealer's place with him, and then on my own when we were busy. There was a building in the center of a little district called Rochdale, which was designated to the university. The building was located on Bloor Street East and it was about thirty floors high. Well, one day we got this call to go there and pick up our acid for the weekend. As Weasel and I walked through the front doors, we were stopped by what looked like security guards, but were in fact the drug dealer's own people. They had dogs, and searched us for wires and guns. They put us on the elevator and locked in the floor. We just stood there and looked at each other.

Once on the floor, there were guys at the elevator to meet us. They walked us to the apartment. As we walked in, at least five guys packing guns were there. One big guy came out, said "hey" to Weasel, looked at me and asked, how much do I want? I told him I wanted 100 hits. He left the room, only to come back with a bulging bag. He set it on the table and told me to start counting. There must have been 1/4 million hits in this bag. I almost shit.

Sitting there, I thought, this was way up the chain for downtown Toronto. Counting seemed to take forever, as everyone was watching me. They had guns and all I had, was cash.

Win; win for them if they just thought what the fuck. Lose; lose for me if I said the wrong thing. We went to Rochdale quite a few times, until one day when we got home to Maitland St., we got gooned on acid and started to tell people they could come over (BAD MOVE). Weasel, Gary and I were sitting around laughing. We heard this noise and got freaked. We took all our acid and spread it all over our carpet. It was deep, dirty, multi colored shag. After finally calming down, all of a sudden the doors and windows to our apartment were kicked in, and this swarm of cops came rushing in. I was stoned on two or three hits, just tripping watching all this.

The cops stripped us and searched the entire place. All they found were rolling papers, an upsetting result, as they thought they had a big drug bust. The rush I got from that was going to stay with me for awhile. They couldn't arrest us, there was nothing for them to find, they had no evidence. We did not recover all the acid, but enough for us to get the fuck out of there.

We got a place out in Scarborough, only to get kicked out for keeping late hours. Finally we found this place near the old Don Jail. We stayed there for awhile with no problems. Drugs and sex was all that was happening around me, and nothing meant anything to me. I was lost in it. We had a good business going. We continued selling drugs downtown and making money. Occasionally we'd visit one guy that we knew when we were short on our acid supply.

This guy, a fucking genius, made his own acid. The first time we got to his place, he was making a batch, and asked us if we would give him a hand. I had never done this before, so I thought, if I'm going to sell it, I might as well know how to make it. Fred had this lab set up in his bedroom. He made acid and then showed us how he wrapped it. On with the rubber gloves, and a mask. Off to the living room coffee table to wrap acid. I was getting off mentally-this was a big thing to do downtown. I thought it would only take about an hour or two, but seven hours later, stoned out of our fucking heads, we finally stopped. Fred was the king of sugar cube acid, since he made it liquid. All we had to do was suck up the acid in little droppers, and then put it on a sugar cube and wrap it up in tinfoil. At first I thought this was going to be a piece of cake but the more I made the higher I got. The acid was seeping through the latex gloves and getting us all high. Leaving Fred's place was the best thing I could have done. I didn't need to get wrapped up in acid manufacturing. We got stoned for free, bought our dope at a discount (as we helped to make it) and left.

The people you would meet in this little world of gay life and drugs were all phony in one way or another. This was one of the attractions that kept me there. No one ever really knew anyone. Everything was being hustled (if it could happen) and everyone was hustling for a living. Drugs and alcohol were the main stay of this life (so to speak). I was caught up in

50

drugs so bad that no one could talk to me on any emotional level because I was dependent on drugs to feel any self worth. I was living in this world of distrust and insecurity.

The table was about to turn, and, instead of me being the underdog in the drug world, I was now in the position to turn people down for drugs. It seemed weird for me not to be the one to grovel, beg or sell my body for drugs. There were people willing to do this for me. A pimp. A drug dealer. An addict. A prostitute, and one lost and lonely child growing up the wrong way as a result of misdirection from the people in my life. The people who would use a child for sex, for a monetary return, or drugs, or clothing, or just good times-ones that would appear as though they would never stop.

I told myself I could operate better on drugs. I guess that after a certain time of dependency, one would act as if they were not using drugs and this is what happened to me. Weasel had gotten to know this guy named Harold, we'd see him now and then. Harold was a big fan of MDA, a very popular drug in the seventies (called ecstasy today). Weasel had known Harold long before I was in the picture. Then one day, after all the shit, what with our place getting raided and learning to make acid, at the new place near the old Don Jail, Weasel and I had this big fight and the landlord found out that some windows were broken and told us we had to move. I had brought this chick home, and told Weasel that she was going to stay with us for awhile, as she was homeless. That sent Weasel into this fucking rage that I never saw him in before. We fought. He hurt his wrist and needed surgery and we got the boot. So Weasel set up this meeting with Harold on the pretense that it was to sell some MDA to him. Harold lived in this community called St. James Town, located in downtown Toronto. He had a nice apartment with an incredible view on the 22nd floor. Harold had this young man staying with him; this of course was a gay relationship of sorts as we were told this young man, named Don, was Harold's son. To me the whole situation was fucked. I don't remember how long it took but Weasel, Gary and I moved in with Harold and Don.

After a few fights with Don over his obsession with me, Harold told Don that he was going to have to leave and that meant only one thing to me. Harold was working it so that he would have a shot at getting to me. I had no control over my life as I was dependent on drugs and the life style I was living and did not want to change. I was still wanted for running away.

51

I was not worried, as my phony I.D. was good quality. I was now, at the age of 14, sleeping with Harold, who was sixty some years old.

Living with Harold was good. I never wanted for anything. If I needed something Harold would get it, or give me the money for it. We had a nice Buick Wildcat convertible and Harold and I would go for drives in the summer and do drugs. Harold was one of Toronto's leading chefs, and he worked in a very fancy restaurant making good money, and he was generous. We had a bar in our apartment that took up one entire wall, and was always full. I was a fourteen year old kid, living the kept life, with needs, and this was ok with me. Weasel, Gary and I would go to the club and sell all that we had. Then we would either go home, or go to the all night movie place called the Titanion Theater, and do more drugs, and watch horror movies or kung fu, only to go home and do more drugs. I thought a lot of my real family, but did not get in touch with them, as I did not want them to know what I was up to and how I was making a living. I would talk about this with Weasel and Gary and Harold, and then one day it was suggested by Harold that I call my brother and see what he was up to. At first I did not want to, but I guess they all could feel my sense of longing. With some encouragement, I made the call.

I cried when I talked to my mother and then my sister Pat. When I got talking to my brother, I told him what I was up to. I thought it would be cool for him to get involved, if he was to hop a bus back to Toronto. By this time my family had moved to Calgary, Alberta. I did keep tabs on my family, but I never showed this side to them. I kept my thoughts, and my feelings, buried inside. Eventually, my brother George said he would come to Toronto and visit me.

When George showed up, it was like old times. My new, wild life seemed to impress George. We went all over the place, with money from drugs, and drugs to do. It was hard for George to accept my sleeping arrangement with Harold. I explained that I was not fucked by Harold, only that I was letting him play with me, and suck my cock, and that was as far as it went with him, and in return I got everything that I asked for and then some. George was most impressed with that fact that through drugs, Weasel and I controlled a lot of people. This precarious power was intoxicating for George. The crew of Weasel, Gary, George and I started.

Up to this point, George had not experimented much with hard drugs, but after a few weeks, he was doing some, and then lots, and we all were going no where fast. I took George to the clubs, trying to explain the gay subculture. I knew it was important he understand the politics of betrayal prevalent in my world. I also knew I'd have to keep an eye open for him. This was the late spring of ' 75, and we all talked of going camping and driving all over. We did have good ideas, but some of them just never came into focus. We did, however, go camping at Ric's old cottage that was near Burkes Fall, Ontario.

Years ago, Ric had taken us to his place, and it held fond memories for us. But this trip was going to be an adventure, as we were all full of drugs and booze, and had it in our heads that it was going to be fun. Shit, just walking in, from where the bus dropped us off, was trying on everyone's nerves.

After walking the five miles to the cottage, we all just wanted to be by ourselves. We had no permission to go there, so we broke in, used everything that we wanted, and then left. We were unconcerned about the mess we left. It was good to go there and spend time out of the city. We did not do much damage to the cottage and what we did do, George kind of fixed, and so there was really nothing to worry about.

Back in Toronto, the world we all knew had not changed, nor had the request for drugs. We had left the dealing in Harold's care while we were gone, and he was not happy. Things were not the same between Harold and me after the trip. After living the old routine for awhile, George suggested that we should take a trip home, that it would do me a world of good to get out of town for awhile, and that it would be good to see the family. I thought this over for some time, and then told George we needed more money than we had, and that we would hitch-hike back to Calgary. At that moment, it definitely felt like the right time. George kind of convinced me to do this, but deep down inside I felt that I had been gone far too long already.

The big problem was to save enough money to do this. We bought some gear, but when the day came to go, we had not saved enough money. So I broke open the house coin vase, and we hit the highway, not telling anyone that we were going to do this. By the time we were near Thunder Bay, we were out of money and having trouble getting rides. Whenever anyone drove by us and did not stop we would curse them to no end. It took us three days and one car theft to get back to Calgary, and I for one was thankful to be home, even though it did not feel like home. You know when you have this feeling inside that something is wrong in your surrounding.

Well, the first night home, I felt this feeling, something like deja vu, but I could not put my finger on it. All that day, we sat and talked of my life with Elaine, my mother, and Pat my sister. George and I had gotten to know each other all over again in Toronto and on the highway back. Things felt good, and we all talked for hours. Soon, it was dinner time and to me, my mother was acting funny and I could not figure it out. There was this knock on the door and I said that I would get it. When I opened the door I almost shit. There were three cops. They said that I was under arrest for theft, and that I was still wanted for running away from Cecil Facer School, and that I was to come with them. All of a sudden it hit me! The feeling that I could not identify was that of the way that my mother had acted when she did this before! She was scared for herself, because she called the cops. As they were arresting me, again, she was saying that it was not supposed to happen this way. Fuck, all she wanted was to feed me first and then have the cops show up.

This fucking killed me inside. I had traveled all over the States, and Canada, arriving home much more grown up than when my family last saw me. My reunion was short-lived. My mother had been contacted by the cops, regarding the stolen coins from a vase, back at Harold's. Harold had called the cops, telling them that I had taken about $1500. In truth it was like $200, but the warrant went out west to Alberta. When we showed up at home, my mother was still willing to turn me over to the law. I was taken to the Crisis Center for juveniles in North West Calgary. The government had their hands on me again, but there was little I could do, thanks to my family. I was seen by this fellow named Mr. Hunter.

Mr. Hunter made the following statement on May 4, 1974:
"The above named thirteen year old was the most hostile defensive young man on initial contact that the undersigned worker has ever worked with.
On arrival at the Crisis Center his attitude was one of hatred. He wandered into every office, opened every desk drawer..."

At this point in time I felt completely alienated from my family. They had turned on me for the last time. I was going to be shipped back to the Oakville Reception & Assessment Center in Oakville Ontario. I had no say in the matter, as I was still a ward of the courts. I was going through drug withdrawals for sometime after this, and again developed an attitude of hatred for the courts and for my family.

CHAPTER SIX

PROJECT D.A.R.E.

I was only fourteen, with no emotional connection to the real world. My feelings were masked by drugs, alcohol, sex and fast money. Once back at the Oakville Reception and Assessment Center I was told nothing of what was to come of my placement. In my life within the system, I was always dealing with what seemed like desk top social workers. They never really talked to me. They made up my life, like it was written by bureaucrats, not thinking of how a systematic structure would affect a child. I had occasional conversations with a social worker named Roberta Roberts, but was never told of what was going to happen to me. I was thousands of miles away from my family and denied access to them. The family I was born into was a hopeless cause, as they did not come to see me! I was told I would be sent back to Cecil Facer School in Sudbury, Ontario, where it would be decided what was to become of me.

I was only interested in one thing, and that was how to get my ass back to downtown Toronto. I felt the child care system of Canada needed to be examined closely. For example, when discussions regarding a child are held, that child should be present for them. They affect the child for life, and who is to say that one's own aspirations, with the proper guidance, are valid or not? The child, at a certain stage of life, will know how to voice those thoughts, but the desk top social worker, caught up in the system (that only follows the guidelines that are set before them by the BUREAU-CRATS), is handcuffed by protocol.

55

D.A.R.E. Means Development, Attitude, Rehabilitation, Education.

I kept hearing of this place, that it was way the fuck out in the bush, and that if you passed a three month course, you were released back to your family. What the fuck did I have to lose? I thought this would be the place where I cleaned myself up and did not think of drugs. Being way out in the bush appealed to me. I put in for a transfer to this place, and waited, and waited. I was going to spend yet another birthday locked up, as I had spent many of them (plus Christmas and New Years), why not another. But to my utter, and I mean utter, surprise I was granted the transfer. I was transferred to Project DARE on August 19, 1975. Just in time to enjoy a birthday, I thought. It was over by November 5, 1975. While I was in White Oaks, I met a man named Bob Turner. Bob was the superintendent for White Oaks, he had known of me since the summer of '69, when my problems with Rob Cedar were happening. I never told anyone, not even him. He seemed the most level headed person (other than Lee Fellow) that I had ever met in my life (up to that point in time). To my surprise, Bob was also the superintendent for D.A.R.E.

Once there, I was given a whole new outfit (for the bush) and a set of runners. New runners, but nowhere to run, I thought. I was one of thirteen boys there to take the course. All of us hoped we could get through this, and go home. The course was divided into phases, each phase one month ahead of the others. The difference in each phase was obvious. Initially, we were told we would have to work as one unit, as this was the only way possible for us to work our way through it. After the general orientation, we all went to our prospective cabins and talked of how easy it was going to be.

Day one: At 5:00 a.m. we were all awakened, rather rudely, and told to put on our swim suits and to assemble in the main compound. Jogging!!! Fuck, I did not even get my morning smoke! The staff member who showed up for work was going to be with us throughout phase one and a new staff would take over for phases two and three. Stumbling off in the dark morning air, we jogged down the main country road. The staff would not tell us how far we were going, only that if anyone stopped for any reason, we would go further. All through out that day, we were told time and again that we had to work as a team, and every day there would be a new team leader. The team leader was the liaison between campers and staff. He would represent us and our concerns. This was a good thing; it gave each one of us a chance to assume some sort of responsibility.

At the end of day one, everyone's attitude had changed. That night we all ached, whining about how hard the first day was. Even though I was sore, I was happy-at least I did not have to think of selling myself for anything. This place taught me I was not going to have to be anything to anyone, only true to my self. I would have to work for whatever I wanted. I started to feel this way after a couple days, and it was a new, good feeling. I got the odd chance to talk to Bob Turner, and this made me feel like I was not alone. I waited for news from my family, and it was no surprise when my birthday card arrived late. It hurt not having some sort of "on time" re-lationship with my family, but I was to blame also. I did not communicate with them as often as I should have.

There were some tough rules that you had to follow at Project D.A.R.E. It was not a free for all of any sort. If you constantly fought, you were sent back to the ordinary system. If you stole, you were sent back. If you did not pull your weight you were sent back. If you broke your leg or arm you were sent back. If you ran you were sent back. Being sent back meant that you had failed, and that the courts would then decide what to do with you.

There was a constant fear of going back. Three months was not all that long, but the adverse conditions we had to endure, in order for us to succeed as a team, were very hard for some of the boys. Some ended up being sent back, as they could not cope with the pressures they had to face at Project D.A.R.E.

I soon moved into phase 2. One night, at the end of phase 1, we were sitting around, reflecting on the first month we had completed. We could see some of our accomplishments - for example, we had built one of the main flag poles everyone could see as they came into the main camp. I was quite impressed with the fact that I had helped build something everyone could see. We built a number of other things in the camp, such as paddle racks for all the canoes onsite.

This was one of the best times of my life. I knew I would never run from this place. I felt comfortable for the first time. I did not have that sense of being exploited for anything, as everyone was treated equally. There were no favorites amongst the staff and, even though I knew Bob Turner from a long time ago, I was not going to use this to my advantage, nor was Bob going to allow me to.

We were all taught about the outdoors, various bushes and the different types of vegetation and trees. The running! Running out in the bush was one of the best things that ever happened to me. Of course, in the beginning it was brutal. Running from the law was one thing, running because you wanted to, was another. You felt good being out there, doing it because you wanted to. It was going to get you closer to being back with your family in the long run.

Once a week, the camp would let us jog towards town. We would receive some money to buy some essentials, such as tobacco, toothpaste, magazines or a new book. We were not allowed to have any kind of pornographic material. This was a different form of "TUCK". There was no need to worry about any expectation of DEVIANT behavior, in return for receiving funds to get tobacco or whatever else. Things like this would cause me to reflect on the past. Previous to D.A.R.E., I would have to let someone have their way, in one way or another, in order for me to receive what I wanted. It started, with the landlord, then at White Oaks Village for Boys with Rob Cedar. People who would consistently touch you in any fashion they could get away with. At D.A.R.E. we had to work for what we wanted, there was no "feel me and I will give you more".

Like my previous placements, Project D.A.R.E. was financed by the government. The only two places I remember ever having any legitimate schooling were at St. Agatha's and Cecil Facer. What was taught at White Oaks Village was suited for children between the ages of 9 and 13. At Project D.A.R.E., we were being taught self reliance and teamwork.

Project D.A.R.E. was located near Algonquin Park, in northern Ontario, set in some of the most beautiful country in the province. In each new phase of Project D.A.R.E. we would eventually have to take a canoe trip, or a backpacking trip, through this country with the counselors. Thorough out the course of the trip, each of us were told to talk with the counselor about our experiences.

These trips (through the out - back, so to speak) would sometimes play heavily on my mind. I was just a kid that had grown up on the streets of downtown Toronto. It was difficult to really identify my feelings. I found it necessary to wander off, sit by myself and reflect upon the turmoil of my life, being sent from one institution to another, the lack of a strong family influence, my experiences with abuse, and so on. I was lost in a world that would eventually lead me on the path that no one should take.

Project D.A.R.E. was similar to an outward bound type program, very tough on anyone put through it. You had to work very hard at everything you did. In the third phase you were taught mountaineering, as well as mountain rescue. It was quite cool. I used to sit around the apartment stoned, watching these programs, and now here I was, doing them. I developed a new relationship with Bob. He knew me as a young child, from ages 9 through 13. He was unaware of anything happening in the basement of the cottages he'd supervised. To this day I'm not sure he realizes what happened.

The last three weeks of Project D.A.R.E. saw each of us completing what was called the ultimate survival course. Twelve kids in the same phases as I had to spend four days on an island, armed only with our wits and the skills we had been taught over the previous months. We were given one match for each day, one pot, one pouch of Bisquik, one packet of soup, our knifes, no smokes or books, a sleeping bag, a plastic sheet and the wilderness. Being out on this island for four days, I concluded that if I could survive on the streets, I could survive in the wilderness.

After the four days on the island, the phase I was in was called O.V.s. There was a cabin owned by Project D.A.R.E., quite a few kilometers from the main camp. One of the staff members, whose name was Tom, slipped off the edge of the trial down a very steep side of the mountain. By the time that we got to him, he was in very bad shape. The training we had received was crucial at that point. We administered as much first aid as possible, until the ambulance was within reasonable distance. It was much easier for us to get him to hospital by ambulance than by air.

We were commended for our efforts in getting Tom in the hands of medical personal. The excitement at graduation time was in the air. Each boy had a feeling that now was his time for the chance to earn praise and respect for three months of very hard work and commitment to fellowship. If there were any fights, or even an attempt at one, the staff would ensure each side was put into a position that encouraged them to talk it out, instead of fighting.

After three months of being out in the wilderness, eating and running hard, and learning about everything, we felt were capable of doing anything. The second to last day at Project D.A.R.E., the O.V.s had to run a marathon, 10 miles long. Participants were timed, in order to receive an award. I was running one mile in a time of five minutes and 26 seconds, one of the fastest times posted at camp. Running the ten mile marathon, I posted a time of one-hour and 29 minutes, not bad, though I felt I could have done better. Not everyone who ran in the marathon finished, but it did not matter, as most of us had already finished the three-month program.

That afternoon after the marathon everyone was given their graduation certificates as well as camp badges and award plaques. Twelve boys graduated. Some were allowed to go home, and some were sent back to group homes, as they had to wait for release from the system. We all had a big gathering at dinner to celebrate the O.V.s finishing phase 3. The boys in phase 1 as well as in phase 2 watched the ceremonies, with eager and frantic looks in their eyes, all of them knowing they would one day be sitting in the same dinner circle I was. It was over, finally, and we were on our way home, or to our next placement.

At Project D.A.R.E., each boy made a paddle, for our trips in Algonquin Park. I dated the paddle, and still have it at my mother's house. It was dated November 7th, 1975. I was so proud of myself, I was going to get home at long last.

The day of departure, everyone said their goodbyes to their new friends. I saved a special goodbye for Bob Turner. It would be a number of years before seeing Bob Turner again.

I was taken to the airport and flown back to Calgary, courtesy of the Canadian government. My family was at the airport to meet me, and the tears started flowing. We went back to my mother's apartment. It was great to see my brother George, who I had not seen since my mother turned us in and I was sent back to Ontario. First I thought about school, as well as looking for a job. It was not going to be easy either way. I'd grown up on the streets of major cities in Canada and the States.

It would be a challenge to be back with my family. I had been gone for so long. Life had, so far, given me very little opportunity to know the people who were supposed to be close to me. It was a feeling I had wanted, for so long, but had been denied me. I was a troubled young boy who didn't really know, or was aware of how a family unit operates. The memories that I had of my family life were short and distant.

Much of my childhood education was limited to elementary school. From the age of nine years, I had been placed in various institutions, where educational structure was aimed at kids much younger. I started to smoke pot, and drink at home, telling my mother I was not a little boy, I was in full control of how much I drank and smoked. I started to slip back into the drug culture, getting carried away, staying up late, drinking, and smoking dope, anything but school or work. It seemed like Project D.A.R.E. hadn't happened at all. I was now starting to get bored with my life at home, and began looking for other means of making money. I started to steal in order to get what I wanted, taking the easy way out.

I got a job at a car wash. It lasted two days. I took a brand new car and drove it into the loading area so that the pulley system could grab the tire. When it was time to exit the vehicle, I did, and it popped into drive and went crashing through the car wash. I was fired on the spot. The idea of going through the school system, like everyone else, just did not appeal to me. I had to have a setup that was hands-on, instead of paper and pencil. I was feeling worse and worse, and all I wanted to do was just leave and go back to Toronto. I tried many times to explain my problems, but I was always told that I needed to be in school or working. All I want to do was trip around; see people, places and things. Once again I was heading nowhere fast.

Something was missing. I didn't know what it was, but my feelings of loneliness and boredom were getting stronger. I started to wish for something like D.A.R.E., a challenge, a purpose, to fill the void inside. For me it was either one extreme or the other. I thought I was old enough to go about life without the guidance of a parental figure or that of a family setting, as I had done for years. I took care of myself, whether in one of the various institutions, or on the streets.

The family situation was getting very poor. We were all arguing over just about everything that came up in our lives. At one point I told my mother that I have my own life to live, and was not about to be told what to do. When my family was out for the evening one night, I got drunk and broke into my mother's safe. She was the manager for the apartment building where she was living. I took all the money, for that month's rent from the various tenants, and ran away to Vernon, B.C., where I hooked up with an old friend. This was just about Christmas time, and I didn't feel any remorse for breaking into my mom's safe, nor for going off the deep end again. I was in it for the excitement. I got together with this girl I used to know and tried to convince her to run away with me, but she would not leave her family.

When I got to town, I rented a room and contacted Susan. She and I got together and talked. Susan was one of my very first loves, and I wanted to be with her. No matter how hard I tried to convince her to leave with me, she would not, but we still hung out together for a couple of days in the hotel.

Eventually, some of my old friends showed up at my hotel, and we started to drink and smoke. One dude said he had a whole bunch of stolen calculators and computer equipment, and wanted to know if I could help him get rid of the stuff. I told him I wanted nothing to do with the stolen stuff, because I would lose the opportunity for the girl of my dreams. Susan did not want me to be involved in that shit anymore if I was to be with her.

I teamed up with this guy (whose nickname was Black-Jack) and his girlfriend, and went to the lodge hotel and got another room. I got a hold of Susan and tried once again to get her to leave town with me, Black-Jack, and his girlfriend. She would not go with me. She wanted to stay and get an education. I could not say anything different to her, because for the first time in my life I was in love. That night at the hotel we all partied and then there was a knock on the door. When I answered it, I almost had a fucking heart attack. The police where looking for Black-Jack. Apparently he was wanted in connection with a recent break - in. The police went through everything we had, and took Black-Jack away with them.

Black-Jack's girlfriend Chris, Susan and I were left in the hotel, and told to stay there, and that they would be in touch with us. As soon as the police said that, the girls and l felt that it was best for us to leave the hotel and go somewhere else. Susan decided she would go home, and said that I was to call her and let her know what was up. Chris and I went to the local hotel. We were sitting there drinking when suddenly, Black-Jack showed up. Chris was just ecstatic, and we all proceeded to get drunk. Later that evening Black-Jack and I broke into rooms above the bar and got Chris to bring some beer. It was just before Christmas, and I sat there and drank, watching Chris and Black-Jack screw around with each other. Chris had made arrangements with this chick that she knew to come over to the hotel and take care of me. She showed up and started drinking. Ann and I had sex. The next day she wanted to be with me, whatever I was doing. That day, Black-Jack and I broke into a garage, stealing whatever we could grab that was worth some fast money. We stole a car, and then the girls and Black-Jack and I decided that we would go to the States and see California.

I started to think of the time I had spent in the States before, and told Black-Jack, Chris and Ann the story of when I was there by myself. Later that night, we left town and headed for the U.S. border. Before I left town, I called Susan and told her I was leaving, and that I would be back for her soon. I did not have much money left from what I stole from my mother as I had spent it on booze and drugs. But the drugs were either hash or pot. We did not do any hard drugs, but drank an awful lot of beer. The car that we stole did not have a heater and that was probably why it was in the garage. While we were on the road, we cuddled underneath blankets and tried to stay as warm as possible. We got to a gas station, and Black-Jack told the guy to fill the car up, and that we need to have some smokes. Then he asked the guy if he could pay with tools or calculators. When I found this out I almost flipped out on him. That was the stupidest thing he could have done, and it got us busted about 40 miles from the gas station. It was very cold, and snowing, and as we drove along the highway we all talked of the sunny beaches in Southern California, and how nice it would be to be there. Then the lights, as the police were pulling up behind us. Black-Jack was driving and it took him a long time to stop. With the snow falling and police lights flashing it looked pretty cool, even for a colored blind person such as me. We got arrested for possession of a stolen automobile.

It was only one month since my release from Project D.A.R.E. and I found myself in front of the courts once again.

These are some written statements prepared by...

Mr. W. G. Heinrichs:
Probation Officer
Probation Services
Provincial Court of British Columbia
Kelowna, British Columbia.

> On December 24th, 1975 it was learned that Jeremiah was charged with break and enter and auto theft in British Columbia and would be held in custody until December 30th, 1975. At this point both the British Columbia and Alberta authorities indicated few alternatives for Jeremiah and Mrs. Douglas was reluctant to have him returned to her home. The charges in British Columbia were adjourned sine die, and Jeremiah was returned to Toronto on January 2nd 1976, and was placed in the Oakville Reception and Assessment Center.
>
> On January 9th, 1976, Jeremiah was transferred to a Ministry of Correctional Services group home in Sudbury, Ontario. On Feb. 2nd, 1976, he ran away and was apprehended on April 5th, 1976.

I had no say in where I was going to be placed, or what was happening at all. Being at this group home was quite different. They enrolled me in college, and I had not the foggiest idea of what to do. I was only 15 years old, and had never been close to a setting like this before. Now, here I was, sitting on the front steps of Cambrian College. Not knowing what the hell was going to happen, I gave it a shot. I went through a course that could determine one's educational level, and found out I had a level of grade nine. For someone who never went to school, this was quite the thing for me. No one had ever told me where I stood in school.

Life at this group home was quite lax. The kids that were there would drink and smoke and do drugs and act as if we were doing everything according to the house rules. We had ample freedom to do whatever we wanted, although we still had to maintain the proper image. That way, no one could send us back to a stricter environment. I tried as best I could for the first few weeks, but it was very hard for me to adjust to a school setting. I had not been in one for many years. I knew I was not suited for this. I could not get into a school system, too much time had passed for me to even cope with the pressures that came with school, let alone the people that made me feel out of sorts.

I started to skip school (I was getting bored with it), and started to do dope with the guys in the house. Soon one thing started to lead to another. We were given a small allowance if we maintained proper marks for the week, meaning chores around the house as well as attendance at school. Most of us got enough every Friday to get drunk, and buy some acid, or mushrooms, or whatever else we could use to get high. Once again, I was stagnating, getting caught up in drugs, so I ran away from the group home.

I left the second day in February, only to be caught weeks later and returned to Oakville Reception and Assessment Center. It was decided that I should be sent back to the group home, by Roberta Roberts (and whoever else she talked with). I just wish they would have at least let me be at those meetings, to see how everyone judged me.

I did not want to go back to this group home. Once again someone else was in control of my life, and I didn't like that one fucking bit, even though I knew I was at fault. I still could not stand the fact that the government had me in its hands (whose ever hands they were, were still dirty in my eyes and I could show no respect for that). On the way back to the group home, we were traveling through downtown Toronto. I saw an opportunity to run, so I did. I ran as fast as I could, to get away from the staff that were taking me back. I had no intentions of being placed in a group home again! It was back to the life of the streets.

I thought I would go and see Weasel and Gary, as well as Harold, to see if I could patch up some of the bullshit that was caused when I left with my brother George. Going back there meant I would be able to get the same drugs I had gotten used to before. The first thing I did was find Weasel. I told him I wanted to get high before I did anything or went anywhere. I was not immediately welcomed back into the house with Harold and Gary. Weasel managed to convince Harold that I needed a second chance. I got some drugs from Weasel and did my thing, for the first few days even prostituting myself for more money and drugs. Soon I tired of this shit. I could not go on turning tricks. I was much smarter than just being a prostitute/drug addict. I now wanted to *sell* drugs, and make as much money as I could, in order to never have to sell myself again. I never wanted to have to resort to that again. Drugs would pay my way. Weasel and I would go to The Manatee and sell from 500 to 1000 dollars worth of drugs in one night. Most of our money we would spend the next day on foolish shit. Cab rides all over instead of taking the bus and to buy clothing and more drugs. Our lifestyle had once again arrived at the point where we were stoned everyday. Even though I wanted to save money, it just never happened.

Even though I was not working as a prostitute, I still kept in touch with some of the bigger spenders. Every so often I would get a call from one of them. Shortly after I was back in my old lifestyle, I met a guy named Darcy. Darcy and I would trip around town, getting stoned and having sex in various public places. I introduced Darcy to Weasel, but Weasel did not like Darcy because he was dark skinned. Not black, just dark skinned, but I guess Weasel was not open to this sort of relationship. I had no problem. Darcy was a drug runner for some people and would be gone for weeks at a time.

One day, while I was sitting in the apartment with Harold, Weasel and Gary, I got this phone call from Florida. It was Darcy. He wanted me to bring him some acid. I asked how much, and he told me he wanted at least 500 hits of micro-dot acid. I was shocked that he would even say that over the phone, so I hung up in his ear. (We had a code word for acid, but at that point he did not use it). About five minutes later Darcy phoned back. I said "are you fucking crazy, saying that shit over the phone?" He apologized. He told me there would be a ticket waiting for me at the airport, and I was on the first available flight to Orlando. I had flown over the border once before (coming back from New Orleans), but I was still a bit nervous, thinking about taking that amount of acid over the border.

I went out and bought a cigar that came in a plastic cylinder. I removed and smoked the cigar and replaced it with acid. I taped the cylinder so it could be inserted it in my ass. I missed my flight, because at the customs booth I could not provide enough identification. So I went back downtown, got all the necessary documents, went back to the same Customs booth, and just smiled to the customs agent. There was no legal reason they could see or find to stop me from going. I thought I would be caught but it did not happen. I landed in Orlando safely, but damn I was one uncomfortable son of a bitch. Never before had I had that amount of drugs inside me, thinking, "what if this fucking thing was to break open?" I'd be dead. As I walked out of the airport Darcy was there to meet me. He asked if I brought the acid, not showing any concern for me, which pissed me off because it felt like I was just a mule.

Once we got to the hotel, the first thing I did was go straight to the washroom, retrieve and clean the cylinder, and give Darcy his drugs. For the next few days all we did in Florida was get stoned and rent dune-buggies. One day we decided we would go to Disney World and just trip around and do acid and drink champagne. We also rented a couple of the small boats you could rent by the hour. We must have had them for about four hours, because we popped a few hits of acid each and then the games began. Darcy was there with one of his other runners. I don't remember his name, but he was capable of grabbing us plane tickets to just about anywhere, free of charge. I watched him walk up to the airline counter, and somehow, he would just end up walking away with a handful of tickets. The last night at the hotel in Orlando, I watched Darcy and his friend make these tickets so that we could fly to New York, then to Montreal and back to Toronto. I was always scared that we would get busted, not just for the tickets, but for the drugs that we had with us as well.

We spent a couple days in New York. Darcy had to take care of some business there. It was nice to be in New York, and being able to see all the sites was great. I was 15 years old and had been running drugs and selling them in downtown Toronto for almost two years. I had a constant fear that I was going to get busted. I was always looking over my shoulder, never feeling secure. I guess this fear kept me going in this direction. It was great to be able to walk around, and spend money, and not have to worry about where it came from. Someone was always looking for drugs or sex. Anyone who entered these fields would never be broke, but could possibly be killed in the process.

The day of departure for Montreal we did some acid, and by the time we were in mid flight, we were all getting off on the acid. Darcy said he had a package of cocaine, and that we were going to do a line in the plane. Before long we were drinking and doing coke, we were stoned on acid flying to Montreal. I tell you, by the time we landed, it felt as though I rolled off the plane and that the ground was still moving. We went straight to the hotel and I had to chill out fast because I felt so stoned.

Darcy's work in Montreal was pretty simple. All he had to do was distribute some of the acid as well as some of the plane tickets to other runners. Two days later we were on a flight back to Toronto. I could not wait to be home, as I missed the club scene, as well as the people I hung with. Weasel was glad to see me back home, although he was a little perplexed that I had been gone longer than I said that I would be.

For the next few days all I did was lie around the apartment and recoup, because I had done a lot of drugs over the last week. Harold, Gary and Weasel all gave me shit, because I was doing too many drugs and not eating properly. Finally, after about four days I came back to life, although I was still going through sort of a drug withdrawal. All I did was eat, but before long I popped some more acid and was back in the game.

My relationship with Darcy was off and on, he was traveling so much that I got wrapped up in my life with Harold, Gary and Weasel. That meant nothing but sex, drugs, and rock and roll. I did not have anyone I could confide in. Most of the people in my circle were really superficial, dealing with drugs or sex and denying.

Soon, I started to get back into dealing drugs with Weasel and Gary in the club, and also at the St. Charles pub, a well-known gay bar in downtown Toronto. I was able to get you just about what ever you desired. I used to deal a lot of drugs out of this bar, and at the same time turn the odd trick. Things were not very good on the home front with Harold. He started getting possessive in the relationship, and I started to resent this. He even asked me if I wanted to be adopted by him.

CHAPTER SEVEN

SEVERE DEPRESSION

I was living in a world of prostitution and drugs, in downtown Toronto, still on the run from the law and always looking over my shoulder to see who was watching me. I was so messed up, I couldn't tell who was being real with me. I always wanted to be loved by someone, mostly my entire life, by my father. I would never hear my father say the words "I love you son." Then there was this guy named Harold, who wanted to have me as his son, not even considering the fact that we had performed many sex acts together. When I heard Harold say that to me, it fucked me up. I left the apartment and went for nice long walk, crying myself tearless.

I was 15 years old, and under a severe drug influence. One day, Weasel told me he was in Harold's will, and if anything was to happen to Harold, Weasel would get control of Harold's estate. The thought was enough to make me get into a fight with him. I felt betrayed and abandoned. Everyday, Weasel would taunt me with this. I wanted to do more drugs, so I would not have to think about what he was saying. He told me Gary was in on a dark idea, but he was scared and wanted me to be there as well.

It seemed like my whole little world was falling apart, fast, and I did not know what to do! So more drugs, drugs and more drugs. Still it seemed as if I could not escape where I was. On one hand I had Harold, who told me he wanted me to be his son, and at the same time have sex with him, while promising security. On the other hand, Weasel was trying to convince me and Gary to help him kill Harold. I'm not saying I did not know right from wrong. But being so fucked up on drugs and street life, something in my head started telling me I should consider what Weasel was saying. He kept talking, and talking, about what he would get if Harold was out of the picture.

One day, Weasel told me he would inherit 60 thousand dollars cash, plus all of his jewelry and personal property (Harold had been abandoned by his family for being gay). Gary and I went out for drinks one day, and he kept complaining about how Harold would pick on him, for being Weasel's lover. He told me he wanted revenge. To Gary and Weasel, the idea of committing murder was justifiable. Weasel would get a lot, and Gary and I would have a share in the profits somehow. How, I was never told.

We would go to club and party all night long doing drugs into the wee hours of the morning. Gary and Weasel were relentless, but I would not commit to helping kill Harold. One day Weasel came straight out and told me he was thinking of killing Harold in order to get what he wanted. I was frightened, and carrying the baggage of hatred for my real father. I wanted revenge on him for abandoning us, and abusing us.

One night in the club I did a bunch of window pane acid, and was really starting to hallucinate. I thought I saw Harry break this guys arm so bad, that the bone was sticking out. I tried explaining this to Weasel; he told me I was just hallucinating, and that I should go outside for some fresh air. Then I started thinking about air, so I turned around and breathed on the mirror, and did not see any fog, and started to freak. Weasel grabbed me and took me outside, and started to talk to me in order for me to come down somewhat. My world of drugs was beyond my control. Harold was not much of a drug addict, although he did more M.D.A. than I did. I always felt that Weasel would spike Harold's drink somehow, in order to kill him. Time and time again I was told how much Weasel would profit. I started to believe it. At one point in time Harold and Weasel got into a big argument over the amount of money Harold was putting out for M.D.A. That was all that he ever really wanted (other than sex,) but Weasel still complained.

I had stopped having sex with Harold sometime in May, because of all the drugs I was doing. I was just not receptive to Harold's approaches. This must have had a damaging effect, because we arguing constantly. Gary and I would do anywhere between two hits to 10 hits of acid every day. Sometimes, it felt like we did not do any drugs at all, we had built up such a tolerance. It was not easy to get stoned anymore.

69

Well, I was out partying with Gary, and he would complain that Harold would belittle him as much as possible, when Weasel or I were not around. He told me how frustrated and angry this made him, and how he wanted to get even with Harold for all the times Harold had hurt him. Gary was relentless, constantly saying these things. I finally told Gary that Harold had asked me to be his son, and still have sex with him and that no one would know. Gary said the only way to get rid of those feelings would be to help him kill Harold. Weasel kept telling me we would not have to worry about money, once Harold was gone. They kept pressuring me to help them, but still I refused.

I was caught up in my own turmoil, and listening to them was not making my life any better. I was so drugged and mentally confused that eventually, I caved into the idea that somehow we would get rid of Harold. I now wanted to be involved in this. Weasel and Gary started contemplating ways of killing Harold. At first they wanted to kill him in the apartment, but I pointed out how ridiculous that idea was. Most of their plans were stupid, and after a while, I told them to forget it. It seemed impossible to get away with killing Harold.

I told them both I had a hard time dealing with this, because I had anger for more than just him. I had it for everyone who had ever touched me as a child. I felt an enormous amount of hatred for my father, because he had left and fucked up my family and my life. They kept saying I needed time to think about it. I told then both that it was not a matter of time, it was a matter of emotions and I could not deal with my emotions at that time, and that they should leave me alone for awhile.

Just thinking about killing somebody was hard enough for me to deal with, let alone my drug problem, alcohol, sex, violence, robbery and everything else. One day I found myself thinking that I had nothing to lose. I started talking with Harold about moving to Vancouver, B. C. At first it was just to go for a vacation. Soon living there became a topic, and we talked of whether or not we could handle such a trip. Harold said that if we were to move to Vancouver, we would have to sell all the stuff that we had in the apartment, to make a brand new start.

The more Weasel and Gary pushed me, the more I would push Harold. It did not take too long for Harold to think the move was a good idea, because I started to have sex with him again, and he was happy go-lucky all over again. Never once did I think that Harold knew what was going on. Weasel and Harold went back quite a few years. Weasel would do his best to convince Harold that it was for the best, because we could make better money out there.

Harold was one of Toronto's leading chefs. He had quite an extensive resume, and felt he would be able to open his own restaurant where we would all work. This became the main focus of our journey to Vancouver. By now it was late May, and Harold felt that he could have a restaurant operational within three months of getting there. He proceeded to put ads, for a complete apartment sale, in the papers. Most of the stuff went in one sale, and the rest was sold off slowly. Everyone was getting excited because we were finally going to leave Toronto and see the ocean and Vancouver. By June we were on the road heading west.

We were four drug addicts traveling across the country constantly stoned. Things were getting really weird. Weasel and Gary both seemed different from the time that we had sold all the stuff in the apartment, as well as when we went to the dealer's place to grab the dope that we would need to last us till we got to Vancouver. I could not put my finger on what was going on with them. As we started out the mood was quite good but I could still sense that Weasel was up to something.

All this time I was living in Toronto and doing drugs and prostituting myself, I had kept in touch with my family. I had found out they were living in Calgary and that everybody was okay. That's all that I would ask when I called. I had called and talked to my brother and told him of our trip to Vancouver. George's trip to Toronto the previous year had not gone forgotten by Harold. Along the way out West, I contacted my brother and told him that we would be in Calgary in about five days. Harold did not want to drive straight to the coast, and wanted to stop along the way and see Canada. By the time we got to Winnipeg, we were all pretty well drug crazed. We stayed in Winnipeg for two days and then headed for Calgary.

Somewhere along the way Weasel and Gary started talking about Harold and his will again. Whenever Harold was not around us, they would talk about the money factor, and how much money Harold had on him. When we popped more acid or snorted more cocaine or MDA, they would always bring up the subject of how to get rid of Harold.

By the time we got to Calgary we were running out of drugs. I told them that I could phone my brother and that he would be able to hook us up with more as soon as we got to town. I met with George downtown, and he showed me where to go in order for me to find the drugs that we wanted. Along the way I got talking with George, and told him we were planning on moving to Vancouver, and that Weasel and Gary had continually talked to me about killing Harold. George did not seem affected by this, saying he wanted to come along with us, not even knowing what the final outcome would be. I told George I wouldn't mind if he came along but I did not exactly know what was going to happen. So, later that day, George showed up at the hotel with his duffel bag (loaded with his gear), as well as his rifle.

Just as we were all getting ready to load up the car in the parking lot, George was waiting there for us. When we did show up, he walked straight over to the car and put his bag in the trunk. Harold was yelling about the fact that George showed up. He was still angry over the fact that nothing ever happened with regards to the coins that George and I had stolen in order for us to get back home. With all the yelling and screaming that was going on, Weasel was doing his best to calm Harold down. George meant that Harold would not be able to succeed in his plan to adopt me.

Weasel was glad that George was coming along with us. Gary was also glad that George was there. He had developed a relationship with George on a brotherly level, because George was not into the gay scene, and to my knowledge, had never had sex with a man. Once we got in motion, Harold started to calm down, and Weasel and Gary both seemed to take the pressure off. I had managed to score a bunch of opium tin foil plates, about a quarter inch in diameter. All we had to do was drop one little plate into a cigarette lighter, and inhale the fumes. We would get really fucked up. I had also managed to get some acid and marijuana on the streets of Calgary. We rolled on, without a care in the world.

We stopped in a small town, went to a Home Hardware store, and bought all kinds of camping gear, and two 22 caliber rifles. We had convinced Harold we should camp at some of the better campsites along the way, rather than staying in hotels, so we could save money for our place in Vancouver. Weasel was most cunning with Harold. Because of the number of years they had known each other, it seemed like Harold was willing to do whatever Weasel suggested.

As we got near Vernon, B. C., I had memories of when I was raped by this guy that lived in a commune with a bunch of people near Mable Lake, not far from the town of Lumby, B. C. We drove around for what seemed like hours and hours for a good place to camp. As we were driving towards the lake, I noticed a nice young doe. I stopped the car so we could take a shot at it. My brother George took seven shots, but it did not go down. I started thinking all those shots would attract attention, so I took the gun from George, put the car in park, and took one shot, killing the young doe. Gary, Weasel, George and I ran over to the carcass. It was still moving and, being stoned as I was, I did not want to have to clean the animal. So George and Gary did, while Harold, Weasel and I sat in the car. They brought the doe over to the car and we put it in the trunk and continued to look for a campsite.

Once we found a campsite, we pitched our tents and proceeded to make dinner while George and Gary cleaned the doe. I watched as my brother and Gary cleaned this animal to the point where it was dead meat. That night we all sat around a campfire and talked, drank and did opium, coke, acid and marijuana. At around 10:30, Gary grabbed his new 22 rifle and handed me the other one. George and I agreed to go along with Gary while Weasel and Harold cleaned up the camp. Gary and I took a bottle of booze with us so that we could continue to party and hunt at the same time.

While we were walking down a country road, Gary kept pointing his gun at whatever moved and would shoot at whatever he felt like. We were still getting drunk as well as completely fucked up on drugs. Gary started talking to my brother about killing Harold. George would not commit either way. I could tell, by the way George spoke to Gary, he wasn't going to be a part of this. I was kind of staggering behind them while they talked. I could not hear all of the conversation, but could feel and see in Gary's eyes this crazy look. The whole thing was making me feel ill.

By the time we got back to camp, Weasel and Harold were in bed. Gary, George and I stood around the campfire, continuing to drink booze and smoke opium using hot knives we had stolen from a restaurant. Gary stood facing Harold's tent. He grabbed a gun and handed it to me, and then he grabbed the other gun and, with this crazed look in his eyes, said "lets do it now." He proceeded to shoot as many times as he could into Harold's tent. I started firing at the same time. I didn't even realize I was firing my gun. Harold was in the tent screaming.

Gary just pointed his rifle at me and my brother and told us to keep shooting. My gun jammed, I could not fire it anymore. My brother took one shot from his rifle, and suddenly there was quiet.

I was in a state of shock, knowing what I had just done was wrong, but feeling strangely good at the same time. I didn't know what to do. Gary was running around in circles, screaming that he finally got his vengeance. Weasel went into Harold's tent and removed all of his valuables. When he emerged from the tent he had blood all over his hands. Weasel was the only one trying to keep everybody intact, so nobody would go over the deep end. Weasel decided we would roll Harold up in his tent and put his body over the side of the mountain. We did it. Weasel felt it would be best to pack up camp, leaving nothing behind.

Weasel took control of the situation, instructing us to do as he said. Once we had cleaned up the entire camp, Weasel told us to get in the vehicle and drive. I was the driver, but I was shaking so hard I had to stop. When I did, Weasel got out and buried all of the documents showing proof of any involvement with Harold.

George and I were very frightened. George was obviously in a state of shock. Weasel suggested we get rid of the car, as well as the guns, and fly to Vancouver. Along the way to the airport in Kelowna, B. C., I stopped the car a couple of times so Weasel could dispose of the guns and anything else linking us to the murder. I was hallucinating severely. I thought I had blood on my shirt and hands. Years later, I was to find out it was no hallucination.

Once we got to Vancouver we looked for a place to stay. It was not easy to find a place for four people in Vancouver on short notice, so we decided to look for a cheap hotel in the Gas town district of downtown Vancouver. We were running out of money. Weasel held what he had taken from Harold. We found a place just between Gas town and Chinatown, with two separate rooms. We tried to go about life as if nothing had happened. For two or three days, I was walking around in a state of delusion. I was two months away from turning 16 years old, and the whole world felt like it was coming down. I didn't know who to believe in or trust. Weasel and Gary were acting like different people.

I was thinking all this time about my dad, and how I felt vindicated killing Harold as a substitute for my father, and no longer had the feeling of knowing my father was alive. All the anger and pain that I held, from years of abuse at the hands of older men, seemed to ease.

The four of us had to get some kind of plan together. Weasel suggested we go over the border (to the states) for awhile, to let the heat cool down. We were trying to cross on a Greyhound bus, but we were all turned back for lack of proper identification. We met with some people who offered to let us party with them in their hotel room. We had some dope and they had some booze. So we went to their room and partied with them.

Sometime in the course of the evening, while sitting on the window ledge, I accidentally knocked a bottle out the window. It almost hit this old man, and this fucked me up even more. The gravity of committing murder struck me. I was all shaky and feeling weird, knowing that by accident, the bottle could have killed that old man.

The next day, as we walked back down towards Granville Square, my brother said "There's our father." I looked him straight in the eye and said "don't fuck around with me". He actually said to me that our father was walking just in front of us. I got him to point out just who he was referring to. I walked up to this man and tapped him on the shoulder, asking him if he was Mr. Douglas. He turned around, looked at me, and shot "Who are you, the oldest or the youngest?" I lost it! I started to cry, feeling completely devastated. This man grabbed me, and hugged me. He asked George and me to come with him to his room, where we could drink and talk.

It was certainly a surreal moment. After all that had recently happened, running into my father seemed almost too much to bear. That night, as we sat around and drank, my father told me he had recently narrowly escaped being hit by a beer bottle dropped from a window above. When he said that, I lost control and started crying. George succeeded in calming me down. We eventually told him I was fucked up because it was I who had knocked the bottle off the window. We kept the murder to ourselves.

For the next couple of days, my father, George and I would eat in one of his favorite restaurants. My father did not get to meet Weasel or Gary. The next day, when Weasel and Gary did not show up in the designated spot we had chosen, George and I started to get very worried. We sat and waited for them to show, to no avail. I was sitting beside George on the bench after having breakfast with my father. Suddenly we were surrounded by cops, in uniform and plainclothes. All of them had their weapons drawn, pointing at both of us. We were hustled to the ground, as you so often see, violently, in front of a big crowd of people, and then ushered away to waiting police vehicles.

I was not going to see my brother again for a very long time. Being as young as I was, it was difficult for the police to place me in a facility suitable for the case scenario. Instead, I was held in a cell, by myself, in North Vancouver, until they could determine what to do. The next day I was asked what we did with our stuff, and where we stayed, so that they could go and retrieve our belongings for evidence. I asked if I could see my brother, but was denied, because my brother was being held at a different facility.

I told the police I had found my father, for the first time in many, many years, and that I had been seeing him for the past couple of days. I asked if they would get in touch with him for me, in order that I may see him.

The police informed me they had spoken to my father, and had later gone back to meet him. The clerk at the front desk told them Mr. Douglas had checked out when he found out his sons were charged with murder. Apparently he had left for some place near Jasper, Alberta. Having heard this, I was crushed once again. I thought maybe he would be able to deal with this situation and come and see me. I really didn't know what the fuck to think. I was so screwed up having to deal with all of this by myself in jail.

My mother was contacted by the police. She was informed that George and I would be transferred to Kelowna, B. C. to stand trial, and that if she wanted to see her sons, she would have to travel from Calgary to Kelowna. I thought, that stupid fucking ass hole of a father ran, like he probably never ran before, and my mother ran to us completely distraught over all these events.

Once my brother and I were transferred, in shackles and hand cuffs, back to Kelowna, we were again with Weasel and Gary. Apparently, because of collaboration, or whatever, they separated us, placing me into the juvenile section, or whatever they called it. Gary had been the first one arrested. He had left a prescription label at the murder scene. Gary led the police to Weasel. Weasel and Gary led the police to George and me. Now George, Gary and I were charged with non-capital murder and Weasel was charged with accessory after the fact. I remember to this day what one of the police officers said to me. "You're a lucky little fucker." The death penalty had been abolished just two months previous to our crime.

My sister was told about what had happened on the day of her wedding in Calgary. She was completely distraught, and told our mother she no longer wanted anything to do with me. When my mother showed up to visit me, I understood how devastated she was to hear that two of her children were charged with murder. It took all the strength that was left in me to walk to the visitor's area and see my mother sitting behind this piece of glass. We each had a phone to use in order to converse.

When I saw her sitting there, crying, I was completely fucked up. I did not want her to know all of the details of the crime other than the basic facts. We talked briefly. I cried and she cried and all I could do to console her was to tell her how sorry I was, that I put her through this. With that, I went back to my cell. I knew that I had done severe damage to our relation-ship, what little of one there was. I hardly knew this person who was my mother. I had been in so many institutions and group homes from the start that I knew everybody else in my world but my own family.

Finally, they put my brother and me together, in a small cell in Kelowna City jail. Instead of having to transfer us back and forth between Vancou-ver, where my brother would stay in Matsqui jail and I would stay at the Burnaby Detention center for juveniles, it was felt I would be better off in that setting.

The following are excerpts from the court records:

BRITISH COLUMBIA CORRECTIONS SERVICE
DEPARTMENT OF THE ATTORNEY GENERAL
SOCIAL HISTORY
FOR
PROVINCIAL COURT OF B. C.
FAMILY DIVISION (KELOWNA)
ON
JEREMIAH DOUGLAS
NO FIXED ADDRESS. AGE: 15 YEARS
BIRTH DATE: AUGUST 21, 1961
ON JUNE 23, 1976 APPEARED IN KELOWNA PROVINCIAL COURT, FAMILY DIVISION CHARGED WITH DELINQUENCY, TO WIT NON-CAPITAL MURDER.
REMANDED IN CUSTODY FOR HEARING JULY 9, 1976 AT 10:30 A. M.
DOUGLAS, JEREMIAH
JUVENILE HISTORY:
FEBRUARY 12, 1970 - JEREMIAH WAS MADE A WARD IN ONTARIO AT AGE 9.
1970 - 1973, RESIDENT AT WHITE OAKS VILLAGE, HAGERSVILLE, ONTARIO AND AT GLENDALE TRAINING SCHOOL (A SECURE FACILITY)
JUNE 13, 1973 - VERNON FAMILY COURT DIVISION:
JEREMIAH APPEARED THIS DATE CHARGED WITH BEING UNMANAGEABLE AND BEYOND THE CONTROL OF HIS MOTHER.
APRIL 20, 1974 - VERNON-THEFT AUTO
APRIL 29, 1974 - ROGERS PASS: THEFT AUTO AND THEFT UNDER $200.00

MAY 7, 1974 - PLACED UNDER SUPERVISION OF GARTH, CHILD
CARE WORKER, VERNON, B.C.

MAY 20, 1974 - PLACED AT CAMP KOPJE AT WINFIELD, B.C.

MAY 21, 1974 - THEFT OF MONEY FROM CAMP OFFICE; WENT
AWOL (ABSENT WITHOUT LEAVE)
APPREHENDED IN VERNON AND BROUGHT BACK TO CAMP.

MAY 24, 1974 - AWOL: APPREHENDED IN WHITE RIVER,
ONTARIO.

JUNE 27, 1974 - APPEARED IN VERNON FAMILY DIVISION COURT
BEFORE THE LOCAL JUDGE; SUSPENDED FINAL DISPOSITION
ON THE CHARGES OF THEFT AUTO, (2 COUNTS) AND THEFT
UNDER $200.

AUGUST 19, 1974 -

NOVEMBER 5, 1975 - AT PROJECT DARE, AN OUTWARD BOUND
TYPE PROGRAM IN ONTARIO.

DECEMBER 23, 1975 - VERNON PROVINCIAL COURT, FAMILY
DIVISION: BREAK, ENTER & THEFT: THE LOCAL JUDGE
INDEFINITELY ADJOURNED THE MATTER WITH THE
UNDERSTANDING THAT JEREMIAH WOULD BE RETURNED
ONTARIO.

EARLY 1976 - GROUP HOME PLACEMENT IN SUDBURY, ONTARIO.

SPRING 1976-AWOL

COMMENTS:

Mrs. Douglas, the subject's mother, states that Jeremiah was
unmanageable at the age of nine and that he was placed in care
in Ontario at that age. As far as can be ascertained truancy from
school and running away from home were the prime problems at
that time.

Mrs. Sampler, a social worker in Ontario who is familiar with
Jeremiah, states that Jeremiah has been in three training schools
in that province. He was initially placed in White Oaks Village for
Boys, as a youngster and then progressed to Glendale Training
School, a secure facility, from which he graduated.

Ontario authorities released Jeremiah to his mother in B. C.
in March, 1973. However, on June 17, 1974 he was committed
to another Ontario Resource, Cecil Facer School, following his
runaway from Camp Kopje and subsequent offences in B. C.

Jeremiah also attended Project Dare, an outward bound type
program in Ontario, from August 19, 1975 to November 5, 1975
at which time he graduated to his mother's home in Calgary,
Alberta. This was followed by further offences and eventually

apprehension and return to Ontario where he was in a group home. It is this writers understanding that Jeremiah was AWOL from the group home at the time of his arrest.

In examining his record in B. C. it is at once apparent that Jeremiah was never placed in a secure facility and it is clear that the dispositions made were largely ineffective. Ontario authorities on the other hand provided four successive secure type facilities from which Jeremiah graduated in succession, and yet the record demonstrates that these programs had little or no effect in changing Jeremiah's long term behavior.

Mr. Hunter, a duty worker for the Department of Health and Social Improvement in Alberta made the following comment on May 4, 1974:

"The above named thirteen year old was the most hostile, defensive young man on initial contact that the undersigned worker has ever worked with. On arrival at the Crisis Center his attitude was one of hatred. He wandered into every office, opened every desk drawer..."

An evaluation signed by Mr. Guerney, Chairman of Cecil Facer School as follows:

"Since Jeremiah's arrival at C. F. S. we have not had a chance to get to know him or trust him. He has run away a number of times using the excuse that he hasn't received a reply about his possible transfer to B. C. After each time he runs he always promises that he won't run again.

Jeremiah displays a polite and pleasant attitude around staff, but shows different colors behind their backs. He is very sneaky and criticizes all the staff when they are not on duty. He spends a great deal of time trying to impress the staff, but we feel that this is an obvious put-on for show.

Jeremiah is very lazy and has to be reminded to carry out his cottage duties.
We feel that Jeremiah requires more counseling and close supervision until we get to know him better."

DOUGLAS, JEREMIAH
PERSONAL HISTORY:

Jeremiah states that he has grade 10 standing in Ontario, although his mother advises that he did not complete grade 7 in Lavington where the family lived in the Vernon area. She states that in grade 2 nothing held young Jeremiah's interest and thinking that he was retarded she had him tested. It was discovered that Jeremiah possessed superior ability and that he was acting out partly because school was not challenging enough.

When queried regarding employment Jeremiah states that he modeled in Toronto for six months, however, he would not disclose the nature of his work there. He did admit to having been approached to model for pornographic films and books.

Jeremiah also states that he worked at a taco stand in Los Angels while AWOL in 1974.

Financially the subject has no assets and has lived largely by panhandling while AWOL.

Jeremiah appears to enjoy good health generally. Mrs. Douglas informs the writer that Jeremiah is totally color blind and this limits his ability to participate in certain occupations.

Regarding the use of alcohol and drugs, Jeremiah drinks mostly beer but tends more to drugs than alcohol. Jeremiah claims that he has used virtually all drugs with the exception of heroin since 1974.

SOCIAL HISTORY:

As far as can be determined, Jeremiah was living in Toronto on his own and with Harold, the deceased, since early spring, after being AWOL from a group home in Ontario. Jeremiah states that he lived with Harold intermittently for approximately two and a half years in what he states was a homosexual relationship.

Jeremiah is presently a ward of Ontario having been reinstated upon his return to that province this year. Ontario authorities are taking an active interest in these proceedings and are prepared to provide facilities if requested to do so.

The subject is the youngest of three children born to Mr. & Mrs. Douglas. An older brother George, age 19, who lived with his mother in Calgary and who was employed as a mechanic is similarly charged and is presently appearing in court.

A sister Pat, age 17, was married Friday, June 18 just before Mrs. Douglas learned of Jeremiah's arrest.
Mr. Douglas, age 51, was born in Scotland and worked as a truck driver in Toronto at the time of Jeremiah was born. He left the family home in 1961 when Jeremiah was an infant. According to Mrs. Douglas, he was caught propositioning her two small sisters. She states that charges resulted and the couple divorced in 1971. There has been no contact between Mr. & Mrs. Douglas since approximately 1968 or 1969.

Mrs. Douglas has followed Jeremiah's progress since he was first made a ward and has had custody of him from time to time. She describes Jeremiah as an extremely independent unmanageable child who does not have a great capacity for feelings.

She wanted this writer to relate to the court that in her opinion Jeremiah must be kept in a secure facility and when asked directly stated that she was afraid of her son. She stated to Mr. Waddell and to this officer that her son should be dealt with in adult court.

COMMENTS:

Jeremiah presents the picture of a young man who has grown up without a fathers guidance and for reasons unknown was unmanageable as a child. He has consistently demonstrated his desire to be free of any guidelines and has used whatever means were available to obtain his freedom.

This writer found Jeremiah to possess a very good memory. To be adept at the art of answering questions and found Jeremiah to demonstrate little or no concern in the course of discussing his life events. Jeremiah recognizes that he has led a free-wheeling and undisciplined lifestyle and commented that he never thought it would lead to this, meaning his present predicament. He did state that he loved his mother and was sorry to see her go through this trying time.

EVALUATION:

The record demonstrates that Jeremiah is unlikely to remain in any open facility for very long. His associations, his travels and his antisocial nature indicate a level of sophistication far beyond that of the average young man his age.

At the same time his young age , his slight build and his homosexual experiences make him vulnerable. Jeremiah will be sixteen in August 1976. At present he is a ward in Ontario and will remain so until the age of 18. It is the Ontario authorities who appear to be most familiar with Jeremiah and they are expressing an active interest in these proceedings.

Writer:
Mr. W. G. Heinrichs
Probations Officer
Kelowna, B. C.
DATED JULY 18, 1976

CHAPTER EIGHT

EMOTIONAL EXPLOSION

While I sat in the cell I knew so well, I thought to myself, I should be placed in adult court, rather than being tried as a juvenile. I felt that I should be because of all facts in the case. I told my lawyer that I wanted to be tried as an adult, because I wanted to be able to do any time that I was sentenced to with my brother. This whole situation that I found myself in, kind of brought my brother and me closer together than we had ever been. I was sitting in my cell one day, and the guard came walking down the hallway towards my cell. I could tell that he had news of the events of my brothers trial, and I could tell that it was not good news, because he would not look me in the eyes, "Jeremiah, sorry but what I have to say to you is not good news."

I sat there waiting for him to tell me with the utmost apprehension. I could not believe my ears, because what he had said was like getting punched in the head, and losing all control. The guard told me that my brother had been sentenced to seven years in prison. Gary was sentenced to seven years as well. Weasel was sentenced to 18 months in prison, for his part of being an accessory after the fact. I started crying endlessly, because I knew I would not see my brother for quite sometime. It was also felt that I should remain in juvenile court, and not be processed into adult court. I do believe that it was the Ontario government that was the main reason for me not being transferred into the adult court system.

I was extremely hateful toward the system for not transferring me, and

I did not even have an opportunity to say goodbye to either my brother, Weasel or Gary (although they were not my main concern at the time). I wanted to see my brother. I knew one thing for sure-I completely fucked up my brother's life. I felt terrible because he had a lot going for him in Calgary. I was transferred back to the Burnaby Detention Center until my sentencing day. One day at the detention center there was a slight riot. I thought to myself, if there was enough noise and confusion, I would be able to escape. There was a young fellow in the cell beside me, and he was bound and determined to break open his cell door. At the same time he would kick on his cell door, I would do the same to mine. After about 2 ½ hours of this riot going on at the detention center, my door finally gave way and popped open. For the first couple minutes I stood there in a state of shock, thinking, I made it.

There was a courtyard in each unit, and each unit housed anywhere from 8 to 10 kids or more in certain units. There was only one door leading into the courtyard, and the rest of the walls were made with 10 by 10 block glass windows. I tried to break open the door leading into the courtyard. It would have been a simple fact of just jumping on the roof and running for cover. I could not break open that fucking door for the life of me. So, I figured I would smash one of the windows and crawl through. There was another young fellow in my cell at the time. I broke open the door, and he pointed out to me that there was a mop and bucket just outside the door. I used the bucket to smash one of the windows. The young fellow in the same cell crawled into the window first, and got stuck at the hips trying to squeeze through. I had to push him through like a plunger. Once through this guy tried to pull me through, but I also got stuck at the hips. Realizing I would not be able to get out, I told this young guy to take off. I ended up waiting for one of the guards to find me in this predicament. Once the guards found me, it just seemed so funny at the time; half of me was in the courtyard, and half in the hallway. The guard and me both started to laugh: how often does one get stuck in a window?

I was later charged with damage to government property and attempted escape and mischief. My court case was to come up at the Burnaby juvenile court in October of 1976. I never did find out what happened to those charges, because I was sent back to Kelowna for sentencing.

The following are more excerpts from the court documents:

JEREMIAH DOUGLAS (DOUGLAS GAULD)

IN THE PROVINCIAL COURT OF BRITISH COLUMBIA, AT KELOWNA
REGINA
VS
JEREMIAH DOUGLAS, a juvenile

DECISION

This is an application brought under the provision of section 9 of the juvenile delinquency act of Canada, were-in the crown seeks an order directing that the above juvenile, who is 15 years of age, be proceeded against by indictment, in the ordinary courts, in accordance with the provisions of the criminal code of Canada. The alleged delinquency involves a charge of on non-capital murder. Three adults, who are alleged to have being companions of the juvenile, are charged with the same offense. Their preliminary inquiry is scheduled for later this month.

At the initial hearing on July 9th, I heard an outline of the circumstances of the alleged offense as supplied by the Royal Canadian Mountain Police in charge of the investigation. I will refer to his testimony in a moment. I also heard the testimony of Mr. Walter Heinrichs, a Probation Officer employed by the Community Corrections Branch of the Department of the Attorney General, I then adjourned the hearing to July 17, so that a psychiatric assessment might be obtained, and the psychiatrist might be available for examination as resumption of the hearing. At the resumed hearing, I also heard testimony of Mr. Turner, a Social Worker employed by the Department of Human Resources.

Before I referred to the positions which Crown Council and defense counsel and have adopted with respect to this application, I propose too briefly reviewed the circumstances of the alleged delinquency. The deceased, who was 56 years of age, had been the homosexual mentor of the juvenile for a period of approximately two years. During his interview with the psychiatrists the juvenile indicated that he did not feel particularly "used" by the deceased. On the contrary, the juvenile considered that he obtained some measure of economic security from the relationship.

The juvenile and the deceased were also friendly with Gary, who is 18 years of age, and one Weasel who is 33 years of age. Gary and Weasel were involved in a long-standing homosexual relationship.

On or about June 4th, after the juvenile and the defendant's

84

Gary and Weasel had convinced the deceased that a trip to the Province of British Columbia would be interesting, the four set out from Toronto in the deceased motor vehicle. To deceased had been persuaded to withdraw 5000 dollars from his bank account, and he was obviously financing this expedition.

Mr. Turner (the Social Worker who appeared as the juveniles guardian with respect to these proceedings) recommended that the juvenile not be transferred to the ordinary courts, but be returned to Province of Ontario, for placement at Hillcrest school. The Superintendent of Child Welfare of this province is prepared to assist in having the juvenile escorted to the Province of Ontario. This position is supported by the closing recommendations of Mrs. Roberts, of the Oakville Reception and Assessment Center, who states," our experience would indicate that Jeremiah needs a structured and predictable environment with psychiatric intervention in a small group setting"

In the absence of an appropriate juvenile resource, I might be compelled to take the position that society will simply have to take a chance, hoping this juvenile will not ultimately emerge from a lengthy period of penitentiary incarceration in a condition which would represent a greater threat to society than the condition which we hope can be achieved through a more appropriate placement. Accordingly, I believe the offer of the Ontario Ministry of Correctional Services must be accepted, and the trial of the juvenile proceeds under the provisions of the Juvenile Delinquents Act. In the event that he is adjudged to be a delinquent, and any disposition order under the Juvenile Delinquency Act does not proved to be effective, he can, of course, be returned to this court to be further dealt with under the provisions of the act (including Sec. 9.).

Dated at the City of Kelowna, B.C., this 16th day of August, 1976.
Signed by:
Judge R. D. Collver
A judge for the Provincial Court of British Columbia: Family Division.
Note: I also asked the court for the death penalty as I had lost all hope. I was told it would be considered. But after my repeated attempts for the death penalty, I was told I was the last person to even be considered, because it (the death penalty) had been abolished on June 1st, 1976 or close to that date. I was the last person to ask for it but I was refused.

I was so nervous, and scared, I could not look at anyone in the court room. My mother was sitting behind me while Judge Collver read his decision to the court. When I did look, I could see how badly this ordeal had taken its toll on my mother. I started crying, as I felt pretty bad for what I had done, and could not see any light at the end of the tunnel. How would she live, knowing her little boy had done such a bad thing?

I was so mixed up; I did not even hear the judge when he handed down his verdict. I was sitting in my chair looking at him but nothing was registering. Finally my lawyer, Tony, told me that I would be transferred back to Ontario, to an institution called Hillcrest School for Boys. I sat there in the court room and did not say anything. I did not want to see my mother but she was allowed back for one last visit before I was shipped out to Ontario. My mother told me I had to grow up, and be responsible, and not be so selfish.

The following is a typed copy of a letter addressed to my mother from the Ministry of Correctional Services dated December 10, 1976.

Dear Mrs. Douglas.

In reply to your letter dated November 29th, 1976 inquiring about your son, Jeremiah. Your son was transferred to this school on November 22nd, 1976 and to this point in time he has been cooperative and willing to participate in all aspects of the program. This school is a maximum security school, and the students go to academic and vocational school the same as they do in the community. In the evenings there is a full program of sports in our gymnasium or out in the play area, to keep the students gainfully occupied and to teach them to socialize in an acceptable manner.

In regards to activity outside the school, the students would have to be here a minimum of three months before they would be allowed to participate in any of these activities in the community, an even at that time the students are carefully screened.

Yours truly,
Deputy Superintendent
Hillcrest School

When I got to Hillcrest School, I was immediately placed in the most secure part of the facility. I was allowed to go to various academic classes and workshops. I was still caught up in the delusion that I was sure somehow I would be able to escape, and go back down to the drug world in Toronto. While I was in jail in British Columbia, they allowed me to have Valium, and I started to get dependent on this, but Hillcrest would not allow me to have any. I was having a hard time coping with anything that was happening around me, and asked for as much counseling as possible, not knowing that my asking for help was going to lead me to a nervous breakdown.

I was getting along with most of the other boys in this facility. I had one major encounter with another boy that was to put me on the serious watch list. During one sports event, in the gymnasium, this kid cross checked me in the throat. I took my hockey stick and broke it across his head, thus leading me to solitary confinement. I do not remember exactly how many times I talked with the counselors at Hillcrest. Even though I attended session after session, I did not feel good about myself or Hillcrest School. I was transferred, once again, to a facility that the counselors at Hillcrest felt would benefit me.

The following is another typed copy of a letter dated January 27, 1977 addressed to Mrs. Douglas from the Ministry of Health.

> In regards to Jeremiah Douglas;
> The above named man was admitted to the hospital on December 20, 1976. It would assist us in caring for this patient if we could have some information about his background and past experiences.
> It would be most helpful if you could visit the hospital in the near future (between 9 a.m. and 3 p.m. Monday to Friday) to see our case historian who would interview you regarding this patience's background. It would be advisable to call or write to let us know when you're coming so we are able to make arrangements for the patient to be available.
> We assure you that any information you can supply will be of great help to us. Please except our thanks in advance, for your cooperation.
> Yours very truly,
> Supervisor, Clinical Record Services
> Oak Ridge Division
> Penetanguishene, Ontario.

I had no idea what I was getting myself into, other than the fact that

I was going to be in an institution structured solely around therapy. I had heard stories of Penetanguishene, that it was one of the biggest institutions for crazy people in all of Canada. The counselors I talked with at Hillcrest did not tell me it was one of the biggest nut houses for some of the craziest people in Canada.

So here I was, going to this place called Penetanguishene, assuming there was going to be other children my age. It was supposed to be a very active program. I told the counselors I would go. They told me my placement was for three to six months, and that I would be returned to Hillcrest School after the treatment at Penetanguishene.

As I was transferred, I was able to see out the windows of the van. When I saw a sign that said PENETANGUISHENE, I started to get cold shivers. The building that we were driving towards looked very scary. It was very tall, up on a hill. Every window on the building was barred.

There were two sections in Penetanguishene. One side was for people who were classified as criminally insane, the other side was for people that were completely gone. By that, I mean they were completely insane. These were people completely psychotic and beyond control, under 24-hour room arrest.

I was put in a cell, without any clothing, after I had been showered with bug shampoo. I was given a gown called a baby doll, so that you could not injure yourself. Everything in the cell was removed. There was only a cement slab to sleep on. At about 1030 at night, you were allowed to grab a mattress to sleep on. This was more than I had bargained for. The seriousness of just the atmosphere in this institution was enough to scare and intimidate me. For four days, we stayed completely locked in our cells, and were only allowed to have one thing, a Bible. Even if we got letters from outside they were screened before we got them .

I was put in what was called H-WARD, deemed the orientation ward for the whole institution. I found out quickly this was not going to be an easy place to live. It was an adult institution. There were some very sick individuals here. We were not allowed to use vulgar language. If anybody had an attitude, or received bad news, there was a group session called. There were four groups at any one time. Each group contained at least 12 people. We would sit against walls in various rooms, on a cushion you would take with you from room to room, and sit around and talk of anything that was asked of us. If it was felt that, during your 20 minutes of therapy per group, there was a possibility for violence, you were immediately hand-cuffed and shackled to protect yourself, as well as the people in your group. This was very, very intense.

They had papers they made you study, apparently psychiatric documents, that would breakdown all of your defenses, so you could gain some sort of help from them. We had to study these fucking papers and be able to read them in verbatim or backwards. Some people would get so messed up by these papers, they would end up either having to be restrained, or the guards would authorize an injection of some sort of sedative. H-Ward was programmed so the people staying for any length of time had to go through the whole orientation program of studying human behavior. Penetanguishene was one of the only institutions that would take people from Federal Penitentiaries, or from the court systems and put them through a 30 day assessment. The way you were labeled was one of two categories. The first label was that of W. L.G., (Warrant of the Lieutenant Governor), and the other was an Assessment.

There were eight different wards in Penetanguishene ranging from A to H, with A, B, C, D, being the most dangerous. E, F, G, H, wards were able to maintain a sense of therapeutic community, based on the daily routine of group sessions centered around one individual at a time. Sessions would last from 7:30 in the morning till 9 p.m. at night. If you did not get involved in the session, it was centered on you.

In the first 30 days, I saw how disordered some people were. I thought I was far from that point. I started to think I had made the wrong choice, and that I should put in my request for transfer back to Hillcrest. My request was denied, and I was told that I would be here for sometime.

I was completely scared knowing this, because when you sat with the group, there was no escaping the intense verbal therapy. You were confronted by patients who had savagely killed other people. Some had killed up to 9 people, viciously. I was talking with them as if nothing had happened. Once the group was centered on you, they took you through every stage of your life, and there was no escaping it. Sometimes the person the group centered on would react violently, or get very emotional, even go into a complete psychotic state. I saw this happen many times. Each time I got more scared. This whole fucking place scared me. At night, you could hear people on the far side of Penetanguishene screaming, like they were being tortured, banging on the caged windows. There was not one night that I was not frightened at Penetanguishene. I could not comprehend the treatments: some included alcohol and drugs. Drugs like Amytal,

Ritlan, Dexmal, Tofranil, Scopolomine (used as a truth serum during the first world war), as well as L.S.D.25 (the purest form of acid). Alcohol was given in mass doses. While anyone took these treatments, they were made aware it was videotaped. It could be used for a group session on the person, once they recovered from the drug or the alcohol.

CHAPTER NINE

MENTAL RECONDITIONING

I was going to be at this institution for awhile. It was a difficult fate to accept. There was no escaping here, including the group or general sessions. These ordeals involved all the guys, with the psychiatric staff and guards sitting in a big void called the Sun room.

The thought nagged that somehow, the system had gone wrong. It fought so hard to keep me within the juvenile courts, yet somehow, I ended up in the adult federal institution best known for housing the criminally insane. I thought, everyone thinks I'm nuts. I'm never going to get out of here (at least not till I'm old) .

The following is another typed copy of a letter from the Ministry of Health, Mental Health Center PENETANGUISHENE, ONT.

> Dear Mrs. Douglas,
> We received your letter of March 3, 1977 concerning your son. We're pleased to hear that your son is writing to you regularly as he has talked of his warm feelings for you.
> Perhaps your son will be in our hospital until he is 20 years old, however, that is not a question that we can give you a definite answer to at this time. His discharge depends on how hard he works in the programs and consequently how well he does. Presently, he is involved in one of our therapeutic communities that require a lot of effort and participation.
> There is no possibility of Jeremiah receiving and education

or trade during his hospitalization. Jeremiah's main objective while he is here is to understand and accept himself. We do not encourage or allow anything that'll take away from his therapy.

Incoming mail is not censored nor do we hold back any letters a patient receives. We cannot stop these people, that you are concerned about, from writing to Jeremiah. This is a responsibility that Jeremiah will have to handle himself if he chooses not to correspond with them.

I can understand that you have mixed feelings for your son at this time and I appreciate your honesty. Jeremiah will be discharge when he makes some changes in himself and it is my belief that he will deserve another chance. He will be a couple years of older when he enters society again and we would encourage him to look after himself rather than live at home. However, some support from you would probably be an asset.

Perhaps as Jeremiah makes improvements that may be noticeable to you in his letters, you'll be able to feel more comfortable within yourself about him. He has shared a couple of your letters with me and I would encourage you to be as open and honest with your feelings as you can be. Talking to someone, who is close to you, about Jeremiah, might be healthier for you than pushing him to the back of your mind until his next letter arrives. Please do not hesitate to contact me at any time.

Yours truly,

M. Mieke R.N.

I was transferred from H-Ward to G-Ward, which was basically the main therapeutic community in this institution. All the wards were about 100 by 25 feet by 30 feet, with 40 beds per ward, plus all the other rooms (and the Sun room) at the very end of the ward, looking out over a big field. All the windows were barred. Some were made with mesh screen, making it impossible to touch the bars. When I got to G-Ward, I was immediately placed in group orientation. This was the most intense place I had been in my life. My being here would result in one of two things. One, it was going to make me a better person, capable of handling life instead of taking from it. Or, I would remain here for a long, long time. The fact was, I had asked one of the counselors at Hillcrest for help, and chose to come here for therapy.

It took time to adjust, but after a few days I started to get into the routine. I was involved in programs designed to teach participants to help themselves and others. The intensity was so dramatic; I often wished I was dead. I even wished that some of the people there would meet a cruel demise. I talked about these feelings during group sessions, and was starting to come to an understanding of my hostility and hatred. It took quite a while for me to open up to anyone at this place, let alone 12 to 40 people at a time. The aim of the therapy: the patients would treat the patients, aided by staff interventions, and alcohol and drugs.

I knew I needed help to turn my young life around. I was lost and drowning in a world too big for me. I was convinced that any enthusiastic involvement in therapy sessions would make me a better person. I asked for all the drug treatments available, as well as the alcohol treatments, and received some of both. It is quite interesting to see yourself on video, in a therapeutic setting completely intoxicated and being questioned repeatedly about the events that led you to Penetanguishene. There was no escape.

It was difficult to probe deeply the events that shaped me. I credit Penetanguishene with helping me immensely to understand myself. I learned there is more to life than stealing, drug dealing and all the other dead-end criminal pursuits. It is not what you do in life; it is how and by what methods you do it..

To talk at length of my Penetanguishene experience would be a book in itself. It would be wrong to exploit the people involved in my therapy, because I would have to expose sensitive information. I will say that I encountered some of Canada's most feared and hardened criminals. Being a 16 year old kid, my placement there was one of the biggest hills I have had to climb.

One day, I read in the paper that a prostitution ring had been busted in downtown Toronto. The accused was nicknamed Blueboy, thus the prostitution ring was called the Blueboy Ring. I had started out in the prostitution business with Doug when I was living in downtown Toronto. I called him Blue and the ring was busted in 1976. It was named one of Canada's biggest prostitution rings. The papers said authorities were looking for his partner, but could not find any documented evidence of him. When I read this, I started to laugh.

I was placed in solitary confinement for having sex with this guy, a blatant violation of the rules. They locked us up in a program called MAP, an acronym for Motivation, Attitude and Participation. I did not really care that I was caught; I had not had sex in almost two years. As I was sitting in my cell, I got to thinking I had never received a visit from any member of my family, nor my relatives who lived in this area. Then I got one, and it was on July 4th, 1978. As I sat in solitary confinement, reading the Bible over and over, the guard came to my cell door and told me I had a visitor. I could not believe his words. He opened up my cell and told me to follow him. We did not go to the main visitors area, rather to the offices, where I met a gentleman named Doug, and a lady named Barbara, who were both from Toronto. Doug worked for the Community Services in downtown Toronto, and Barbara worked for Juvenile Resources in Toronto.

I did not pick up on Doug's lifestyle until I met him again. They asked me various questions about what I would do if released, and if I would go back to my family. I told them I would not go home, that I would try to live my own life, letting time take it course with my family situation. Even though I was at one of the biggest mental institutions in Canada, my family relationship was still in a very vulnerable state, and only time could heal the wound. Barbara and Doug advised me not to communicate any of our conversation to *anyone*, because there was no telling what could happen. I thought, "Oh fuck, what has gone on here, and why should I not talk of this?" I'll never know the answer, because they did not give me reasons for their visit.

About eight days later, lying on my cement bed reading the Bible, I was actually praying for a letter from my family. The guard came to my cell door and said, "Grab your letters and your Bible and follow me." I had no idea what was going on, thinking perhaps I was being transferred to a different cell, or I was out of solitary confinement. As we passed by the other cells, I asked the guard where we were going. He told me I was free; all my personal belongings were at the front of the building. I was to get dressed, in my own clothes, and get out of here (as soon as fucking possible).

I was in a complete state of shock. Not knowing what all of this was about scared the shit out of me, but I did what I was told. I got dressed, grabbed all of my personal belongings and headed for the front doors of Penetanguishene. There were (and still are) people that had done similar to what I had done, and had been in for 30 years or more. I was walking out the front door, after two and a half years, scared beyond belief. I called my mother in Calgary and told her I was coming home. I asked her if she could wire me some money for the trip. She was happy to send the money. Of course, I lied. I had not intention of going home.

As I walked towards the door, Doug was standing there waiting to meet me and take me to Toronto. I was going back to the same area of town where I'd lived with Weasel and Gary. Doug worked for what was called the Triad Foundation. I knew one thing for sure. Doug was a homosexual, and the group home I was taken into was for young gay men.

How some gay foundation even knew of me remains a mystery. For one thing, I never, ever, talked to anybody about my sexuality during my stay at Penetanguishene. Barbara would not give me a complete or definite answer to any of my questions regarding my release.

I am by no means homosexual. In my life, all I wanted was a close family and a relationship with a woman. Barbara could not explain how a release was set up, into the center of the gay community in downtown Toronto. I never asked for it. I did not even know it was going to happen.

Scared and lonely, I found myself back among the elements that led to previous disasters. After becoming so self aware, I was scared. I had learned to trust people with my feelings. I was not worried about how they were received. Penetanguishene was a therapeutic community; now, I was walking the streets of downtown Toronto. I would not have to worry about anything. I was free, although officially on probation until my 18th birthday. It was now July 20th, 1978. I did not have long to wait.

Being scared, lonely and free was a complete reversal of my previous situation. I was never scared while I was out before, and never lonely: I was a drug dealer, with lots of people around me all the time. I had never been free. I was always on the run from the law in some form or another, and now my life was different.

Everyone at the group home thought I was completely gay, because I had done numerous years in jail. It was hard for me to explain, because they were all gay themselves. Where the funding came for this group home I do not know. I was under the impression it was funded by the government, where Barbara worked.

The group home was situated in the downtown core on Irwin Avenue just off Yonge Street and one block from the club where I dealt drugs. I found it very hard not to get caught up in my emotions. I was back in the same area, and did not last long.

Shortly after my release, in the downtown core, I started to smoke marijuana again. The buzz from smoking my first joint in years was so intense that when I got to the group home I went straight to my room and got very sick. This group home was outstanding. How the system did this seemed fucking unbelievable.

Doug owned a house with his mother Rose. There was also Doug's uncle Albert, who lived in the basement. Together, there were at least six to eight people living in this house at any one time. Doug would make all kinds of sexual advances towards me. Although I had kissed him, when I was released from Penetanguishene (in front of all the guards and any of the other patients that might have been able to see), I kept refusing his advances. It did not seem to fluster him at all-there were many other kids in the house.

I could not believe, for the life of me, that the system had fucked up so completely to put me right back in the same fucking environment that had caused the problems I had just worked out in Penetanguishene. Nobody would give me a straight answer to any of my questions, and this really messed me up.

I did not last long in abstinence, and found myself peddling drugs to enable me to go to a straight club, or a bar like The Gasworks, or Young Station, popular bars for straight people. I only had to stay in the group home until I was 18. At that point in time, I would decide what I was going to do. From the time that I was released in July, till my birthday in mid-August, all I did was look for schooling and a job, but once I started to meddle in dope for people, I was making fast money again, and starting to lose sight of everything I had just attained from therapy.

I had bumped into some of my old friends from before. To me, it seemed I was not good enough to be around them. I tried to pay it no attention. I would go down to the old bar called St. Charles, drink a few beers and watch all of the people I use to know, noticing how different they had become. The guy I smoked my first joint with (after getting out) asked me if I wanted to sell dope for him. I said, why not, I need the money as much as anybody else.

Before long, I was selling pot in various bars and nightclubs. I started to develop a clientele, and had a regular connection that was never out of drugs (or so it seemed). I was doing well, as far as the money situation went. There was a new club, a bisexual bar, opened up in downtown Toronto, right beside Maple Leaf Gardens. It was quite interesting to go into this bar and see a lot of seemingly sexually compatible men and women. I got to know one chick named Jane. She became a very good friend of mine till later in life.

There was a Y.W.C.A. located right across the street from Maple Leaf Gardens, and Studio Two was located kitty corner to both places. Jane lived in the Y.W.C.A. Everyday, I would go over to her place and we would roll up a couple of ounces. We would sell them in joint form, in order to make a lot of money. Since she lived right across the street from the club, it was quite easy for us to come and go at will. My situation at the group home was not improving. I was getting caught up in the drugs again. There were a lot of women I associated with, because of drugs. What I desperately wanted, more than anything else in the world, was a female companion. I got to know a few women intimately. I had never enjoyed having sex with men. It did not seem right to me, probably because of all the shit I'd been through.

I was almost 18 years old. I was capable of leaving the group home at 18. I had served out my sentence, under supervision, until I was 18 years old. Let the games begin, I kept thinking to myself. Doug was rather reserved about my leaving the group home, because he felt I needed more help. Barbara was a different story; she wanted me to do whatever I wanted regardless.

I was getting into the downtown scene again. Not once did I look back, and think of the things I had gone through to find myself. I was gravitating back to the same way of life that led me to do harm to everyone, including myself, without really caring. The way I looked at myself was; I had gotten much more powerful in the art of verbal persuasion and manipulation. Knowing the facts of my life, and how I went about handling them, was not easy to rectify in Penetanguishene, and now I found myself using it to my advantage, to get what I wanted, whenever I wanted. I wanted very much to be able to help people with the knowledge I had found, but ended up using it to my advantage. Helping other people was going to be something that just started to happen to me. The transition took forever it seemed.

The fellow I got my drugs from was named Robin. He was quite cool, and there was never any pressure on anybody about drugs, sex, bar talk. He seemed like the reserved old hippie type, and we got along just fine. I was capable of keeping up my end and never being late with the money. Robin would front me dope, and over the course of the weekend I would proceed to pay him back. Things were going really good for me, although I was leading myself right back into the same old shit. Now it seemed easier. I think someone wrote that I was very cunning. Never having been given an education that was suitable to my intellect, my education was in the art of manipulation. I used it.

One day, I went down to the St. Charles bar and started drinking. I met with a bunch of my old friends and a party was going. There was an older fellow there, his name was Bart. He seemed like a decent sort of guy, with money. He was buying people drinks, and gambling with them at the same time. I started to get involved in the game. Before long, I was winning, and Bart was down 500. I didn't mind, I was there to party. As the evening wore on Bart asked me at one point if I would like to go back to his hotel room and have a few more drinks, and gamble some more.

I went back with him and got drunk. When I woke up in the morning, I had all this money in my pocket. Bart was sitting in his chair, drinking whiskey. It was only about 10 in the morning. Bart told me that I had to go home, and that he would give me a call. I thought, sure, no problem, and left. When I got back to the group home, I counted the money. I had almost seven hundred dollars. I almost shit! Doug told me my time in the group home was over, and that I should find a place to live. I did not know where I was going to go or what I was going to do. I turned 18 with no problems, other than being broke and almost homeless.

Doug said he would give me at least three weeks to find a place to live. I thought it possible to sell enough pot to save for a damage deposit on an apartment, somewhere downtown. I got a call from Bart, about two days later, asking me if I wanted to go out drinking. I told him I would meet him at the bar. We started to drink quite heavily, and before long, I was doing some cocaine. I had told myself, when I was released from jail, I would not put my feelings out to anyone, because I was scared they would find out what I had done. Bart asked me if I wouldn't mind looking after an apartment he was going to rent close to Young Street and Wellesley Street, basically downtown central. I thought about it for a while, as we established some of the ground rules. There were some things I was not comfortable with. One of the biggest problems: Bart is uncannily similar to Harold.

Bart and I gambled and drank. Man, did we fucking drink!! I told Bart I would accept his proposal, on the grounds that there was nothing sexual. We rented an apartment behind the Gasworks Bar on Yonge Street. This was pretty cool. We were central to everything going on in our lives. Bart was off for three weeks and we hung around a lot, because there was nothing wrong with what we were doing, (so I thought).

Bart and I would take a cab wherever we went, even if it was from the apartment to the St. Charles bar, only four and a half blocks away. One time, Bart got the cab driver to stop in front of a bank. I sat in the car and waited. When Bart came back to the cab he started talking to me about making a new start. He knew that I was financially strapped. He handed me one thousand dollars cash, plus 15 hundred dollars in traveler's checks, telling me *this* was a good start. Now I had good money to carry me through until I found a job. I took the money, not thinking about any consequences.

A few days, later Bart had to go out of town, and I was finally alone in my own apartment. I got in touch with an old friend named Peter. We got some people together for a party, and I did some acid and speed. Not at the same time, but enough to know the difference. The stone I got was incredible. I hadn't been this stoned in years. I felt like I could do all kinds of incredible things, and later that night we rented a car and decided we would drive all over town just for the trip of it. Driving around town was incredible, out of our minds on all kinds of drugs. I did not have a driver's license yet. I had just been recently released from the government, and did not want to have one then. Peter asked me if I wanted to drive, and I said, sure, no problem. I jumped into the drivers seat, unconcerned with the fact I was drunk, stoned and without a license. It didn't seem to matter to any of the people in the car. As I was driving east on Queen Street, I got pulled over by the police.

Someone in the car handed me a license. Back then there were no pictures needed. I looked at the drivers license quickly and the police asked me to accompany them to their car. Sitting in the back seat, we started arguing rather heavily, and one thing led to another. Before I knew it we were fighting in the back seat. I was stoned on speed and acid, and not easily subdued. We fought quite heavily until the back door opened, and we tumbled into the street. I could hear one officer calling for backup. Before I knew what was happening, there was a swarm of cops around me. I could not stop fighting. Apparently one of the police officers sustained a facial injury, from the corner of his mouth to the corner of his eye. It was a giant cut. When I saw this, I immediately stopped fighting, but it was not over.

As the police walked me down this hallway I was punched or kicked by various cops as we walked by door ways. There was not much I could do; I was cuffed with one cop on each arm. As we got closer to the cells, I saw the sergeant standing in the middle of the hallway. As we approached him, he was saying, so you're the stupid fucking asshole that put four of my officers in the hospital. I just kind of looked at him. Then, as he was preparing to kick me in the chest, using the two cops for full impact, I used the two cops for support and kicked the sergeant right in the fucking balls.

I was taken to the lower cells, and the fucking shit was beat out of me. I don't think I had been beaten like that ever in my life, and when I was shipped over to the Don Jail in downtown Toronto, I was put into the jail hospital, barely able to walk. I started to panic, because I was locked up once again.

I got in touch with a lawyer from the Legal Aid Society, who managed to obtain bail in the sum of 1500 dollars for my release. I did not have that much cash left, and could not find my travelers checks. I did not have a phone in the apartment yet, so I had to contact another friend of mind in order for him to get in touch with Bart, so he could post bail. Once Bart came to the Don Jail and saw my condition, he immediately posted bail. When I was released, I went straight to a doctor I knew. He gave me some narcotics for the pain, telling me it would take two maybe three weeks to recover.

Back at the apartment, I explained to Bart exactly what had happened. I felt bad, because I was trying to stay out of trouble, seemingly to no avail. Bart told me he had to leave town for a week or two, and that I should maintain a low profile to recover. It took about four days for me to receive my traveler's checks, after reporting they had been lost. It was not a total loss, but detrimental to my staying out of jail.

When Bart returned, he did not seem like his old self. I could not put my finger on what was wrong. A few days passed and then Bart told me he did not want to live in Toronto anymore, asking me to move to Hamilton with him. I had one month to vacate the apartment and find somewhere else to live. There was no possible way that I was going to move with Bart to Hamilton. My friends were calling him " the sugar daddy that walked".

I had lots of friends, but the only person I called was Jane, because we had worked together almost every night, selling drugs.

Jane had introduced me to a girl named Sherry, whom I had met only briefly before, while Jane and I sold drugs at Studio Two. She told me Sherry was looking for a roommate, but the catch was that Sherry lived in the same building as Jane, which was the Y.W.C.A. for young women, and I would have to be very sneaky. I agreed, and before long, Sherry and I became a couple around the club scene. Sherry was pretty cool, because she preferred to sit and drink if she was going out in a straight bar, and only went to bars where Jane and I sold drugs.

We spent a lot of time together, and as I got to know Sherry, I found out that she had cystic fibrosis. Not knowing what this all meant, I was drawn

100

closer to her. One day, as Jane and I were selling our stuff, we went home and were informed that Sherry had tried to kill herself. She was tired of taking the drugs, and using the various medical machines. When we got to the hospital, Sherry refused to see Jane and me.

It took about three weeks for Sherry to come around. Things started to get back to normal, although I sensed a stressful difference in our relationship. Thinking about relationships and all that was involved; I started to think of my family. I called them every so often to find out if everything was all right. Once I knew, I would just go about my life without that crushing feeling of knowing they did not want me.

I was still facing charges, for assault causing bodily harm, to Toronto Metro's finest. I started to get this real squirrely feeling, because the charges were coming up and I did not want to spend my summer in jail.

I was standing outside the Gasworks Bar smoking a joint one night and got busted with 13 joints. I was released on my own right to appear, and I continued on with my life as if nothing happened. I was still selling drugs and turning the odd trick if I thought it would help out. I was not worried about getting a sexual disease from either a woman or a man. I would always use condoms, just to be safe.

I had tunnel vision once again, and was only into drugs, sex, and rock and roll. It seemed like once again, I did not care for anyone that was not in my immediate circle. I really didn't even give a shit about what was happening to me.

Sherry used to work the streets as well, and this was also a big strain on our relationship. She could do it with men, and I would go to bed with women and men and get paid for having sex with both. Things were not going very well for us and we broke up. I moved in with Jane and her girlfriend. It was very difficult because Sherry and Jane lived in the same building. I would often see her and this was really hard, because I loved her. She was having a very hard time with her drugs and all the medical bullshit in her life.

Despite all the counseling I had received at Penetanguishene, it seemed I could not even help myself in a relationship, let alone live in Toronto. I started to think one day about traveling back down to Florida. There was nothing for me in Florida, other than freedom from going to jail in Toronto, and my memories of my first and second time there. I met with a former cell mate from my arrest for marijuana, and we got to talking over some beers. I told him of my plan to go to Florida in order to escape going to jail. Rick was my friend's name, and he also did not want to faces charges in Toronto. He thought it would be a good thing to go to Florida.

I did not tell Jane or Sherry of my plan to take off to the States, and when the day came, I just left them a note telling them that I loved them both and that I would be in touch...

CHAPTER TEN

EVASIVE ACTIONS

I packed what I thought would be sufficient gear for the trip to Florida. I contacted Rick, telling him I was ready to head out for the border. Getting over the border was another project altogether. At one point, I was turned back from crossing the foot bridge over Niagara Falls, so I thought the only other way to get across was to hide on the railway cars that went across the bridge. Rick and I found a spot where we would be able to jump on a train and hide, before they did the security check of all cars. Hiding in this little hole on a grain car was fucking hard to do. I had to cram myself into a small hole quickly, as did Rick, before the border guards checked the train. It was one of the best adrenaline rushes I'd ever had. Once we got over the border (about 10 miles), we jumped off the train and proceeded to hitch-hike south.

Once we got to New York City, we were both highly impressed by the magnitude of the place. We had asked a few people on the way into the city where the best place was for us to get some food, or turn a trick to make some fast bucks. We were directed downtown, near West 42nd. We walked around endlessly, looking for something to do. After a few hours, we were sitting in front of the Empire State building, looking around, when some guys approached us, asking if we wanted to buy a joint. It was not unusual for this to happen. We had our back packs, and looked like transients, so obviously these guys did not feel threatened in any way, so we accepted.

We sat there and smoked the joint with these guys, feeling comfortable with the fact that they were not trying to rip us off.

These guys seemed genuinely decent. They offered to help us, to keep us from ending up in the gutter. They offered to let us stay at their apartment overnight, and, in the morning, they would drive us to the south side of town, where it would be easier for us to hitch- hike to Florida. They said just getting out of New York was hard enough. Only when we were on our way, did I feel comfortable. New York is a very dangerous city, if you're on the streets and unfamiliar with the area.

Once Rick and I got to Florida, our whole world seemed to change. I wanted to find a job and chill out for awhile. It took me a while to get accustomed to life in Tampa, Florida. Once I felt comfortable, I was able to go out and start turning tricks, in order to get a place to live for a while. Rick and I both did this. We got a half decent place. We worked the streets, not taking any of our clients home, but rather to a hotel room at their expense.

About the second week in December, I went to the usual spot to meet Rick but he did not show. I hightailed it back to the apartment that we shared, and discovered his belongings were gone. I did not know what to do. We were both on the run from the cops in Canada, which made going to the police impossibile. I searched all over for one week, and found no trace of Rick. I was getting scared, so I decided to go back to Toronto. I left around December 16th or 17th. I had some money, but not much. I started hitch-hiking back to Toronto. Along the way, I ran out of money, and started to get hungry. I got picked up by two guys heading to Detroit, MI.

They were driving a beat up old truck, and had their doubts as to whether or not the truck was going to make it. They knew of my financial situation, that I had very little to contribute, and by the time we were close to Detroit, they were broke as well. They decided to steal purses from people going into a mall to do their Christmas shopping. There was no way that I could do that, so I starved myself, thinking I would be would be able to get something to eat at a mission in Detroit.

By the time I got to Detroit, I was very sick. I was looking for a home-less shelter that would offer me some food. I remember standing, looking at some of the buildings. The next thing I remember is lying in a hospital bed, with my hands cuffed to the bed and an I.V. going into my arm. When I came around, I told the nurses I was from Toronto, on my way home for Christmas, and that I had just hitch-hiked up from Florida.

The nurses told me that some pedestrians witnessed me passing out and that I was having what looked like a seizure of some sort. I was cuffed to the bed for my own protection, and the fact that I was without identification did not help matters.

Once at the border, I had difficulty proving I was a Canadian citizen. Because I had no identification, I had to contact someone in Toronto that could send money (for a bus ticket) as well as identification. The only person I could think of was Doug, back in Toronto. It was Doug who freed me from Penetanguishene.

Back in Toronto, all my friends were happy to see me. Doug and Barbara stressed I was in trouble, and that I had to clean up, so I could do something right. Christmas and New Years came and left in a flurry. I was staying wherever I could for the time being, and it was getting close to my trial for my possession charge. I started to get nervous again. I was dealing drugs again with Jane. The game started again, and I was getting caught up. Early 1979, I left for Florida again, with a guy named Steve (my age, and also in trouble with the law).

Steve was surprised at how easy it was for us to get over the border. Our plan was to go straight to the citrus belt of Florida and work in the orange groves, but our trip was phenomenal. We had no problem getting to the south side of New York. Steve and I both did not want to go into the city, so we stuck to the highway and maintained our course south. It took us about two and a half days to get to the Georgia border. It was very hard to hitch-hike on some of the state highways, because it was illegal. We had to stick to the merge lanes in order to hitch-hike.

One afternoon, we were sitting underneath a bridge. It was raining, and hard to get a ride. We casually stuck out our thumbs and, to our amazement, this girl pulled over, offering a ride. This was a hitch-hikers dream: to get a ride from a nice looking chick, going nowhere in particular. Her name was Linda. Late into the ride, the car was having little problems, and Linda asked if we could take care of the car in return for a room at the hotel she planned to stay in for the night. I thought sure, why not. Steve was in like a dirty shirt.

Not realizing where I was, other than it was a city called Macon City, Georgia and not knowing anything about this area, Steve and I immediately became aware that people looked upon us strangely because of our long hair. Once we got to the hotel, Linda rented a room, and Steve and I proceeded to work on her car. Once Steve and I had fixed a few of the minor problems, Linda offered us dinner in the hotel restaurant. Steve and I quickly got cleaned up and went with her.

Sitting in the restaurant, it never occurred to me something was wrong. I was soon to find out there was. Linda bought us dinner and beers, and then more beers. I started to get quite the buzz going, while Linda and Steve seemed to be hitting it off. We all started to dance later in the evening. Linda was paying for everything with her credit card. To me, it didn't matter; Steve and I were just travelers and she had offered. About 11:30 at night, the manager approached us, stating it was illegal for two guys to dance together (as Steve and I had done during the course of the evening). We told him we would discontinue, there was no problem.

About an hour later, the manager came back with 5 state troopers. I did not know what was going on at first, suddenly the police and hotel staff surrounded us. There were a couple of detectives as well. We were arrested for fraud. As we were leaving the restaurant, the detectives asked all us how long we had known each other. I told the detectives that I had only met the girl six or seven hours ago, when she picked Steve and I up hitch-hiking. Steve was a little drunker than I was, and he told the detectives he had known her for six or seven months, though he meant to say hours. The detectives looked at Linda and asked her how long she had known us and she said she had known us for two and one half years. When she said that, I almost lost control, because I knew she was going to use us as scapegoats for what ever the charges were. The detectives would not listen to us that night. We were all drunk.

The next day, some detectives came to ask Steve and me some questions. We did not hide anything from them, because we did not want to go to jail in the States. To me it seemed like Steve and I were stuck in an old Burt Reynolds film. This was Macon City, Georgia, the heart of Red neck territory. One detective informed Steve and I we were looking at some serious time behind bars. Linda was charged with grand theft auto, stolen credit cards, possession of stolen property, and we were accessories.

For three or four days they kept us locked up. One day the same detective came back to the cells, and to our immense relief, told us that Linda had come clean, and we were off the hook. She admitted she picked us up hitch-hiking. We were released, given an escort to the county line, and told never to come through Macon City again. Steve and I never looked back. We decided to take a little tour, and not head directly for Florida. We decided to go to Nashville, TN., just to trip around and see some of the sites that made Nashville famous.

We were low on money, and panhandling was very hard in the States, although we did manage to survive. Once in Nashville, Steve and I pawned the camera I had taken from Jane, in order for us to eat and maybe grab a couple of beers. Walking around downtown Nashville was quite a trip. We bought a six pack and some sandwiches with the money we got from the camera and sat down beside an old building, not knowing what it was. We got slightly buzzed and joked about being at the Grand Old Opera House. We were actually sitting against the Grand Old Opera House, we later found out.

That night we headed out for Florida. Around 7 or 8 p.m. we got a ride, heading towards Chattanooga. This guy was drinking beer and offered us one. We gladly excepted, as it was very warm outside, and soon there was no more beer. I suggested that he stop at a store, and I would buy another six pack to replace what he had given us. We were heading east, on Interstate 24, and there was a service road that ran parallel with the highway. I noticed a store and suggested that we go to that one. The guy exited the Interstate, and there were gas stations like a regular highway junction. But instead of going to the gas station, where you could buy beer, the guy went underneath the bridge, onto the service road and headed back west towards the store that I saw before. We got to this store and I went in and bought the six pack of beer.

We sat in the parking lot drinking and talking about where we were from, and this guy was telling us little bits about his life. About an hour passed, and this guy said it was a better idea that we stick to the road and not wander too far, as this was Red neck territory as well. The guy seemed rather normal, and at one point even offered to let Steve and I sleep at his house with his family. We told him we would be safe on the Interstate, and that we appreciated the offer. We kept on drinking.

As we headed back east towards the intersection he had taken to get off the main interstate highway, instead of going back under the bridge, this guy went straight past the intersection on the service road. Then without warning, he pulled into a driveway, jumped out of the car, and ran up to front door of the house. He started banging on the door. It opened and he ran inside.

Just as fast as he ran into the house, he ran back out with a shotgun. There was another man behind him with a rifle as well. Steve was sitting in the front seat of the car, and I was in the back seat with the backpacks. When Steve saw the guy running out of the house with the shotgun, he jumped out of the car and ran. This guy ran up to the car and held the shotgun to my head. He started to yell that if Steve did not return, he was going to blow my fucking head off. I was trying to hide behind the backpacks, but the guy demanded that I get out of the car. The other guy with the rifle was yelling "let's just shoot him." The guy with the shotgun kept yelling for Steve to return. Slowly Steve started walking back. I was standing in front of the car with the backpacks on my shoulder, facing these two guys with guns pointing at me.

Once Steve was in front of the car with me, this guy started yelling that we had threatened to kill him and take his car. He must have been some kind of weird psycho, or something, because this was all happening for no reason. Steve tried to shake the guy's hand, and when Steve moved to do this, the guy used the butt end of the shotgun on Steve's face. It slashed his face from the edge of his mouth to corner of his eye. The cut was deep, instantly there was blood all over. This guy started yelling that we had five seconds to get off his property. Steve and I started running towards the main intersection of the Interstate, and this guy was shooting at us as we ran. I had ripped off my t-shirt, using it as a compress on Steve's face as we were running.

I thought for sure we were both dead, but we kept on running. As we got near the gas station, people started to look at us. I ran with Steve right into the gas station and started yelling for help. People in this gas station just sat on their stools and looked at us. I let go of Steve, jumped across the counter, and ran to the phone to call the police and ambulance.

We were taken to Chattanooga General Hospital, where they performed surgery on Steve while I sat with the cops. Steve and I had given the cops fake names, so we had no problems with the law, other than the fact we were hitch-hikers with little money. About three hours later, Steve was released, with his face all bandaged up. He looked like shit. Being continually interviewed by the state troopers was not easy. They were very unforgiving. At one point, the police suggested we were A. W. O. L.

By the time we did make it to Tampa, Steve was in bad shape. I went and did a trick for thirty bucks, and when I came back to where Steve was waiting I could not find him. I looked all over to no avail.

I stayed in Tampa for some time. I found a job as a male dancer at the Tiekei Saloon in downtown Tampa, and made my money under the table.

From what I was making doing tricks, I was able to live well. I started to do speed again, and this time, a lot more than I ever had. I did not have to pay for it, just drive a car around and use fat women.

We would find a woman who was way overweight, and take her to doctors throughout the gulf. We would get Preludes, better known as Pinks, by the script of sixty pills. We could sell a pill for five or ten bucks. I was losing a lot of weight, as I was doing five, some days ten pokes a day, not having to pay for the high.

I met a guy named Allen one night out on the strip, and we hit it off right and became good friends. We would go all over the place, selling drugs and women, if we could find some women to pimp. Allen had a girlfriend, who let him take her car whenever he needed it.

Inwardly, I was feeling very lonely. My good friend had disappeared. I felt alone. I called my mother in Calgary. But that made me feel worse. My brother was still in jail, and my sis would not talk to me, nothing would change with them.

Allen kept telling me he had some friends in Gainesville, Fla., friends who would score us a pound of mushrooms to sell and use for a good time. I said 'why not.' So, off we were, on our way to Gainesville with his girlfriend's car (without telling her). Once in Gainesville, we found out that Al's friend got busted (or moved). Once again, we didn't know what to do.

We saw a hitch-hiker, stopped and talked with him for awhile, eventually asking him where he was going. He told us that he was going to New Orleans to screw around. Al asked the guy if he knew where there was an Albertsons all night food store and the guy said "yes." Al looked at me. I knew he had something on his mind. He said, "How would you like to go to New Orleans, and trip around for awhile?" I thought what the hell. We got what we needed to make fake hash, went to the hitch-hiker's friend's house, and cooked up a pound of this shit. With our fresh batch of hash, and little fuel, we went to the gas station, where we proceeded to trade one half ounce for gas. We were on our way.

Allen and I would sell this bullshit hash to just about anyone. We made sure to get our asses back on the highway as fast as possible. We never got caught, even though we knew some people would eagerly want to see us hurt. We did not care who bought it. Once, we sold an ounce for some guy's new script for percodan. We scored more than thirty pills. The poor guy we traded had just suffered a broken elbow, and wanted to smoke rather take pills. Al and I still had a number of hits in the car to poke with, and this was the first time I was to boot percodan. I would get a rush just *thinking* of sticking a needle in my arm, and the sight of the blood mixing with my drugs was sometimes a high in it self. After doing these percodan, I was so high we could not drive for awhile.

We slept in the car when it was late, drank beer all day long, never worrying about anything. We had money coming in on a steady basis. We had left all our stuff in Tampa, but it didn't matter; if we needed more clothes, or whatever, we would just buy them.

Once we got to the border of California, Allen told me that he wanted to stop at his family's house to say hi. I didn't mind, as it was going to give us a chance to freshen up and hit the road again. It was nice to meet his mother and father. They were both very kind. We had made a point of telling them we were going to San Diego for work. We were actually going to Monterey, Cal. When we got there, we visited some of Al's friends, and then decided we should head south for some drugs we could move some how. Allen and I never once thought about the car, or whether his girlfriend would report it stolen. At one point we had stopped to get something out of the trunk, using a knife to open it. While I jacked the trunk, and Allen sat in the car waiting, three cops exploded out of nowhere. The cops jumped the cars, pulling shiny 45 hand guns and yelling "FREEZE". I froze alright. The top cop barked out orders, saying, if we moved we would have very uncomfortable holes in our bodies. That was all I needed. It seemed that, some how, my past was always catching up to me, whenever I saw a gun.

We were both charged with car theft. I said to myself, you did it good this time-and now you are back in a U.S. jail. I gave them my real name. I knew there were no warrants for my arrest in the states. I had to laugh at the irony of my situation: this was the first time I could use my real name and not get busted and thrown in jail for a long time, like in Canada. I don't know if the judge bought our story about the car. We told him we had purchased it from Allen's girl, but Allen had cheated on her. As a result they had parted on bad terms, and we felt she was trying to get revenge on him. He bought it, and let us off after three days in jail. Allen and I even tried to get the car back, but the police in Monterey had different ideas. We couldn't even pay for the towing at that time. We looked at each other, and hit the road. Hitch-hiking down to San Diego sounded good to me, and that was where we were heading, when Allen suddenly went A. W. O. L.

I was sitting on the beach, and Allen had gone to make a phone call. He never came back.

I went to this town called La Jolla, and just bummed around watching people, hoping I could pull a trick. Money was getting thin. After three days of nothing, I met this older gent named Russ. He knew before I asked him for money that I was hustling. Russ took me to his apartment and said I could take a shower. We would grab a bite to eat and then do some talking about me.

I was on the level with Russ. He treated me with respect, which I found comforting. We sat in his living room, over-looking the strip that lead to the beach. You could walk to Black's beach from Russ' house in ten minutes. I thought it was handy, as I wanted to go look at some beautiful bodies. Russ and I had just started to kiss, when his roommate came walking in. He fell silent when he saw us. Russ introduced us. His name was Bill. Russ and Bill had lived in the area for some time, trying to pick up the good looking guys and pamper them. Russ told me if I wanted to stay for awhile, he would be able to find some work for me, as well as a place to stay. I thought it over while I walked around the beach. I phoned Russ and told him I would take him up on his offer.

The work Russ was giving me was at his cabin, in this little town called Julian, not more than an hour away from the beaches and the desert. The cabin was located on a beautiful meadow, with lush forest surrounding it. The town was not more than a fifteen minute walk. I was told that Russ had tried to find some young man to do this for some time, but every time he did, the guy would stay for a day then take off. I found this out from Cal, a friend of Russ' that owned the antique shop on the outskirts of Julian. I met Cal about three days after arriving at the cabin. Russ also left me fifty bucks. He bought beer and food to last me for a week and left.

Russ would phone every day to see how I was doing. I was working on his land, getting paid, with the odd fringe benefit. Cal was also gay, enabling us to start on the right foot. I could relate sometimes when I found out the person's true nature. About a week or two went by, while I worked hard on the land. Suddenly Russ showed up with this young guy named Kie. Kie was about twenty-two, good looking and bisexual, which would work out well for us later.

Russ asked Kie if he would stay up here with me for a while and help, saying it would be less lonely for me. Kie said that he had some things to do, but would come up on the weekend. I was getting to know some of the people around town, and became friends with most. One time I walked into town, and was hitch-hiking out after messing around. I got a ride with a girl named Leigh. She had a young boy, no more than a few months old, named Mil. We talked and I told her I was staying by myself, and that I never got to meet very many people. I told her if she and her old man would like to go out for dinner, or come over for a few, it sure would be nice. She said that dinner sounded fine, she would pick me up in town at six. She asked me what I was doing now. I told her I was just picking up some pot from a friend at the antique shop, but if she wanted to stick around I would grab a toke and come out to get her high before she left. She stayed! I could not figure her out, a good looking woman who never once mentioned her old man, even when I asked the both of them out.

That evening when I went to town to take them out to dinner, I was in for a surprise. Leigh and Mil showed up, but without her man. I asked right out where her boyfriend was. She told me they had broken up. I did not expect this, and it showed! She told me I did not have to do this, if I felt uncomfortable. I told her I would be happy if I could still go to dinner with them. This was the beginning of the best few month of my life.

I finally got to be myself. I got close very fast. She lived alone with Mil, something she did not like. I spent the first night at her house. Soon she would not stop seeing me. I wanted it this way, as I was now receiving the missing link. The very thing that I wanted all my life was to have a woman love me, the way I was.

Leigh and I would spend all our time together when we were not work-ing. I did not think Russ had a right to know about what I was doing. I figured that since the work got done he could not say anything. I had Leigh over for the first time, and Russ phoned. I guess he assumed something was wrong, saying he was coming up for the weekend, and hopcd I had the place in order. I thought to myself, somehow he had gotten wind of the fact I was bringing a woman there; I started to worry that he would not let me stay, since he was totally against women.

I told Leigh I would not be able to see her that weekend, as I had to go th L.A. on business. I did not want her to be there, if anything was going to happen. When Russ arrived, I realized why he wanted the place clean. Russ had made plans to spend the weekend with Kie and me as his little toys. Needless to say I was more than annoyed by this, as I wanted to spend the weekend with Leigh. But when he got doing drugs and drinking (one hell of a lot), it sure made me willing to let someone suck me off. I would not know sometimes what mouth I was in, as we got so fucked up.

Saturday, Russ met with two owners of the antique store in town. Both of them were gay, so Russ immediately invited them to dinner, while Kie and I had to cook. Russ was showing off his little harem. At least, that's what it felt like to us. That day I realized I was very attracted to Kie, as I was not feeling alone when it came to the uncertainty of total gay life. That night turned out to be more than I had expected it would. Before long Russ was giving Tim head in the living room, and then the drugs broke out, and the booze and I was in there with Kie giving me head, and Rex (Tim's lover) giving Kie head. It was not long till Russ said that we should all go into the bedroom and get more comfortable. It was a night that I will not forget for life.

For six hours all we did was suck and fuck each other and get higher all the time on pot, ludes and booze. When the final volley was reached, we all went our separate ways for the rest of the night. My night was spent in Kie's arms.

The next day, I could not wait till Russ was out the driveway. I was on the phone to Leigh. I told her to come over; there was someone I wanted her to meet. Kie and I had done a lot of talking, and he knew that I was involved with her..

The first words that came out of Leigh were, why did I not want her to come to the cabin all weekend? I was not ready for a question like that, so I had to do some fast talking. I said the owner of this cabin had told me he wanted me to pick some things up in L.A., and that he wanted to spend the weekend at the cabin without anyone bothering him. Leigh bought it, but this was the start of losing the woman I loved, and always will. Time went on, and Russ found out that I was seeing a woman on a full time basis, and that she was spending a lot of time at the cabin. He phoned me one day to tell me he felt it was time I pushed on. I did not want to leave the area. I was in love, and told this openly to Kie. Leigh and Kie hit it off really well, and it made me think.

I asked Leigh if she would move in with me. Leigh said the magic words. Then out of the blue she asked Kei if he wanted to live with us. What a relief, as I had planned to ask if Kie could live with us. I did not have to worry about not being with her now, as I told Russ I would be out of the cabin by night fall.

I found a job with this guy named Van, doing carpentry for seven-fifty an hour. I was getting quite accustomed to this new way of life, and it felt better.

I told my family I was in love, and that we had a son. My sister finally started to talk to me, the best thing that could have happened. I was now one hell of a happy man.

I was getting to be known by the young crowd, which added to my happiness. I was called on to help others, and in return I found that they helped me. I made friends with a guy named Al, who was more or less one of the heads in town. We started to have him over more and more all the time, only later to be let down by his friendship. I had told myself long ago that if I ever found the woman of my dreams that I would never do anything to upset the relationship. Well, one night we had the gang over to do some drinking and toking. I got real drunk and asked Leigh to drive Al home, as I did not want to drive. She said she would, and that she would be right back.

Al lived about three miles from our house, and after about an hour I started to get real worried. I told Kie I was taking the truck, in order to make sure nothing had happened to her. I drove right up to Al's driveway and saw our car. I walked up to it, opened the driver's door, and saw Leigh sitting in Al's lap. I did not know what to say, so I just shut the door and walked back to the truck. Leigh called for me and I turned around, saying I would talk about this matter at home. With that said, I drove home and had a couple of beers before she arrived.

I told Leigh that I did not like what she had done, and that I could only let it go, if she never let it happen again. I thought I was doing the best thing, as I had fallen in love with this woman, and I was not going to let anything destroy it. But, after about three weeks, Leigh was starting to really upset me. Every time we went to the mall to shop, or sell mistletoe, (as it was near Christmas) she would say I should go and take this girl, and that girl, out, and then we would be even. I kept telling her that I did not want to get even, as I did not hold being with Al against her.

For the next few months, all Leigh would talk about was me going and getting some sex from another girl. One morning while I was taking a shower, Leigh was throwing all of my stuff out in the rain. I could not take it any longer. I told her I was going to move back to Canada. I would write her, and if she wanted to, she could come and live with me. I left, and stayed with my boss for a couple of days. I tried to sort all the shit out between Leigh and I over the phone, but it didn't work. I told Leigh I would stay in touch and that I would come back any time, provided we start fresh, but this was never to come around.

I moved to Hollywood and stayed with a friend of Russ'. I tricked again so I would have pocket money.

Sally was a very religious person, so when she would ask how I got all the new clothes, I told her I had a job working nights, and I would be home late at night. She never suspected anything, which was a relief. I stayed with Sally for about two weeks, then told her I would be moving over to Phoenix, Arizona. In reality, I was going to live with a trick. I was going to get a job working with him. After staying there for about three weeks, I felt I should move on. I was playing pool in a bar when I got to talking to a guy looking for a hooker who had ripped him off. I thought I might be able to help, but eventually he gave up and asked me what I was doing. He asked if I wanted to come and stay with him in Redondo Beach. I told him I would, but only for about a week, as I wanted to spend my summer in Phoenix. When I did leave, I would buy some smoke from him for the road.

I had a good time with Len. He would go bike riding with me, and we spent most of our time together. The reason we got along so well was we did not have sex. We just related to each other, and I felt quite comfortable visiting with him. When it came time to leave, Len gave me an ounce of good pot, and told me if I was ever in the area that I should drop in. With that, I was off, on the road again.

CHAPTER ELEVEN

GOING HOME

I was sitting on the highway, waiting for someone to give me a ride, when a young guy drove close enough to see that I was holding a joint up for a ride (this tactic worked most of the time). I got a ride with a fellow named Rick all the way to Phoenix. On the way, after a few beers and lots of tokes, Rick said that he had a deal for me. He would give me one hundred bucks if I helped him move into his new place, as he and his father were opening a new shop to sell some kind of parts. I thought, at least I will be in a new city with some bucks. Rick then went on to say that I could stay with him, if I found a job doing anything. He would cover for three weeks, until I found a job. I jumped at the offer. Rick was straight, and I knew we would have a good time. Once again I found myself longing to be with a woman. The only way I was going to accomplish this, was to go out and get involved with the world again, instead of running.

I got a job, and Rick and I went out and bought a car (actually he bought it with the odd suggestion from me). Rick told me I could use the car we used for the drive from L.A. I started to feel the way that I did when I lived with Leigh. I had the choice of now picking up a lady, or nothing at all, with the freedom to come and go whenever I wanted. This made me feel great!

Rick and I would often go to the bars to drink and pick up women, but for sometime, I never was able to. I would think of what happened, and I would end up gun shy whenever I met a woman. I could not talk about

116

this with Rick, as I felt embarrassed to discuss this with another man. I felt the best thing, was to tell the women I did meet how I felt, and take my chances.

I was always in touch with Jane in Toronto, but only in letter form. I lost her number and she had moved. But I felt safe when I thought of her, in the sense that I could trust her more than any woman I knew. I loved my mother, but could not trust her with my feelings, in the way I could with Jane.

Well, my idea worked, and I fell in love with this beautiful girl named Sun, who I met one night at the bar with a friend from work, named Mike. Mike and I could not believe that I was going to walk out of the bar with the best looking woman working there. I was never going to hear the end of it. Sun had long black hair and a beautiful smile that could make water boil. She had a body to match. That first night with Sun was the best in years, and I was not going to stop going to the most popular bar in Phoenix (Called at that time "Scene West" located in Tempe) not far from my place.

Mike and I got to be real close friends, and this bond has stayed with us to this day. We spent a lot of time together when we got off work, as Rick had gone off on a business trip. Mike and I partied hardy, and I was using Rick's new car, even though he told me to park it and not drive it. But I could not resist a new Mazda RX7, and we drove it to Tucson, Arizona, just for fun. Things were going good all the way around, and my relationship with Sun was going strong. I started to feel full of life, knowing that what I did was for the good and enjoyment of two, not just one.

Mike and I would get tanked almost every night. We would work out, sparing with each other. One night we got shit faced and got a little rough with each other. I caught a spinning back kick to the inside groin, and a few hours later had to go to the hospital to see the doctor. I was swelling up like a balloon. I got to the Mount Sinai Hospital, where the nurse told me it was necessary to have my lymph node removed, as it was ruptured. I consented to the operation, telling the nurse I wanted to watch the procedure. She said it was not a serious operation, but to proceed correctly they had to freeze my groin. This was a very intense situation for me to watch. I was cut open, right beside my life line, so to speak. After she removed my lymph node, she dangled it in front of my eyes, saying it looked malignant and was going to be shipped to the Texas Research Institute. I would be notified of what the out come was. I asked her what she was talking about. She told me that I might have cancer! I told her to sew me up as fast as she could. I had to get home.

Mike was waiting for me in his car, sleeping, as I walked out of the hospital. I told him what the nurse had told me, and could not believe the way he acted. He felt that he had brought it on sparing with me! I tried to say he had nothing to do with this. If I did have cancer, I contracted it through life, not him. I did not know what I was going to do. I phoned home and told my mother the news.

My mother wanted me to come home. There was no better place I could think of being. I told Sun I was going to return to Canada, and, if she wanted to, she could come with me. I asked my mother to take us in that we were in love. I told her Sun wanted to be with me.

I said goodbye to my friends in Phoenix and, with my mothers help with the plane fare, we both were set for the beginning of a new life in Canada. After not seeing my family from 1976 till the spring of 1980, it was one wet reunion. My mother and brother came to the airport to meet me, and I cried almost all the way back to their place.

My mother was pleased to see me, so much so that she cried when we started to talk about our lives since we last saw each other. Her fears continued when we talked of what the doctors had said on the phone, when I tried to find out what was going on with my lymph nodes. Tests that were to be done were sabotaged by the fact that my sample was misplaced. I was told I would get a call from the hospital as soon as possible. I went out and got a job, working with the mentally handicapped. Soon after that the news broke. I was sitting at home, drinking a beer, when I got the call that took all the pressure I was feeling off me. I did not have cancer. I had nothing to worry about.

I went to my doctor for a complete exam. He gave me a clean bill of health. Now I wanted to start having fun like I use to. I changed jobs and got into the restaurant industry. I saved enough money to move into an apartment with Sun, but we had to take on a roommate after awhile. Work was good, and Sun was having a good time. We never really wanted for anything, as I would bring home tokes and sometimes a bottle and we were happy.

The novelty of being back near my family lead us to start arguing all over. My family still felt a lot of resentment towards me. I held onto some resentment towards them, but the only thing to do was not drink with my mother. Somehow we always ended up arguing. My brother and I were at each others throats more than once, but we settled down after awhile.

I met my next door neighbor, named Monk, who worked at the same restaurant (Lucifer's on Seventh Ave. in downtown, Calgary, Alta). We got along well, and drank and smoked a lot of drugs. I got right into dealing, so Sun and I would have extra money. Monk lived with another guy who worked at Lucifer's, named String. String, Monk and Sun and I got along well and partied a lot together. We soon started to do acid, which brought back a lot of memories of my past. But it seemed as though I was more in control than I was before, and I never let that change. (Although I have stopped doing heavy drugs, I do smoke pot).

The good feeling I had going ended when I started to suspect Sun of cheating on me. I soon broke up with her. I was once again a single man, with no one to worry about, and this was starting to suit my life style.

My reunion with my sister was emotional and intense. We both cried in each others arms. I know there will always be some resentment from my family for things I've done. In spite of this, I saw my sister. I knew, right then and there, that I was still loved by all.

I was happy by the fact that I was working, making honest friends, and living well. I had sent Sun back to Phoenix, and even though I thought of her often, I did not plan on seeing her for some time.

Monk and I got involved with some people up in Red Deer, just north of Calgary, in the drug business. It turned sour on us after one deal. Monk and I went to Red Deer to do some trading. We soon determined we would not make anything from this, so we decided to steal their drugs, go to Calgary, unload them and have a good time. String's mother told String we were in trouble over drugs, from reading the cards. String relayed the message even before we told him what we had done, which made us more than a little nervous. Eventually, we decided to go to Vancouver and lay low. The people we took the drugs from left some bullets stuck to the door of a party house where we met, definitely a signal for us to cut town for a while. We caught the next train to Vancouver, telling our friends we would be back late that summer.

Monk and I stayed at the Regent Hotel on West Hastings. We sold the odd bit of pot, but started to think of going down to the U.S. I wanted to see some friends there, and this would be a good trip for the Monk, since he'd never been to the states. We started our trip to Phoenix, and what a trip it was. Once we got to Reno, Nevada, we got picked up by two girls. Monk got to spend the night with one, while the other took off and I had to sleep in the car. Well, in the morning I had something to raze Monk about. When we got back on the highway, this girl gave Monk thirty bucks and said it was a good night. "Well I never knew you had it in you," I said and he said, "Well neither did I" and we both laughed.

We met up with another hitch-hiker, also headed to Phoenix, who said we should team up. I said no. It was much too hard to get a ride with two people, let alone three. We agreed to stay in touch as we traveled along the same road. If one of us got a ride with someone with enough room for another rider, we'd ask them to pick the other up. We got to Redondo Beach, California.

Len was glad to see Monk and me. It had been quite sometime since we had last seen each other. Monk and I stayed there for about three or four days. One afternoon we saw Len had received a rather big shipment of mushrooms, tie stick, and just some regular bud. I thought that it would be nice to go back to Calgary with better drugs. We took what later weighed out to half a pound of tie stick, a half a pound of some good bud, and, to top off our shopping list, close to a half pound of mushrooms. We hit the highway fast, and found a ride with a fellow who should not have been on his own. By this, I mean he was somewhat different. After about a hundred miles, I told the guy to let us out, as he was getting stranger by the mile. I wanted out of his car fast. I started to remember people telling us of the Hillside Strangler in Southern California, as well as the I-5 Killer (Interstate number 5). All that I could think of was this guy, who for no known reason changed his attitude to pure hatred so fast, and his voice so suddenly, it was definitely scary.

After the guy stopped, Monk and I felt relieved. We sat down and smoked a big bowl of pot before we started to hitch again. We got a ride just outside of Sacramento with a young fellow and his younger brother. To be honest, I don't remember his name, so I'll call him Sam and his brother Joe.

By the time we were nearing the border, we got caught in a fire that raged on both sides of the road. The smoke was so thick you could not see out the windows. We stayed that way long enough for me to smoke a joint. I was slightly worried once in awhile, you could see flames that stood at least 15 feet tall. We sat for half an hour, maybe more. The smoke cleared enough for us to see about fifty cars that looked damaged as well. Everyone had to go for a wash. Sam, Joe the Monk and I all thought it was quite the experience. From that point on, all the way to Seattle, the Monk and I got shit faced. We rolled out of the van when we hit town, only to find out that we still had a ways to go before the Canada-U.S. border. I suggested we look for someone who wanted to buy some pot, in order to straighten up before we got there.

As fate would have it, it worked, but only for awhile. Once we got closer, I thought, how the hell am I going to get this shit over without getting busted? It was raining and we could not walk around. There was only one thing to do and that was to walk right up to the customs office and hope like hell they wouldn't search us. I did not think it would work. Being the doubtful one, I got the honor of doing the job.

No one in Calgary knew we were on our way back. This was for our safety, but also we wanted to surprise everyone if we got over. I put all the drugs in one bag, and put the bag in the front of my pants like a small belly. I put on a rain poncho, and so did Monk. We walked into the office.

There was a female customs officer on duty. She asked me what I was doing in the states. I told her I was camping with my friends. Monk told her the same thing. She asked us if we had anything to declare. We both said no. I thought we were busted when she asked two more times. I told her I had something to declare. I looked at her and said "I have a hangover and a sun burn, and I'm going to get our friend back." I told her the friend we were camping with thought it would be a good practical joke to take off while Monk and I slept. She laughed and said she hoped our luck was working, and to have a good day. She told us to walk, and that we did. It took two rides to get home, and it felt good to be back.

Once back, I soon settled into a peaceful co-existence with my family. I lived with my mother, for awhile. When I found a job, I moved in with a guy I had worked with previously named Stan. I started out as a prep cook, which was just fine. I was not fast enough yet to work on the line.

I was working five days a week, enough to bring home the bacon and pay for the odd party. All of us knew each other. Our group included Stan, George, Monk, String, TAC, Sid, Vincent and me. We took over an old building in downtown Calgary, calling it the Frankenstein place. It became known as the Frankie's. We would have some good times together. There was one special woman who won the hearts of every one of us. Her name was Lady Di. She worked with Monk and me for some time.

One day, while Stan and I were downtown, I met a beautiful lady who I was later to love the way I could never love another. I leaned over and asked her if she had a rolling paper, as we sat on a bench on Eighth Avenue Mall in downtown Calgary. She said no. Another person had one. I went back and asked her if she would like to smoke a joint. She said "Yes". Her name was Ann. Ann worked for the government. She said she was going out of town for the week-end. I gave it my best shot, and she took my number, saying she would call.

My life was going to change. My job got better when I got some line cook experience. I could not get this Ann girl out of my mind. I thought of her all the time.

One day, while Stan and his brother were sitting drinking with our next door neighbor, Stew and I got into a fight, which just about destroyed our friendship. The next morning, Stew wore a cast, with a broken wrist. He had given me a black eye. We both laughed had a beer, and discovered our friendship was intact. The next day, we were both embarrassed. Ann came over to buy some smoke, and when she saw the shape we were in, she laughed. I thought I had lost the girl of my dreams. I was shocked when she didn't care after we told her what it was about (being drunk and rude.) I invited her to accompany me to a party on Friday. When she said yes, I knew it was going to that kind of night.

We started out drinking a number of beers then dropped acid. I had not done LSD for sometime. I was starting to lose interest in drugs (except pot). The party was rocking. There were drugs, smoke and more to drink than you could imagine. Ann and I thought it would be good to hide her purse. Despite our extra care, someone found it, and stole all her money. I confronted the guy who had let us stash it in his room. He told us he did not go into the room. We never found the money, and left the house, vowing never to return.

We went back to my place and talked for a long time. When we kissed, I felt my heart go to my throat. She seemed to know there was something between us. We made love for the longest time that night. In the morning, I told her I wanted us to see each other as much as possible, that I was most happy to have met a person like her. We spoke daily after that. I was feeling better than I ever had in my life. I tried comparing this relationship

122

to my previous ones and could not. It seemed to me that nothing could destroy this. Murphy's Law was not going to let me off that easy.

I went to work like I did every night, and was told that I was being laid off without notice. I was finally doing it right, and the rug came out from under my feet again. I got a job as a security officer at the Calgary Stampede, in order to pay for the camping trip I wanted to take with Ann and her friend Sal. Sal was introduced to my brother, so it was to be a foursome.

I was not going to take being laid off without notice, so I got the Labor Board in. I was paid for two weeks of severance. I felt at least I stood up for what was right. I had also moved in with Ann, which was going good. I did not get to see much of her for the two weeks that the Stampede was on, as I was working 12 to 14 hours a day and it was night shift.

I had applied to go back to school, to get a degree in Forestry. I liked the idea of being outdoors, working in that kind of environment. Still, old habits die hard, and I was living proof. I tried at school, I really did. Some of the time I would do good, and some of the time I just could not. I had a very interesting English teacher who told me I should write, as I had done some good work in his class. He was the only teacher that I got along with, and I tried.

I got to know a lot of Ann's relatives. We all got along. There was one relative that asked if I could do some work on some of his houses. I told him I was good with tools and I would do the work, but it would cost him. I was going to school, but I could do it after school and on week-ends. Matt offered to let Ann and I move into one of his houses. We would only have to pay half the rent, and that was only two hundred and fifty dollars. A month later we moved. I was now going to school, taking care of the grounds and general up keep of three houses. I was tired, but I felt good with what was happening, for the first time.

I was still peddling the odd bit of pot to keep Ann and myself in smoke, and it started to lead to problems. I spent the Christmas holidays with Ann's family, and was not without pot. When we got to my mothers place, I was never without pot there either. One thing led to another, and I started to sell the odd gram of coke for him, then a quarter ounce, and I got a gram from him later that night. The friend I was selling for came over at six-thirty, and demanded his coke. I told him I had to go get it. He freaked out and jumped on me. I was barely awake when he did this, and not ready. So he got the upper hand. All I saw was a shiny object. I thought it was

123

his keys coming at me. Later there was a cloud I could not see through, no matter how hard I blinked. He gave me a cut that just about left me blind. The cut was right at the corner of my eye. I had previously rented my sister the suite above Ann and I, and when she heard the noise, she came running down stairs. She saw me and started to scream. I had blood all over me, and could not see. Blood was in my eyes.

I ended up with six stitches. I told myself I was not going to get involved with drugs. I was not getting anywhere, with them or my life. One of Ann's cousins and I had planned on going to the interior of B.C. for a canoe trip. I was still not over getting cut, but I wanted to get out of the city. I was not doing anything of value. School was the pits. I was cancelled from the program (because of lack of attendance) and I didn't care. I went on this trip, and Ann was not amused. She thought I should not run from anything. I told her I was not running, I just wanted out for awhile. Inside, I was running, but the way I was feeling, I could not admit she was right. For two weeks, I did nothing but contemplate my life. What was going to happen when I got back?

I came to the conclusion I would sell drugs part time, get a job, and start over. I wanted to just take off, I wanted to keep going and not falter at everything. I went job hunting, filling out applications with no luck. Ann did not understand. I will never be able to tell her that I am truly sorry. I can't blame her. Her patience was running short. I was not doing much of anything. I tried to get in touch with Jane so that she might come out and break up the monotony.

Jane wrote me, saying she would like to come out for a couple of weeks in the summer. This must have upset Ann; she thought Jane would try to take me back to the old life style. Ann read the letter. Jane had mentioned that she wanted to get high.

My relationship with Ann was on the rocks, as a result of getting slashed. School was non-existent. Money was scarce, but drugs were always there. She did not like living with a drug dealer, a person with no ambition. I did not have much to look forward to. I was just stagnating, not doing anything of value. I tried to talk to Ann about Jane's visit, but it was not going over well.

The night Jane flew into Calgary, I was really excited. It was almost five years since I had seen Jane. Ann reacted to the fact that I was seeing someone who was important in my life, and I felt good. We went to pick them up at the airport, and when we met, I could not believe the warmth I felt from Jane. This was something I had forgotten! We sat in the parking lot and cracked open a bottle of wine. Then the car would not start. I was seen by the cops, who asked what was wrong. I told them we needed a jump to get us on our way. The cop looked inside the car, saw the bottle of wine, and I was had.

I was fined for having open liquor, which set the evening off to a bad start. Jane had made arrangements to stay at her friend's place for the night. They were not going to stay in the city for long, as Jane wanted to camp. (Jane came out with her new girlfriend, and wanted to spend as much time with her as possible). Ann and I had a drink with Jane and her girlfriend Tammy. When we left, I told Jane and Tammy to contact me so we could spend the next day together.

Ann and I, along with our friend Cher, started to talk of moving to Deer Run in south Calgary, where my sister lived. There was an open condo for rent, and I told Ann if we were to move there, I would get a job, not deal drugs, and try as hard as I could. After we got moved in Jane phoned, asking me to take Tammy and her to Banff, Alta. It was only an hour and half to Banff. Why not? I went over to where Jane was. She was waiting for me. We put their gear in Ann's aunt's car and drove out to Banff.

I took Jane and Tammy to the place where Ann and I had camped. I thought they would like some of the area. I sat with Jane and Tammy, had a few drinks then told them I had to get back to the city, as I had to drop off the car. I was talked into another drink, and then I told them I had to leave. I said that I wanted to stay, but I was in love and did not want to ruin it. (Meaning that things were not going too well for Ann and me right now.)

I will swear, on a stack of bibles, I only had three small glasses of wine. On the way home I started to hallucinate, and I could not understand why.

CHAPTER TWELVE

STARTING OVER

Time period for this is spring of 1983. Ann and I found it impossible to live together after the way I came home from seeing Jane off at the Park. I came back just loaded, and I still do not know how I got so shit faced from three small glasses of wine. Maybe Jane thought if I was loaded I would spend the night with them, at their camp (nothing sexual). I assumed she had spiked my drinks as I was never known, even to myself, to get loaded on such a small amount of liquor. I acted like an ass, and when Ann went to my sis' place (that was only next door), I was not about to stop and walk away from my lady leaving me. I walked up to my sis' door and took a good swing at it. My sis came out and told me if I did not stop, she would call the cops. I stopped, but would not quit trying to talk to Ann. Ann came to the window, and said she had called the cops. I knew it was time to go to bed. I walked over to our place and smashed something, with no real intent to do damage, and fell asleep. In the morning, I found I was not dreaming that this had happened. My hand was bruised badly, and I was all alone in our house. I could not get a straight answer from anyone.

I was now going to have to start all over. This I found harder than anything in the world to do. I was in love, like never before and had slipped again. I was living in the basement of the house that I use to take care of for Matt. He was the only one in any position to help me find a place to stay, and only as long as I got a job.

I went to welfare and got put on assistance. I gave Matt what was his for renting a room with nothing but a mat on the floor. I went from good to complete shit and I could not help it.

I started to look for work, and saw Ann the odd time. There was still a chance of getting back together with her, and that was all I wanted. I got a job at the Cove, in downtown Calgary, as a prep cook. I was to be trained as a line cook, so I would be able to take a night shift once in awhile. I was starting to pull it together again. Sis saw the change, and allowed me to move in with her, as long as I paid my own way and did not have any loud people over after work. (I was on the 5:30 to 1:30 or 2:00 shift). I did not care what shift I had to work, as long as I still had a fighting chance at getting back with Ann.

I was seeing Ann once or twice a week. She showed she cared, and that gave me strength to do what I had to, but this was not going to work. After awhile I saw that we would not be getting back together, and I was once again taking the only way I could think of. I went back to drugs, and drinking, and using the money that I could front from my checks. I was able to keep myself high. This lasted until I met this stripper that worked at the Cove. The Cove was the only place where, after a certain hour, you could pick up a girl on lady's night. Since I worked there, I was given lots of chances. When I did, I started to get back on track.

My job was going good. I got a raise and was always there for work, as I liked the people. I made lots of friends at the Cove. This was important to me, I was tired of being alone. I was working with Lady Di again, and it felt good. She would come into the kitchen and get me stoned. I screwed up her orders sometimes but we would laugh it off.

I never once gave up selling the odd bit of drugs, and this came in handy sometimes. I did not have anyone to see on a regular basis, and this was not always satisfying, but you have to make do. Judy, the girl I met, was only interested in one night stands, and I was looking for something more steady. Our relationship only lasted tor a week. I had the same emptiness I felt when I was just getting over breaking up with Ann. I wanted a girl, but I just could not slow down my restless pace. I was a bit more concerned about myself, and what was happening in my life, so I put off looking for a steady girl. I was still having the odd bit of sex with men, but I never let anyone know this. My way of life showed to everyone that I was straight. What ever I did, no one knew, and this was good.

My goals were starting to change. I liked the way things were heading.

Since I was living with my sis I started to slow down, and not go out drinking or blowing my money. I went to church the odd time. This was a first. I was going with my sister and her kids. Her son, Fred was a year and a bit, and Cathy was two or three. I felt great going with them and meeting with all my sister's friends. I started to get involved with people on a more open and honest basis, and this felt good.

I was still doing some drugs, at some of the staff parties after work, for example. I still was in touch with some of the people back east, through Jane. I was never going to give up her friendship, and always left the line open. If I was ever going to come back, I would bring drugs or something.

Whenever I did talk to Jane on the phone, she would ask me to come back for a visit, but the thought of going brought back memories. But the reality of it was, I was still wanted by the police in Ontario. I was walking around Calgary as if nothing was wrong. I told her that I would think on it.

The summer was going good. I was working steady, had good friends and good family. What more could a man want, I was saying to myself???

While I was at work one day, Lady Di asked me to drop by her house so I could meet her brother Paul. I went and met him and had a very good time. Paul told me if I was ever in Toronto, to get a hold of him for drinks. Most of the Cove staff was there, which made it better because everyone knew each other. After that party, every night at the Cove we would all sit around getting shit faced, till the management would tell us to leave. Winter was just around the corner, but I was feeling good, with no depressions or down time. I was getting along with my family. My mother had since moved back east, to be with her family. It seemed to me she was doing what I had done. I went away for a long time and came back, and now she was doing it. George moved with her, so it was only Sis, her kids and me out west. I was doing the best I could to help sis with the kids.

I found out one night (at work) we were going to have new management changes as soon as possible, to improve the crowds. This was going to be the worst move of my entire life even to this day. I really did not care if the management changed, so long as I had a job. Bill, the new entertainment manager, seemed like a fairly good guy, although my first impression of him was a big time hood. He made me feel uneasy. I watched him whenever he came into the kitchen. Bill and his wife, Sonya, got the Cove off the ground. In the first week Bill was there, starting on Wednesday to Sunday, the place was packed every night, at least four hundred people a night. The way he did it, was to offer free dinner to anyone who bought drinks. It was a hit. In the kitchen we worked fast and hard.. It was getting cold now, and I wanted to buy a car but could not afford it. Work would not give me a loan, and I thought I would have to wait.

One night, after work, the girls had rung out their tabs, and we were all sitting in the kitchen. One girl, very close to Lady Di, came in upset, saying someone had stolen her payout to the club. No one could find the envelope, so the club was holding her responsible. After everyone looked for it, the staff and Jewels had a long talk. We concluded that one of the d-jays had the opportunity to take it. All the weight went from Jewels to the d-j, named Ted.

No one could find him. Rex was locking up, and since he lived near me (about 15 miles from work) and I did not feel like walking, I asked him for a ride. We sat for a while after everyone left and had a drink, trying to figure out how to find the money. Finally, we went outside and looked through the garbage bins. We found all the charge card slips, and concluded that what the staff had said was the truth. We went out to some of the night spots (where the restaurant people go) and found Ted. He had a room in the York Hotel on Seventh Avenue. We thought we should check it out.

He was in his room. We talked Ted into letting us come in and talk.

We related the story of how the Cove was robbed, and how we had to talk to everyone, including Ted, that was at work tonight. He said he had to take a pill, and went to the dresser. He reached in, and faked a cough. Thinking no one was watching, he stuffed the money down his pants. I said, "Put the money on the bed before I flip out and hurt you." Ted started to cry, saying he wanted the money for his family, and that he was sorry for doing it. He put the money on the bed. Rex and I looked at each other and smiled.

The next day when I got to work, the manager asked me what happened. I told the story, saying I was very happy to have taken part. Now, would you consider loaning me three hundred and fifty bucks for a car? He said he would think about it. I knew I was going to get the loan now, and tried to think of where to get a car. Just as shift week was coming to an end, Tim the night manager came back and gave me the money. I was happy as a dog in shit. I was going to get a car!

I don't know if it was Fate, or the Almighty, or even Murphy's Law, but

I was doing something right, and feeling good about it. Bill said he knew where I could pick up a junker that would last the winter, and then I could buy all sorts of things. I did not catch it immediately, but soon realized that my first impression of Bill had been right.

Bill told me I did not have to work late. He said I should spend the day with him and Sonya, and their family, at the ranch out in Okotoks, Alta. I said that I would like to, and then got out, as we had reached my drop off point, as he was giving me a ride.

The next day, we went to the ranch and met Bill's mother Lilly and his dad Mr. Sands. Then I met the one I was told so much about, their daughter Autumn. We sat around, talked and drank a few beers. When we wanted to smoke a joint, we would take a walk. Bill asked me to go for a drive. I knew that now he was going to lay his cards on the table. The first thing he asked was; if I had a chance, could I unload about thirty pounds of pot? How long would it take? I told Bill I could do it. It would take me about two or three days. Then he asked me if I could move something more valuable, fast. It was cocaine.

We agreed to call the coke Uncle Emilio. I told him I had not moved coke since I got slashed, but I could do it, and that if I really wanted to, I could do it, no problem.

We would need at least one good deal, in order to buy our own product. Back at my sis's place, I sat in the living room, drank a beer and smoked a joint, trying to decide what I should do. I knew it was good money. I could buy some things for Christmas. I did not see Bill for a couple of days, as his mother was ill and he wanted to stay near. I went to work, as I always did. While I was cutting up cabbage on the meat slicer, I was thinking of how nice it would be to score some coke and have some fun with some women. I was so wrapped up in this trail of thought I sliced a part of my finger, and was bleeding like hell. I wrapped up my finger and was taken to the hospital, where it was necessary to have neurosurgery.

I was put on workmen's comp. My first cheque wasn't due for sometime. I thought I should accept Bill's offer. The car I bought through Bill and Sonya turned out to be a lemon, so I got rid of it. Bill promised me a new car when our money became solid. We sat down to make a plan, to rid ourselves of all the coke we were going to bring in.

I just so happened to know a few people that were into coke. Bill fronted me $200, to have on hand to impress the invited customers. I talked to a few people at the Cove, and was able to put together a deal for a half pound of powder. Soon, my sister started to wonder what was going on, and said I should level with her. I told her I would later. I still had to find out where this trail was going to take me, hopefully not to jail.

Bill and Sonya had found a house in Mindapore. They knew a fellow that lived in north Calgary named Ree. He was a friendly guy, and we got along well, becoming friends. Bill and Sonya wanted me to move in with them. I talked it over with my sister, telling her I would still help in any way possible. I decided to move in with Bill and Sonya. Once I was settled in the new place (actually owned by Ree) Bill suddenly became dirt cheap. I was later to find out they were related.

At first, I could not understand how: Ree was oriental and Bill was Scottish. I found out Bill had married Ere's sister, ending up with two kids and a divorce. But that never stopped them from keeping in touch, especially in the interest of drugs.

It was a very comfortable house, good for all that was needed for a party. I moved in with everything I owned, thinking nothing could go wrong.

It was about one week since the Cove. I wanted to find out what the word was on the deal. As I was driving there, I began thinking about what I was really getting into, and the long term implications of my choices. I had a lot to lose, as well as the potential good times. Greed and stupidity got the better of me, and I went into this full force.

Bill got about a pound and a half of Peruvian rock, capable of blowing anyone's brain. He took me to the den to show me how he worked over his friend Uncle Emilio. As I looked at Bill, getting prepared to do things, I laughed as Bill took the time to put on a little apron and plastic gloves and a little mask over his mouth and nose. Why you ask? Who the hell knows. I never did find out!!!

Bill cut his friend with vitamin B, and did it three to one, to ensure that the word got out there was good snow in town. It took time to have everyone call it Emilio, but it worked. I got the deal all set with this beautiful blond chick. She was eight ounces of Emilio. I was ready to do it, when Ree asked to talk to me. As we drove along in his $18,000 dollar car, he related his vision of the future, calling this a solid start for the organization. I told him there was nothing to worry about, that it would go down just the way we planned.

I met up with Liz (the girl that was buying) in the dressing room at the Cove. She was also stripping now and then. I walked into the room, and not a word was said till I saw the money. Liz sat in her chair, and with casual exhibitionism, showed me some of the sights but nothing serious. I grabbed the coin. She asked if I would like to count the money, I told her I wanted her to count it for me, but first she should do a few lines with me. Her reaction was fast and full of smiles. Liz started to call me cutie, saying I should come over to her place one night and do a cook.

When we finished counting the money, and I was satisfied that there was $18,500.00 there, I told her about what was going on. I told her that we would be going for a drive, and that she was to bring the money. She would be dropped off with Emilio during the ride, Liz took no time to get ready for this and before long, we were in the car driving a route that I had worked out with Ere. Once I got to a certain point, Ere would follow me. I was to pull into a parking lot and wait, as Ere was going to be right behind me. I was to keep going, watching to make sure it was not a set up. After a few minutes, Ere drove up and parked a little way from my car. I took the money in a newspaper and walked to his car, leaning in to the window and taking the paper he had for me. We would meet at Fourth Street Rose for a drink. I walked back to the car. She kissed me, and then I drove her home. I was never so awed by a person, as I was by the way she seemed when I gave her the paper. She got an intense look in her eyes, so intense I thought she was going to cry.

I met up with Ere and Sonya. They had been sitting in the car, counting money. They gave me the "thumbs up" sign. I thought they underestimated me. I started walking to the bar, to wait till they got there. Sonya asked me if there was something wrong. I was cold and wanted a drink. They both told me I had done a beautiful job, that I should be happy. I would be happy when I started to see some of the coin or a car. We all laughed, had a few drinks and went home.

I was doing Emilio everyday. I started out carrying one gram at a time. I went from one to five, or ten, and always gave away the occasional line. I also used it to get some satisfaction and enjoyment with women. I would talk to some of the hookers on the strip, get them high before we had sex, then pay them with Emilio. This worked to bring in some new customers. I was into this, but started to find out I was getting no where with Bill. I started to stay with him more when he went out. I was asked to do everything shy of the laundry and the shopping.

I told Bill I wanted to get more active, to go and see some people I knew, which I thought was a good move. So I phoned a woman I had known for sometime, and talked Emilio to her. She said it would be good to come up with an ounce, and that I could spend the week. But this was too close to Christmas, and I told her that I would rather send it to her. She said it would not work; she wanted to have it brought up in case anything went wrong. So I was off to Yellowknife, N.W.T.

After consulting with Bill, I was sent north, staying for the Christmas I was supposed to spend with my sister. I told Sis I was very sorry, but I would be back. I promised to do something special. She seemed to understand. Sis and her kids told me stories of what there was to know about the N.W.T. Sue and her husband Clayton did the odd line of Emilio, and we all got shit faced, I proceeded to cook up some Emilio, something I was doing to much of at that time. Sue and Clayton had not done Emilio this way before. They liked it and bought more, putting in orders every week. I was afraid to go there with the coke. I did keep my eyes open for anything that might be trouble.

I was glad to be back in the city. I wanted to relax, and not think of work. (I'd call it when I was away.) I was not back long enough to sleep twelve hours, when Bill came in and told me I had to go to Toronto. He couldn't, because Lilly was sick again. I still felt for him in a strange way.

I was on the jet to Toronto before long, and proceeded to get blasted on the trip, I was having trouble drinking, as I was not eating anything (from all the Emilio). I wanted to puke badly, so I went to the can, but instead of getting sick, I pulled out my little bag and started to snort my face off. When the plane landed, I was happy to breathe fresh air. I felt confined in the plane.

I told my hotel to send a car to pick me up. I thought; why not take what was offered to me now, while I'm on my own. I got to the hotel (on the airport strip), called Again Motor Hotel. Bill told me this was the best place to stay. I got a message from Bill, as soon as I was in my room. I was to contact the fellow named Joel. He wants to talk to Uncle Emilio. I was off to my first meeting, and got the desk to get a car ready. I was going to be chauffeured. I felt out of place. I had not been in Toronto since 1979, only long enough to spend Christmas there. Now I was back, and this time, I came with a friend that was going to make me, and the company, lots of money (I thought).

It felt so funny being chauffeured around the city I had grown up in, on my own. I started to play the role of a big time drug dealer, and went every where in a limo. Bill had such good Emilio; I could get anything I wanted with it. I started to go downtown, but I only stayed long enough to see an old friend I had not seen since the late seventies. Doug was glad to see me, even though he knew right from the start I was doing no good. I could not lie to him. I told him what I was doing, and he said I should be careful, as there had been a lot of busts lately. I thought he would tell me I was not the same as I was when I was released. That maybe I was going back and this would really fuck me up. I wanted to hear those words, but they were never spoken. I left Doug's house with false pride about myself, and I did not even dwell on it.

I knew a guy in Calgary who was trying to set up a deal in Victoria, B.C. When Bill phoned me one night, I told him I was sure Lou was good for what he promised. To my surprise, Bill had installed a conference line. Lou, Bill and I all talked over what Lou was setting up. Bill and I finished the conversation, and I reassured him.

My mother and brother were living in Toronto at this time, so I thought I would contact them, and do something special. It was almost New Year's, and I had not seen them for sometime. They came to the hotel and we had a few beers. I told them to come to my room, and we would have a beer there and talk. Once inside the room, my mother asked me what I was up to. I told her I would show her, on the grounds that she do nothing, say nothing and not ask many questions. She said okay. I told her she was going to meet the nickname that she has had for so long. I pulled out about seventeen ounces of almost pure Emilio. I told her there was enough coke there to make way over $50,000. She could not believe I was doing this again. George sat quite still. He asked the odd question, and I told them both we would do something together soon. I said goodbye to them, and promised we would get together. I took off to meet this guy Joel, as he wanted more. Again I went in style, I was all fucked up again, and refused to acknowledge it. I was having fun. I got to go where I pleased, and was not told how to run the company while I was away. This led me to some *heavy* partying.

Downtown was a heat score, and I knew I would only have trouble. I thought it would be nice to talk to the Uncle I had not seen for well over ten years. I was shocked to see he had broken his leg, and was hobbling around. I told him we did not have to go anywhere, and that we could sit around and do a few lines and talk. But beer was on order. Soon we went to this bar down the street and drank for awhile, then went back to his place. I got stupid again, and did another base (cook) with Red and his wife, although she did not partake. It was still cool with her. The next morning, I went back to the hotel and was phoned by Red. He said he and his wife Connie had an argument and that I had best get out of that hotel, as she said she was going to set me up. I left, and thought to myself that I should go to the next best hotel. So, I got a room at the Hyatt Regent, and it cost me $117.00 for one night. I was now more than a bit nervous, and did not want to see Red or his wife. But no more than two hours after getting the room, I got a call from Red. He told me that he just knew were I went, and still wanted to go out (as the boys and not have to worry about Connie.) I told Red we could get together later that night and go for drinks, but for now I was going to be busy.

I had nothing to do but sleep; even that seemed impossible. I wanted to get a woman, and do some serious love making. I phoned up this call girl place, told them what kind of lady I wanted, and started to drink. I did a few snorts by myself. When she showed up, I did not want to do it. I just lost my nerve. I guess she could sense this. She asked if anything was wrong. I told her no, and that she should come in and have a drink. We got talking, and then the phone rang. I was not expecting anyone. It was security for the hotel. They told me that there was a man sitting in the lobby, and I had better come down and straighten this out. It was Red. I told him to wait for a bit, as I had a client in my room. Security did not say anything, once I told them who this fellow was. I went back to my room, told my lady of leisure that her time was up. I gave her two hundred and said goodbye. Red came up, and we talked of what the hell I was doing. I told him I was involved with some heavy people. I was now a runner and seller of high grade coke. This was the wrong way for him to see me. I should have just told him the same story I had told my mother and brother. Now I was up shit creek.

In the morning, I left that hotel. I had gotten in touch with Lady Di's brother Paul. We had gotten along well when he visited Lady Di in Calgary. He told me it was okay for me to stay at their place. I would not be so paranoid about hotels. I talked to Bill every day, but did not tell him about the hotel change (till later.)

I sold Joel eight ounces of Emilio, and then started to see the money a day, sometimes two days late. I told Joel I wanted money up front from now on. He tried to argue, but I would not let him.

Paul knew I was selling Emilio, and that started me basing again. I had run out of my personal, and did not care about opening up an ounce. I thought it would last me for the last time I was going to be there. I started to do some heavy partying with Paul. Joel started to fuck up again and told me I was going to have to wait for at least a week for the people that he fronted it to. This time I gave him supreme shit.

I told Bill this, and he hit the roof. I was told to send all the money, and I was to apply more pressure to Joel. Bill also told me about some other people I should look up, so I did (selling only about two ounces). I asked Red if he could unload any Emilio. He said he would send the guy to me. It was only worth two ounces (and a possible order for more later).

I was talking to some of my friends back in Calgary, and they told me the Monk was in Toronto. I should look him up and party. Well, the big night was here. New Years Eve in Toronto! I had dinner with Red, and what a dinner it turned out to be. I left Emilio at Paul's place, plus all my money (which was now over forty thousand), went downtown, and hooked up with my uncle. Red and I went to a nice restaurant and had a great meal. I was feeling good. I was with someone who had known me all my life, and had the same (well, almost the same) attitude as I. After dinner, we started to walk towards Bloor St. and Yonge, looking for some women and a place to party for the build up to the new year. I saw these two ladies standing by a bar. They were drinking a bottle of wine, waiting to get in. I thought, well that looks like a start. I suggested we try this bar, and see what happens. Red said he was game, and we stood behind the girls.

I asked them if they would like to sit together, once we got in. They said yes, much to our surprise. I told them I would buy the first bottle and then would set the pace for the night. I ordered the best bottle of champagne, and from there, the service was outstanding. Kelly and Dawn did not seem to mind that we drank fast. Once they found out we were doing Emilio, I do not know why, but when you do coke, you can drink like a fish and stay relatively sober. I started to do Emilio right at the table. I gave the little bag I had to Red, and told him go right ahead and do what he wanted, then pass it on.

Kelly and Dawn were not sure at first. We waited till later, and hit it again, after a few bottles. Then Kelly said she would like to try some, as she was getting buzzed off the drink. I gave her the little bag, and cut one of the straws that was on the table. She took one hell of a snort, out of the bag, then passed it over to Dawn. Soon, the night was closing, and everyone in the bar sat quiet for a moment. Then one hell of a party started. We all danced and choo-choo trained around the bar. There must have been forty people doing this, while the rest danced at their tables or on the dance floor. I was all fucked up. I snorted at least two grams in that bar, not counting what Red and the girls did. I thought, what could be better??

I wanted this night to last forever. I pushed away all thoughts, and partied. I ended up going home alone, but started to do it all over again. Paul and his roommate Ron sat with me in the kitchen, while I based about three grams. I played a couple hundred games of darts in the time I was there.

I was in touch with the boss in Calgary, and was told by Sonya that Bill's mother Lilly was in the hospital. Bill was getting all fucked up, and was over-doing it with Uncle Emilio and the strippers from the Cove. Sonya was starting to worry that Bill might do something stupid.

I phoned the hospital and talked to Bill. He wanted me to come out there as soon as possible. I told him I had to wait till Joel paid me for this guy I fronted through my uncle. It was worth about five thousand. I had a blow out of a party before I left. I took home all kinds of stuff for Sonya and Autumn. Paul drove me to the airport. I said my goodbyes, and promised I would come back again.

Throughout the flight home, I was going through withdrawals, and had to go to the can a lot to snort my face off. I was not basing, I needed more to get me off. When I landed in Calgary, Ere was there to pick me up. I asked how Lilly was, and he told me she could die, anytime. She was just holding on. Mr. Sands was taking it rough. He realized what was inevitable, and stayed by her side day and night, crying like a little boy.

When I got home, Sonya told me Bill wanted to see me as soon as I landed. I told her I just wanted to change, and then I would drive down. Ere did not stay long, and was soon off back to town (we lived about fifteen miles from town). He wanted to make a deposit. I could not tell Sonya what happened in Toronto, but filled her in on some of the highlights.

I did not know why, but I had the worst case of the willies than I ever had in my life. In spite of all the herculean partying, the call girls, the clubs, hotels, booze and mountain of blow I had burned rough in Toronto, I still managed to come home with 60 grand. I was 22 years old.

CHAPTER THIRTEEN

UNGLUED ONCE AGAIN

When I got to the hospital in Okotoks, just south of Calgary, I was stunned by how everyone looked. They looked ragged. Lou had been with Bill (most of the time I was in Toronto setting up deals) in Victoria, B.C. and elsewhere. He told me Bill had not been true to his word, regarding his commission for setting up the deals. I told him not to fret; this was a trying time, but business was not on hold.

I looked at Bill, as he sat crying beside his dying mother. I had just started to get to know her. Bill's father, Mr. Sands, looked as if he was going to have a breakdown.

I went to sit by myself for a minute, and Bill came over to talk to me. He said this was too much for him. He had just spent time overseas, and did not get to spend the last years of his mother's life with her. He could not say what needed to be said, and did not know what to do. I told him it would be best if he sat down beside her, told her everything, the truth. Bill looked at me, as if to say, fuck you, who the hell do you think you're talking to? But I knew what was on his mind. He asked me if I had brought any Emilio, as he needed some right then and there. I told him I did, and that I had to go to the car. When I got back to the room, Bill asked me to get some coffee and put Emilio in it for his father. I told him I would not spike a drink. He did, and for awhile, he and his father seemed a little calmer.

Lou and Mr. Sands left and Bill and I got into the bag. I went into the room and saw Lilly laying there. I put her hand in mine, and told her to

138

fight, and that we all were pulling for her. Bill told me a little later that he had to get the hell out of there, as he was going batty knowing there was nothing anyone could do. We got into the car. I asked him if there was anywhere he wanted to go. He said he would let me know when to stop. As we drove, all over the south end of Calgary at three thirty in the morning, Bill had his little bag out, and was snorting his face off, crying at the same time.

I told Bill it would be better for him if he went home and saw his wife. Sonya could be of more comfort than me. Bill told me he did not want to go home, he wanted to escape and not have to see what was going on right in front of him. He said it hurt too much. I often thought what if my mother had died when I was on my own? Bill told me he wanted to go see his little sweetheart Patricia, a striper at the Cove, and get fucked up. I told Bill we should get home, as Sonya would be worried, but Bill did not want to go home. So off we went to Patricia's apartment. Bill had a couple of ounces in the car, and once we go to her place, Bill pulled it out. He got Patricia to base it (she did it good), which seemed to make him happy. I knew this was not right. It was four in the morning when we started to base, and base we did!! From four in the morning, till ten thirty that night, we based Emilio, getting really shit faced. Bill gave me a chain, worth a lot of money, and told me never to take it off. It was in reference to his mother. I told him it would never come off.

I knew that Bill cheated on Sonya, but I could not do anything about it. Once Bill set his mind to anything, it got done. That was the only good quality about Bill I can remember. I knew he want to be alone with Patricia, so I lay down on the couch (I had enough Emilio). They went into the bedroom, and once every half hour Patricia would come to base up some more Emilio for the two of them. I thought to myself, how the fuck can he keep going and going? I never did find out.

About three in the afternoon, I asked Bill if he wanted to go home. He got mad, saying I was trying to rush him. I told him I was only thinking that if we did not make contact with someone soon, we would never know how Lilly was doing. That was the wrong thing to say. Bill got all fucked up when I brought up the subject of his family. I was learning just how valuable family really is, being close to my family once again. Bill did not want to go and started to do more Emilio. I got on it, and then we did not stop till we ran out of Emilio. Bill wanted me to get more, but I told him that it was time to go home.

By the time we left, it was ten thirty, and I knew what was going to happen. Sonya was going to flip out. We did not even phone home. Patricia had the phone unplugged. Ere was going to give Bill shit! Mr. Sands was going to chew on Bill's ass (and then mine), and no one was going to understand me when I said I tried but could not get him to leave. Sonya told me just before I left the house that I was to take care of Bill, and not let him go off the deep end, but I did, and now I felt like shit.

We walked into the living room, and there sat Sonya. Sonya told Bill that his mother had died, at five thirty in the morning. I thought at once about the chain, and Bill let out a yell and started to cry, and Sonya did the best anyone could do at the time. We all sat quiet for sometime, and then, just as I thought everything was okay, Sonya hit the ceiling. She started to yell at me for not phoning. Bill did not say a word, so I just absorbed it. I told Sonya that Bill wanted to go for a drive, and that I drove for almost seventeen hours while Bill cried and napped for short periods. All the time, telling me he did not know how to handle it. What else was I to do? I told her, turning it around so I was to blame.

Sonya then turned on Bill, demanding where he got off doing that, at such a hard and trying time for a lot of people. Bill told her he just had to get away from everyone who reminded him of family. The arguing lasted all night. In the morning, I thought we were going to hear more, but Bill came out of his bedroom dressed in his best suit. Sonya was dressed in her best clothes. All the family was going to get together that day, to spend some time mourning. I had only met a few members of the family, and I felt a little out of place. Lou was going to be with me, and we were going to go out for drinks later, since the family was going to have a closed family session.

Lou showed up, and we all went to the church. Lou and I sat in the back and got some rather uncomfortable looks. We just sloughed them off; there were other people there that looked like drug addicts. As the ceremony started, I found myself looking back at the times I was with them. Midway through the ceremony, I started to get emotional again. I thought that I was responsible to her for some of son's actions.

As the ceremony came to the end, everyone was told to go to the Westward Hotel for drinks in Lilly's memory. Within two hours, all the people started to get drunk. Some started to cry, and others left as they did not want to hurt anymore. I was hurting as I thought of Lilly.

Bill gave me a few hundred dollars, and told me to pick up some booze. Some family members would be coming over to the house, later that night, for drinks. He wanted his father to stay drunk for the next while. Bill was still going for the deep end plunge, if you know what I mean. I knew that day and a half that we spent partying when his mother passed away was not the end of it.

I had left the car at the hospital, and I told Bill it would be awhile. Lou and I wanted to go out, since the family would be getting together for awhile first. We would be at the house in about three hours.

When Lou and I left, we went downtown to the bar called Cannery Row. We sat there and talked of all the deals Lou had set up for Bill, and how Bill was treating Lou while I was back in Toronto. I found out that Bill and Sonya had broken up, in another of their episodes. I had heard from Sonya they had done this a few times, and one time Bill had tried to kidnap his daughter Autumn. Also, Bill had been seeing almost all of the dancers at the Cove. Now I knew where this trip with Bill was heading! It was going to go sour, and it was going to all happen at once.

When Lou and I drove to get the car, we had some Emilio cooked up, and the car was full of booze. We started back to Calgary, and the cops stopped me. Lou kept going, and I told the cop I knew the car was not road worthy, but I had to get it home. Lou was driving close, so I could use his headlights. Then the cop started to think, as he saw Lou stop, not far up the road. I got some tickets, and was told to get the car home a.s.a.p. The cop took off fast, and stopped Lou. I pulled over and we all started to talk, but the cop told us to shut up. He felt he could make a major drug bust. He was looking at the booze, and he also found the pipe that Lou and I used to smoke some hash (we did not get into the Emilio yet). We both were sweating as he told us we either throw the pipe away or get busted. We told him what the booze was for. He seemed okay, so we threw it away. (The pipe, that is.)

When we got back to the house, Bill gave me shit for taking so long. He would not listen to me until he was finished yelling at me in the bedroom. At once, everyone started to drink and drink. I saw Bill going for the Emilio, and then Sonya. I did not want to do any, but Bill called me in to the bedroom once again, and told me he was going to do a few lines and talk about the people at the party. Well, when he said that, I knew he had something in mind. I did some, and he did some, and then he said he wanted me to spike all the drinks, so the people could stay up longer, and keep his father and some other family members comforted. I told Bill that I would do no such thing, and that he was fucked for even suggesting it. He told me I owed it to him to do this after all he had done for me. He also told me he needed it, he felt really alone. I still told him no. He got angry, saying things could get tough for me. I said I would do it. He told me he was sorry. He took it all back, and he needed me to help him through this. I told him I would not spike all the drinks, only a few, and he could do the rest. I spiked my drink, Lou's drink (I even told him that I did. He said Happy New Year), Sonya's drink and Bill's drink with Emilio. They had done it before, so I did not need to worry. I did not spike any of the families, or Mr. Sand's drinks.

About two or three hours later, one of the guests started to yell at Bill. He was saying he never got the kind of buzz on booze as he was getting from it now. He started saying Bill had spiked the drinks. Then I saw it coming. The whole house left and Bill blamed it all on me. I did not say a thing. I started thinking how I could stop all this Emilio trade. It was proving to be one big, shitty deal.

Bill would not talk to me all the next day. He was planning something, but would not say what. Bill treated me as though I was not trustworthy, and this upset me. I started to think of the perfect way to stop Bill before he did anything stupid. As far as the house went, Bill owed four thousand plus to the phone company and thousands to Ere. I wanted five thousand for myself, and Lou wanted three thousand. Everyone wanted money and Bill was broke. I knew he was planning something.

Bill told me he had to fly to Miami, to see about setting up a deal with some new Emilio. It would be big enough to pay everyone once the shipment was done. I went along with it. Bill showed me how to import Emilio from Peru. He said one day I would be going there to do this. So I watched. The next day, he told me I was to drive him to Great Falls, Montana so he could catch a direct flight to Miami, and be back in Great Falls in fourteen hours. He said it would be best if I stayed in the states till he got back. I told Bill I was game, and that I would like to take Lou with me for company. He said it was okay, and that I should ask his sister Sam if she wanted to come with us, as I could always use a piece of ass. Lou and I got some Emilio and hash for the trip, careful to hide it from Bill. He would've flipped out.

Once Bill was on his way, we decided to go skiing. The car we had did not make it up the mountain. We had to phone Ere back in Calgary and ask him what to do. Ere told us to come back to town. I could take his new car. Skiing was out, but we had a blast driving back to Calgary, smoking Emilio with hash and not worrying about the law.

By the time we got back, Bill was due in Great Falls in less than ten hours. I knew we did not have much time to do anything. We made one stop for some more Emilio (that I had taken when Bill was not looking), and cooked it up for the ride. Lou and I went back to Great Falls and Sam stayed at home. Lou and I tried to cross the border, but we were turned back because we could not prove that we did not have criminal records. This slowed us by one hour. We had to drive to the Kimberley, B.C. crossing. When we did get there, Bill and his friend Smokey were there and upset, till Lou and I explained what had happened.

Bill explained that Smokey was one of the new members of the company, and that he was going to act as the controller. I knew as soon as Bill said that, things were going to be a lot different. Lou and I were going to get used even more. Bill told me he was bringing back over two kilos. He wanted everything to go right this time. He needed to pay for some of the costs of Lilly's funeral, as well as all of us and the house. I only had to set up the deals, I was not going to have anything else for awhile. He found out I had brought some hash over the border. This upset him, since he was carrying over forty thousand on him at the time. I told him that was bullshit. I helped to get this whole company off the ground, and I could walk away any time. All I wanted, if I did that, would be what I came in with, plus what I had obtained since I had been here. As I was saying this to Bill, I was just waiting for his reaction, but he did not give me one. Instead he just looked at me and said I was right. He said I was going to be in charge of the market retail.

That did not stop the feelings I had at the time, but I told Bill we would pull together and do this right. I knew then that this was not going to last. I had it in my mind to stop Bill when he was out of the country. The only way I could do this was to get the help of the R.C.M.P. I kicked the thought around for awhile, and decided I would give Bill about three weeks to see how he was reacting, and decide what to do.

For the first three weeks that I gave Bill to change his attitude, I wanted him to run it just like a business, not a free life with nothing to show after spending money on hookers and free coke. Out of all the Emilio he brought back, we never got paid. The rent never got paid, and the phone was cut off.

Sonya and Bill had another argument. Sonya went to stay at Mr. Sands, and Bill and Smokey stayed at the house. I went and stayed at Lou's place. Bill did not like the idea of me staying somewhere else. That meant he had to cook for himself and Smokey. I felt the change and it was very sudden. The next day I met Bill at the Relax Inn on Macleod Trail.

Bill and Smokey had rented the room to work the Emilio. Smokey, Bill and I all worked for about two hours, until I told Bill I was going to see a girl I had sold a half a pound to, to see if she wanted more. It was a front, so I could get away from Bill.

For two days, Bill acted like a rag, with nothing good to say unless we had money in hand. I was at my limit with Bill, but it came to a head when I got an ounce from Bill and could not account for it. We yelled at each other. I'm sure Bill felt the change in my attitude. I turned cold towards Bill and the whole fucking set up. I felt the end was near in our relationship. I had ended a lot of things in my time, but never an operation this size. I went and talked to my sis. After I left her, I knew what I was going to do would be for the better of a lot of people. Bill was not only capable of murder, but also of depriving one of any sense of well being. Bill was almost a master in the art of belittling people, and this he would do to you on your first encounter, if you let him.

I asked Lou when I got back home what we would do for smoke. Our habit had grown quite a bit. We were smoking about an ounce a day, depending on what we had. Bill was quite strong in the area of not giving me any Emilio, but he would give Lou some and this was the last route we took. I set it up with Smokey that Lou would come to the hotel to pick up an ounce of Emilio. When Lou left, I got a call from Bill. I hung up on him and waited for about an hour. Just before Lou got back, I called the city cops. I told them they could have two kilos worth of coke, and that there was more at the house, and then I hung up.

Lou walked in the door with the ounce and we sat sown and started to base it. I can only tell you that the feelings I was going through at the time were so strong, I can't possibly relate. When I took a toke, I felt so good I did not care if I was dead or alive. I was so high on Emilio, and the rush I

144

got after calling the cops was unreal. About thirty minutes later I got a call from Bill. He told me Sonya had phoned him at the hotel room, telling him the house was raided and that the cops where looking for all of us. Bill told me he would kill the person that set him up. I told him I wanted a piece of the action. I had all my paperwork at the house and I was wanted for the same shit. I tried to act convincingly.

Bill wanted to see Lou and I out in Banff. Bill told me I was to bring money for an ounce I got, and for the ounce Lou got, and to be in Banff in two hours. I had the willies so bad I could have shit.

When Lou got back he was just freaked at the way Bill sounded. Lou had no idea I was responsible for this. I told Lou we had to be in Banff in two hours, and we had to have the money for at least one ounce. We sat down to get stoned, to try to calm down.

I thought I had lost the case right then and there. I thought of Bill and Smokey getting away. On the way to Banff I told Lou that I had to phone Calgary, as there was someone I had to warn not to go near the house. So we stopped, and I called the law again. I told them Bill was going to be in Banff, with two keys, and that if they wanted him, they better act fast.

When we got to Banff, I could see the look of fear and anger in Bill's eyes. I was put to the test. Bill thought I was responsible for what was happening. I tried to turn the table as best I could, and it worked. Bill started to calm down. I was just as shaken looking as the rest. We all calmed down and went to a restaurant for lunch. Bill told me he wanted me to take care of Sonya and Autumn, to use the money from the two ounces to put me, Sonya and Autumn on a plane for Vancouver, B.C. We would stay there for a few days, and then fuck off down to Miami, Fla. I told him I was going to need a few days. I had fronted some, and the one Lou got is going for $2500 tonight. We would be in Vancouver by Friday.

Bill and Smokey left to go to Jasper, and then on down to Vancouver. Lou and I went back to Calgary. I was to meet Ere, who was also freaking out because his office got raided. I phoned Sonya and told her I was busted with an ounce.

It had been four days since Bill and Smokey left, and I could not think of anything else to say about the ounce. Doing what I did, and then having to play the part, was so different that I was in awe most of the time. I thought it great that I could act. I had previously phoned the cops and told then that they could have two kilos or so of coke, and nothing happened. I phoned back, and the city cops told me this was to big for them to handle, and that the case was turned over to the R.C.M.P. I was to get in touch with them as soon as possible.

I phoned the R.C.M.P. and talked to Corporal Jerry Smith. He told me he wanted to get together, have a few drinks and talk. I told him on the phone I wanted some sort of guarantee I would make it out of this, with a name change and a safe place to live. This was not a nickel and dime operation I was to reveal.

I met Corp. Smith and another constable, Jim Standard at the Brown Derby Bar on 10th Ave., in downtown Calgary. We all introduced ourselves, and they bought booze first and started to ask questions. I stopped them in mid sentence and told them my demands for all that I would give them. Jerry and Jim both looked at each other, and then at me, and said if what I produce will results in anything substantial, I would get compensated accordingly.

I was slightly drunk when we left there. I was scared now, as the ball was started and now there was no way of stopping it. Jerry and Jim agreed that my trouble had just started. I hit them with the story I told Bill, about my getting busted with an ounce. I told Jerry and Jim that I needed fake documents, stating I had been busted. They agreed, and said I could pick them up in the morning. Relieved, I went back to Lou's place. I told Lou not to worry about the ounce. I was getting some fake papers from a friend I had in the cop shop, and he too felt a sense of relief.

Bill said he would see me when he got back in town and that was to be in a few days. When he did show up, he was just as fucking mean, if not worse. This was the only time I ever saw Bill show any sort of feeling, other than grief when Lilly passed away. I told myself it did not matter, I would do the same. If drugs weren't involved, he wouldn't care. As it was, Bill went out and got me an appointment with one of Calgary's top drug defense lawyers. I thought, oh fuck, now I not only cooked my own goose, but I put my head in my ass at the same time. I did not want Bill to get his hands on the fake documents. The lawyer would determine it was shit right off and tell Bill, and then I surely would bite the big one. I phoned Jerry and told him what Bill had done and that I did not know what to do. Jerry told me it was my ball and I was to fix it and make it work.

That night, after I showed the paper to Bill, I went back to Lou's place and we started to base up some more Emilio. I went out that night and spent a lot of money, telling everyone I was busted for an ounce, and I was to see a lawyer first thing in the morning. I told some people I was thinking of taking off to the states. I went back to Lou's place, smoked some more Emilio. I picked up the document in front of Patricia and Lou, at his sister's place. I set the bogus paperwork on fire, and told them that if anything was to come of this, I would take off to the states.

It did not take long for Bill to find out I was out the previous night. He asked me to meet him at the lawyer's office. I thought of jumping on a plane, to any place far from Calgary.

There is no possible way to relate what I was going through while I was driving to the lawyer's office. I was there before Bill. As I waited for him, I was shaking so bad I thought I would blow the whole ball game. All the time I was going through this, Jerry and Jim kept saying I was to play the part right to the end, so they could get as much on Bill as they could. When Bill did show up, I suddenly felt this rush, and then nothing. I was just there, and I did not feel anything other than hatred towards Bill.

I went through the whole charade as if I was the guilty one. Then I told the lawyer the whole story of going to the Port-O-Call Hotel to sell an ounce, and I was busted in the elevator on the way to the room. It seemed plausible to me, and it went over as if nothing was wrong. Bill tried to reassure me that it was nothing to go up on an ounce of coke, and that I might not even get time. I told Bill I would not go to jail, at any cost, and that I would take off to the states or some other country, but I was never going back to jail.

The lawyer said I had nothing to worry about. Smokey stayed in Vancouver and wanted Bill to go back out there. Bill left with Sonya and Autumn. I guess when the going gets tough, the tough get going. Bill told me he thought it was Lou who had set us up. Bill was going to put a contract out on Lou! I almost shit. I knew Bill was mean, but not crazy. I told Lou this, and that I knew some people that would be able to help us.

I had to tell Lou I was the one who started this. I had one hell of a time getting to the point. I was taking Lou to all kinds of bars, to make him receptive to what I was going to tell him. Jerry and Jim told me not to tell anyone, but when my friend's life got involved, I had no choice.

I told Lou I was the one putting an end to this bullshit company. He said he wanted in; he wanted the same kind of guarantee as mine. The law would change our names, and give us a new place to live. That we would never have to worry about Bill or any of the people we knew.

CHAPTER FOURTEEN

THE ROYAL CANADIAN
MOUNTED PROCRASTINATORS

At first my relationship with the law was fruitful. I would talk to Jerry and Jim and walk out of the office with five hundred at a time, usually once a week, if not twice.

Both Lou and I spent a lot of money, and had lots of women and drugs. I lost what ever sense I had that what I was doing was right. I was doing the same thing, only now I had to buy my own coke.

I still did what I had to, to survive, but it turned by accident into an occupation. By this time, Lou was making travel arrangements in order to move to Ontario. The boys, Jerry and Jim, called us in, asking us if we thought Bill could do what he promised, or if it was bullshit. At that point we had our first argument about the size of the company. I told them this was not just penny-anti, and that we were not fooling with life. It would slide through their fingers, easier than sand, so it was in their interest to be on top of Bill and Smokey's every move.

Bill had already gone to Miami. Smokey was back on his own turf, without a care in the world. Sonya and Autumn were with their family back in Caracas, Venezuela. Ere was still under investigation, and I was told by the boys I was to pump Ere for all the information I could get. I was to feedback anything that was of value. While drunk and stoned one night, Lou and I decided to stop taking drugs and make some money out of this.

Jerry and Jim called us in one day and told us a new member of the team was going to be joining us soon. We met at the same place, and got to know this new fellow named Andy. We talked about Bill Sands and Smokey Blue, as they were called. The only person with any contact was Ere, and he told me that we could meet once a day to talk about what we were going to do.

We would meet at the Manhattan Bar on 11th Avenue SW, very popular with the fast paced crowd. At one meeting with the boys, it was decided I would wear a wire taping system to one of these meetings with Ere. I was staying straight and working at what I was doing with Jerry and Andy, as Jim was transferred to a detachment in Northern Alberta. I agreed to wear the wire and set the stage, with Ere ever so unsuspecting.

Ere said Bill was now in Peru, and that he was going to be gone for awhile. Any deals that could be made, we were to do them together. The time that I did spend with Ere we talked openly and never hid anything. Still, I did not feel comfortable with him alone. I made damn sure our meetings happened in a public place.

Lou was readying himself for the trip back to Ontario. I knew that I would never hear from him or Sam again.

I was scared I might get some flack from any number of Bill's friends, and did not want to chance it. I got in touch with Tac, telling him I need a place to stay, as I couldn't live at home. Tac said I could live with him, and share all expenses. I moved in, which lead me to tell Tac what I was doing. We talked of making it into a small occupation. I did not really plan this, but once into it I found it hard to get out. I had found the thrill I always wanted, and it was too good to let go.

I needed money badly, so I set this deal up for two thousand hits of black moon acid. I talked to Andy and Jerry, and they got it approved with Edmonton, where the head office is for K Section. (R.C.M.P. C. CALGARY DRUG UNIT). I was to meet them at the Sandman Inn on Seventh Ave. And Eighth Street, at ten thirty or so, to finalize the plans.

I met the guys, but there was a stall that took about an hour. I had to sit with these guys outside, as we wanted to smoke some joints. Here I got another rush that felt good. I was smoking dope in front of the cops! Under surveillance! I was told by Jerry and Andy I was to do the deal in the washroom of the Unicorn Bar on the Eighth Avenue Mall. I went with the mark. Along the way I asked if I could get four thousand, instead of just two. For some reason, I attract people with a drug background and I could get whatever I wanted, anywhere. I started to feel like I could go anywhere, working as an agent to the R.C.M.P.

Tac was my eyes and ears while I was with these guys. He kept in sight at all times. Once in the Unicorn, I told the guys the first round was on me, and I would then walk across the street. I'd hit the bank for four grand and be right back. By that time, the stuff would be there, and I would not have to sit and wait. They all agreed, and beer was served. We talked about what was going on, and where I was taking this stuff. I must say, I can dish out some good bull. In the back of my mind I was laughing, as I knew exactly where it was going - to jail, with him and the rest of them.

The followng is an excerpt from the Calgary Herald. Bear in mind all names have been changed:

> **The RCMP drug squad's first LSD bust this year yielded one arrest Thursday and the seizure of 4,000 "hits" of the hallucinogen estimated to be worth $20,000 on the street. The bust was one of the largest seizures by us in recent years, said Sgt. Len Thomas, acting head of the drug investigation unit. A suspect was arrested about 1 p.m. Thursday in possession of the hallucinogenic drug called "Black Moon" and distributed on a blotter, Thomas said. In January, city police noted there had been an alarming increase in the abuse of the drug in 1983 when 37,108 "hits" were seized. In one bust alone last year 11,200 "hits" worth $56,000 were seized, police said. In 1982 there was only 1,305 "hits" that were confiscated. Staff Sgt. Ron Wood, head of the city police squad, said about 14,000 "hits" of LSD have been taken off the street thus far in 1984. "It appears that LSD use continues to increase", Wood said. The relatively inexpensive drug cost about $5.00 a hit has made a comeback since it's heyday in the late 60s, particularly among teenagers who cannot afford more expensive "highs." Although LSD is cheaper than other more common drugs, it is a lot more dangerous, police say. Although RCMP drug investigators have concentrated on cutting the supply of cocaine to the city, the LSD seizure is considered important because it occurred relatively far up the drug distribution chain. "Certainly well above street level," said Sgt. Len Thomas. "It's a lot of LSD."**

I was in the washroom when the bust went down. I was pissed off, as they did not read my signal right and I almost lost the case. As it was, I was made out to be just what I was saying. I was a buyer and these guys never knew what, or who, or how they got stung.

I sat in the office with Jerry and Andy. They freaked, as I did not tell them I had gotten two thousand more than they expected. I was quite happy with the way things worked out. I had some money that was going to take Tac and me to Vancouver, B.C.

I got a few hundred from Jerry right off. This took us there, but things did not work out and we were on our way back. In all my life, I never thought I would ever see who I saw on the city bus heading for the train terminal. It was "The Weasel."

I was shocked, and angry at the same time. I did not know what to say. I must admit, Weasel was my next target. I stood there looking at him, thinking this. I wanted to see him out of my life for good. I figured I might as well go with the flow, and see what happens. Weasel asked me and Tac to come over to his place. We would get high and talk. At first, I was leery. I did not know if I could trust him, but the idea of smoking some pot kind of hit home. It was close to our departure time, and we did not stay long, only long enough to smoke some MDA in a joint and then exchange numbers. I did plan to sting him when I came back to Vancouver.

I don't know why I felt this way. Maybe it was because I had grown up awful fast with Weasel, and that long lost feeling of security only home can provide. By the time Tac and I got to the train station, we were well on our way to getting high. Weasel gave me a gram of MDA for the ride home. Tac and I had rented a sleeper cabin for the ride home, the only way to travel. I had gotten out of drugs, but could not resist this freebie.

I did do the odd bit of coke when I was with the person I was working on, but to this day I have not done more than twenty bucks worth. I am a beer drinker and pot smoker well before I will ever do a chemical again. But things could change, I thought. Tac and I spent another week or so in Calgary before going back to Vancouver. The Weasel had made some plans for a deal for me. I was still waiting for my money to come through from the Bill and Smokey operation, but Jerry and Andy said I would be waiting a while yet. They said I should do something else, and not count on living off that type of work. I could not see myself giving up the high I got from this, so off we went to Vancouver. To do the deal Weasel was getting together for us.

When we got to Vancouver, Weasel was waiting for us at the train station with a big smile. Weasel had been trying to set a deal up for a half or full pound of MDA. Taking him down would be the best form of punishment for what happened eight years ago. Weasel did not suspect anything, and this was what made our trip so much of a rush.

Weasel introduced Tac and I to two guys who were to turn us on to one guy that could fill an order of forty thousand hits of acid, or half a pound of MDA. Their names were Paul and Walter, both rather strange fellows who liked their drugs and young women. Walter wanted to be someone of status, and he put the image out rather well. Paul was rather more reserved, and did not talk much. I was sitting back talking about the times with Weasel, and how much we were both into drugs and did not see any other kind of occupation. These guys, Paul and Walter, took our hook. The deal was going to take a few days. Tac and I had scrounged about a thousand bucks to do this deal. We had to show we had money to spend. Weasel was working during the day, which allowed TAC and me to use the phone and do our deal with the R.C.M.P. in Vancouver.

Our contacts with the Vancouver R.C.M.P. were Const. Robin, and Const. Leach. They wanted names and an address, and we gave them what they needed to start the ball rolling. I went to welfare and told them I was not working, and had just come from Calgary on the promise I would have work. They gave me three hundred and fifty, a big relief since we were running out of money. The next day, Robin and Leach phoned, telling us they had five bills waiting for us that afternoon. For a few hours work and intrigue, Tac and myself were back over a grand. Walter came over that night and said he would be able to introduce us to the guy who would do the deal. He said we had best be on the level, and there would be no weapons seen or brought, for that matter. I told Walter we did our work without the aid of stupid weapons. The meeting was set for the next day after dinner.

All that day, Tac and I walked around talking about what we were doing. We thought it best to take these guys off their turf, and onto ours. We drank a lot that day, and when it was time to meet Walter's friend we had a nice glow on. It worked to our advantage. The guy's name was Stewart. He was the lead guitar player for a heavy metal rock band. We walked in while they were in session, with some cold beer to break the ice.

Stewart knew what was up, and said we should get together around noon the next day. He would have a price by then. We could work our end with the money to ensure there would be no delays. I was getting the rush I felt whenever I did anything like this.

It felt like I was doing something positive, something giving. I had taken so much from life, and taken one life.

I felt a pushing on my arm. Tac was shaking me awake. I was sleeping, dreaming, but I swore to myself I would do what I dreamt, no matter how long it took.

We met Stewart, and he drove us all over the fucking place looking for this one guy. He couldn't track him down. We sat in a strip joint in Gastown, getting slightly loaded. Stewart said he would phone up later. I thought, you son of a bitch. I wrote it off as he was just checking Tac and me out.

I phoned Robin and Leach and told them what was going on. I was to make contact with the supplier in the next few hours. They told me we could do a flash of cash if need be, and from that point on we were going to be followed. I was in a state of emotional hunger. I wanted to see this whole deal go down without a hitch.

I waited with Tac at Weasel's house for Stewart to phone with news. We were really high strung at that moment. Only one thing wrong with this work- you never get sick pay!!!

Stewart did not phone that evening, and we just sat around and drank. The next day he told us we needed to do a flash of half the money, set at thirty five thousand dollars, some time that day. I told Stewart that was impossible, as I just don't keep that kind of money lying around. I told him we would be able to tomorrow at two in the afternoon. I wanted to go out tonight and see if I could get laid. Tac was still more or less a silent partner, keeping quiet when we were in a meeting with Robin and Leach. I told them we had to flash half the money. They said no problem. I would have had difficulty telling Stewart I could not come up with the money after all. It was arranged so we would do the flash right behind the building Stewart played in. Everything went as planned. Robin introduced me to a guy who was to be our man from Calgary named Larry. Larry was with the Vancouver Drug Unit of the R.C.M. P. We talked before we went to do the flash, and got to know the whole scenario. Larry was to tell Stewart that we did not have all that much time before we had to get back to Calgary. We would do this deal here but if not, we would do it in Calgary. Stewart had said his band was going on a road tour, and their first stop was Calgary, so it would work out either way. The flash was set. Larry informed Robin and Leach and they had the area under surveillance.

Tac and I were dropped off at the entrance of the old warehouse Stewart's band had converted to a studio. We got Stewart, and all of us walked around to where Larry was with the car that was bugged and had more eyes on it than could be seen.

Stewart did not say much for the first few minutes. Then, he let loose, telling us we had fucked up and he would talk about it later. Then he counted the money. I did not know what to say, and Tac looked a little uncomfortable. Larry finally saved the day by saying that he could not help but take out all the money. Stewart looked at me and asked me if I had told my man only to bring half the money. I said yes, that I did not know he brought all of it. Larry said he brought all of it in the hopes of getting the deal over with-he didn't like Vancouver. Stewart lapped it up, and said it did not matter, only that he would have liked to see half. There was no water spilled, and we were able to get his voice on record, having negotiated a deal for forty thousand hits of acid. This helped to confirm what Tac and I had set up.

From that point in time, the deal was only to take two days, as Stewart said his people needed a bit more time to fill the order. That night Tac and I got drunk, thinking we were on top of the world and nothing could go wrong. We knew it was an awful risky business, but this job we were on right now was going to pay our way to a vacation, and we were happy. None of us got in touch with each other for one day. The next day, Stewart came over to Weasel's house with a hit of acid. He called it the tester. We were to get in touch with him later that night.

Tac and I looked at each other and smiled. We knew we were going to do the tester, and not give it to Robin or Leach. But this was a treat for us. Neither one of them knew about it. This would turn out to be the turning point if my life. I never thought I would ever have a bad trip on acid, but this stuff almost killed Tac and me. The stone I got from this acid was like the stone I had in Toronto one time, when I thought the figurines were talking to me, telling me I was going to die of a drug overdose. This scared the shit out of me. I got violently ill and could not stop puking my face off. I started to throw up blood. This was it, I kept saying to myself.

I was hyperventilating and sweating like no tomorrow. Inside, I was thinking you really know how to fuck things up, don't you? This is probably going to kill you, and you never really lived your life. Tac tried to console me, but that rarely works when you are fucked up on acid. I took the shit at 11:00 p.m., and till ten thirty the next day I was puking my face off and not thinking properly. I told Tac I had to get the fuck out of this place and back to Calgary, back to safety.

For awhile, I felt good, but I started to reflect on my life. I became so dammed depressed, I did not know whether I was coming or going. I tried to pull myself together, to get set for the flight Tac was working on to get us home. I was okay for about an hour, but once we were at the airport I started to peak on the acid again. This one hit me with so much force, I honestly thought I was going to die. I told Tac he had better call an ambulance, and tell them I was overdosing. For the first time in my life, I was scared of drugs and did not know what to do. When the ambulance got there, I told them I was stoned on acid. I was going to die, the way everything was going so black.

They took me to Richmond General. I told them I had done some bad acid and I need to come down real fast. I couldn't take this much longer. All I wanted them to do was give me a shot to knock me out for a few hours so I could come down.

Tac got a hold of Robin and Leach and told them I was in the hospital for a drug overdose. They freaked out, to the point where they were calling me and Tac every name in the book. They gave me a shot at the hospital and I was under, without a care in the world. Looking back I could have killed myself, and it would not have mattered.

When I came too, Tac was standing there, looking at me. I told him I was through with chemicals, and wanted to be back in Calgary. Tac had left a note for Weasel to tell Stewart he was to phone us as soon as possible. I was still not altogether there, but we did make it to the airport and home, with more difficulty than I care to remember. I was so relieved to be back in Calgary, all I wanted to do was kick back, smoke a joint and relax. That acid trip was going to be the last one, I said to myself!!! I started to feel as though the work we did in Vancouver was of no value to us. It would be two weeks or more to see if we could do the deal. Tac and I played the waiting game.

About two weeks went by, and then Stewart showed up. Money started to flow once again, as we were supplying information to the Calgary Drug Unit, with the same two guys I worked with before. Andy was glad to see me, but you never know, do you? I often just felt used, and not for my own comfort.

Jim was still his non-committal self. I introduced Stewart to this chick I did a deal with (actually the first one for Bill's company). Liz and I met in the Cove, and I told her about this guy from Vancouver, and that we were working on a deal. I wanted her to show them a good time, though I did not mean by supplying sex. Being back in town, I was still portraying a fast pace (when it was not all that fast). I wanted to make Stewart believe Tac and I had a lot of things to do.

Stewart, Tac and myself talked one time while driving all over Vancouver. Tac and I lead Stewart to believe we would throw some money his way, as sort of a sponsor for his band, if everything went well.

I mentioned this to Liz, and that was the biggest mistake I made. When she was left with these guys, she opened her mouth, and the whole group assumed if Stewart did this drug deal, the band would make it. The guys flipped, and then word got back to me that while Liz was talking her little head off, the guy who brought the acid to Vancouver was listening to every word. He did not like it either, and that was going to be the last work I did for a few years. I did not think I could keep it up in Calgary. I had done too many people there, and Tac felt the same way. We thought Edmonton would be a good place to relax. Tac could get the rehabilitation that he needed. He had a bad back, from a work accident. Workers' Compensation was going to pay for a hotel room, TAC was going to fix his back, and I was going to write.

I still no idea when I was going to get paid for the deal with Bill and Sonya, but I knew I could phone them anytime to see what's up. I thought I was going to get a chance to relax. Just when the fun began, Tac and I found ourselves sitting in the bar, looking for work. Since we were there, it couldn't hurt to look around.

I found myself in a motel room, trying to write a book, not knowing where it would lead. I never did finish, as I was called from Calgary. They told me that my money was in for the Bill Sands job. I was to come to Calgary as soon as possible. I did not have any money to get there, so I told Andy (Calgary Drugs) he would have to send me some money so I could fly down.

I got in touch with a constable in Edmonton. He gave me $100.00 for the flight. It was August, 1984.

I got my money, what little it was. I bitched till it was heard, but it did me no good. The Government decided the work I'd done wasn't dangerous, that it didn't warrant a name change. In total, they gave me over two thousand dollars.

I thought, you fucking ass holes! You not only use people, you shit on them later and throw them away, while I'm here to make a statement. I was betrayed by these well respected Law Enforcement Agent Provocateurs, The Royal Canadian Mounted Police!!!

No matter what I said, it would not be heard in Calgary. I was forced to drop the issue. I took my money, bought a second hand jeep and headed for Toronto. I thought I could get some sort of work there for a few days. From there I was going to Halifax, N.S. Tac and I formed a partnership, and since Tac's father was once a cop in Halifax, we thought he could help us out.

I was going to try to talk to this fellow I got to know from White Oaks Village, back in '69. I had been in touch with Lee in Toronto. Since I was headed there, I told him I had worked on my book, and wanted him to read it and tell me what he thought.

Tac and I said goodbye to everyone in Calgary and with his girlfriend in tow, left for Toronto.

By the time we arrived, we were at each others throats. We were broke, with no clue how to make it to Halifax. I looked for work, but I just did not like Toronto. To me, Toronto represented my time as a hooker/dealer. It will always have negative connotations for me.

I decided to seek retribution from the R.C.M.P. I had been used, abused and thrown away. I just couldn't let them get away with it.

I talked to a member of the NDP party, named Mr. Lauric. We talked for an hour, until he told me he could do nothing for me. He said I should find someone in the right field. I phoned a member of the Liberals and was told the same thing.

Things at the home front were not going over well. Tac's girlfriend, Sidney, started getting into my mother's best things. All hell broke lose, and my mother hit the roof. She told us to leave pronto. I had a falling out with Tac at that stage. My mother had helped us out, spent all the money she was saving, when we ran into jeep trouble in Northern Ontario. She took time off work, came to where we were stranded, and basically bailed us out.

Tac and I went to the welfare office to get some money, to help out my mother, and to pay for the trip to Halifax. Once Tac had his money, he told me he was going on without me. I hit the roof. He said Sidney did not want to stay here any longer. They had to leave. I could not believe what I was hearing from Tac. Needless to say, they went on their way, and I stayed with my mother.

I was not getting anywhere with the politicians. The thought crossed my mind to go public with the story. I went to a reporter at the Toronto Star, Dan MacDonald. We went out for lunch a few times and talked. He told me stories of different people, in the same business I was in.

There are only about five or six people who were treated the same way. There will probably never be any justice for us.

For three months I stayed there. I even got in touch with Lou, who I happened to see driving down Bloor Street one day. We talked of meeting Dan, and set it up. Dan told us the story could fly, if we got in touch with some of the others guys. Dan would help us, but each one of us had to keep a low profile, so as not to attract attention. In other words, remain unanimous to each other.

Two weeks later I got a call from Dan MacDonald, telling me there was no way he could publish the story. I did not know what to do. I thought I should go back to work. I did not have any money, and I wanted to get out of there badly.

I found two girls selling guns downtown. I thought I could make a few thousand dollars on the deal. I approached the drug unit and told them I wanted to work on these two girls. I also wanted to get paid well. Guns were risky and new to me. They reassured me I would be compensated accordingly.

I was out with the girls the night I was stopped by the city cops and arrested for warrants I had out from 1978. Still, I knew I would have no problem getting off. I was released the next day. I thought of running to Alberta, since they would not deport you. (That law will change soon, I'd bet.)

I did not want to stay there and neither did my mother. I sold my jeep for good money. My mother and I returned to Calgary.

I wanted to go back to cooking, as I liked that sort of work. I also wanted to be near the mountains, to go camping. Toronto did nothing but remind me of all my wrong doings. I'm sure if I had stayed there, I would have ended up in trouble. There is nothing but crime in that city for me, and though I would fight it as well as I could, I would never win. Not lose, but not win.

We got to Calgary for Christmas and had a good time. I was living with two friends I got to know through Lady Di's old man. Steve was Justin's brother and we got along fine. We drank and partied together one hell of a lot. I lived with them for about two months, until I told them I was going to move to Vancouver. Vancouver didn't have what Calgary had: people like Bill Sands and the treacherous R.C.M.P.

I decided to stay with Weasel for awhile, till I could find a place of my own. It was to be a new beginning.

CHAPTER FIFTEEN

NOBODY GOING TO SLOW ME DOWN

I left Justin and Steve in Calgary and moved to Vancouver in March of 1985. My intention was to have some fun, and not put up with any bullshit from anyone.

I got to Weasel's house at five in the morning. He was waiting with coffee brewing and a nice warm joint. I wanted to live a low profile life, and not have to worry about a damn thing. I also wanted to get involved with the community, and do the things I always wanted to do here.

I mostly wanted to see what the city had to offer young offenders. I believed I could have a positive influence. For years now, people have come to me with their problems, and I have tried to help them as best I can. At this point, I had a nagging feeling something was missing. The best years of my life I wasted, doing drugs and not living!!!

Saying good-bye to my family was not the easiest thing to do. It seemed as though it was all I had done for the past twenty-five years, and I wanted never to say that again.

I soon realized living in Vancouver was not going to be as I had planned. It's a cold city, making it hard to get close to people. This society has worked it's self into a state of utter distrust. I had thought, "Oh wow, now I can go out and practice what I preach" help some people if I could. I merely went to different places, met old friends, and shot the shit. The few people I did meet happened to be Weasel's friends, and they were, and still are, utterly directionless. I got the chance to help a few people by being there when they needed someone to talk to, and that felt great. I thought to myself, I'm doing it. I'm not out for my own gains, but for others, and for awhile I was at peace with myself. Then I met this guy from my past, and things went a little haywire. His name was Edmond.

I took another challenge and bought a motorcycle. I was downtown in a gay bar, as that was where I stopped in for a drink once in awhile back then, when I felt like being a hooker and I happened to see Edmond. We talked for a long time, and I found out he had just been released from the penitentiary.

Our relationship was twelve years old, even though we were in touch only occasionally. It did not seem as though all those years had gone by. Edmond was still into drugs. Since he was just out of jail, he wanted to get high. He asked me if I could get some drugs. I told him I could find some MDA. We both did a hit and the feeling hit me that I was full of shit, that I would never amount to anything. I analyzed my life whenever I did drugs, and this is what almost always led me into a depression.

Edmond wanted to get out of town for awhile. I left everything I could not take on my bike, and, along with Edmond, set out for the southern interior. We set our sights on Penticton. We both had less than fifty bucks to live on, and not enough for a camp ground. We decided to pick cherries, to earn money to live on for a day. When we got there it was like an oasis. I was in heaven.

Picking cherries, starting at seven in the morning, was just not my bag, but I stuck with it so I could eat and drink and because if I worked hard enough, I could even buy a few joints. I busted my ass, everyday, so I could go to the beach at three and smoke and relax.

After the jacking action I had seen while in Vancouver, I swore I was never going to stick a needle in my arm, or anywhere else for that matter. But, I got right into a rowdy crowd at Saha Beach, and my drug use went way up. I saw things these kids were doing that reminded me of me, and I could see some of them going astray. I must state at this point that I have not injected any drugs since the early 70's.

I got to know a few cool people. There was one girl I liked and we talked about all kinds of things, but inside me, I knew I was not going to settle down in this area. I did work there, and was happy, but the employment in that town was seasonal and I could not see me doing nothing for great lengths of time.

I met this older chap by the name of Marty. At the same time, every night, I would meet him near Okanagan Lake and we would kill a forty ounce bottle of rye. We would talk of all the different things we had experienced. I told him why I was here and what I planned on doing.

Work had all but come to a stop, and I was wondering if I should return to Vancouver and get a job. It was getting on to the end of a lazy wasted summer. I left the city on the spur of the moment, and now I was out of work. I went back to the city to pick up my welfare cheque, and headed out.

The money I had was gone in three days. I tried to work, but there was none. To this day, I still do not feel at home in that city.

Edmond started to become a real jerk. All he wanted to do was hurt people and rob them, as I was soon to find out.

Edmond and I were down to our last few dollars. I lucked out and found us a job. He looked at me, and said he was going to leave tomorrow. He'd had about all the fruit picking he could take. I told him it had been his idea, and now he couldn't take it. I worked for the day while Edmond just loafed around, and then it came time to go grab a bite and hit the beach. When I got to the beach, Edmond wanted the money I had worked for so he could get some drugs! At that point, I knew I was going to be on my own again. I was not going to give up what I had worked for so someone else (who had not worked), could enjoy the benefits. Then it hit me. I was becoming an adult. I was not going to have to steal, or rob, or do anything wrong to get what I wanted. What a feeling: I told someone what I was saying to myself for the last two years. I did not really care what Edmond's reaction was. I was the one that counted. I knew I was nothing more that his enabler.

The next day I went to find Marty, and became very upset when he didn't show up. The previous night, after our argument, Edmond found Marty, got him drunk and robbed him. It had to end like this. I told Marty to call the cops. I was going to turn Edmond in. Marty was nursing a bump on his head where Edmond had slugged him. Marty told me he did not hold anything against me, as he felt there was something wrong with Edmond. He had taken a chance and was proven right.

Marty was the biggest influence for me at that time. His wife had passed away a few years before, and Marty had been a heavy drinker ever since. There was only one time I went to his house and we did not drink. He asked me things about my life, and I could not hold back the pain I

162

was feeling. I guess he fit the father image I had in my head, but I knew it would never be. I just liked the time we had together.

I was getting to know a group of guys, and a few girls. We all partied on the beach, or in this guy's condo (that eventually got ruined). This one guy, named Animal, and his brother, Dillon, were the ones I was getting my tokes from. One time, they brought over an ounce of oil. What a treat, as I had not seen oil for a long time. They were the ones that liked to get rowdy and rough. All together there were eight of us.

Bob, Chet and Randy were all from Vancouver. The girls were Susan from Penticton, and Ann from Vancouver. Between all of us, we did a lot of shit, and did not give a damn about the law. Some did hard drugs, and others simply smoked pot.

One time, Bob asked me if I would ride him into Vancouver for his welfare cheque. It was that time of the month. I told him I would, as I had to get my cheque too. I was scared of my bike. It was a 650 cc Yamaha Special. It was the first one in my life, and I took my time whenever I went anywhere. I had fallen off a number of times, being drunk. We got to Vancouver about three in the afternoon and went to Bob's parent's house. I felt out of place, as they argued about his lifestyle. He was taking care of his life as he saw fit. I was like that, but I did see Bob as soon to be among the socially unaccepted, or behind bars. I left early, went downtown to get my cheque, and got some stuff for the bike. Later on, Bob told me he was going to try to buy some acid, so he could make a fortune selling it in Penticton.

We went downtown, and Bob found what he was looking for, fast. This surprised me-I thought I was good at finding drugs!

We were drinking beer, when Bob said we should do a hit, to see what it was like. I was starting to get drunk, and said "what the fuck" once again. I took a big hit and got fucked up. Bob wanted to drive my bike. I told him no fucking way, I was too high. We spent the night, had breakfast and then set out on our way. Before we left, we took a hit of acid, thinking it would be a gas to bike to Penticton stoned on acid. I wanted to be young again, and do daredevil things. I felt old, but, I was only 25 years old.

When we got there, we were both exhausted, but the word was out that some acid had arrived, and people were all over the place looking for it. I had to sleep, as I could not relax. I went to my tent and passed out. When I came to, I thought, now I am going to sit back and watch what happens to the town. The third night back, almost all the acid was sold by Bob, Chet and Randy, who had been stoned on the stuff since our return. The fourth night, there was a big bash at Saha Beach. There must have been at least three hundred and fifty people, between the ages of 9 to 35. Things got out of hand. The public washrooms were destroyed. Sinks ripped off the walls, toilet paper throughout all the trees at the beach, and along all the electrical wires, and then set on fire. The town R. C. M. P. could not control it. There was even more people showing up from Kelowna, by the hundreds. I got drunk, minded my own business and was not bothered by anyone. I could not believe what I saw the next day.

People had taken the park benches, put them into those Smithrite garbage cans, and set them on fire, only to have it burn like a fireplace. The law and the fire department had one hell of a time trying to get close enough to put them out. There was not one clean spot on the entire beach, nor any fountains for drinking. No washrooms and the concession stand was shut for some time. Bob and the gang found an abandoned house, and we slept there once or twice. I was getting restless, ready to move on again.

Susan and I became involved. She sure looked good to me. Susan was going to be with me and go to school. This all seemed fine and dandy, until I saw the way she lived. I told myself I could not possibly take care of her. I was having a hard time of it myself. I told her I was falling for her, but it couldn't work. Times were hard, and I didn't think I could make it any better.

I eventually went back to Vancouver and settled down with a beautiful woman. Before this, I did some work on some people I wanted to set straight. I moved back in with the Weasel. We agreed to respect each other's space. Weasel was in love with me, and I had to be very blunt with him. He did not like women, and would sooner have seen them dead, than have anything to do with any of them.

For one month I stayed there, seeing all kinds of people in all kinds of jams. Al was sixteen years, heading to twenty-five fast. Kim was sixteen, pregnant, going on forty. Both were drug abusers. I could not help but speak up when they were arguing in Weasel's house, to act like their mediator. I do not have all the answers, nor am I capable of giving more than what is asked.

I do not want to be another statistic in the subculture anymore. I really do not care what anyone's reaction is when they ask for drugs and I say "No." I want to live, and see people live outside the drug oriented culture.

It takes someone who has experienced some sort of turmoil in the fast lane in life to help someone who's life is threatened.

Her name was Cat, and she was the best thing to happen to me. She worked behind Weasel's place. This was a bit of a problem, as I was spending my last few days at his place.

Cat and I started to date. One thing led to another and we moved into a place together. She had a roommate who was quite the girl. Her name was Deb, from Hope, B.C. Her family lived along the Fraser Rive, which created an opportunity for the three of us to make some money running salmon caught in the nets off the banks of the Fraser.

Deb was from the Hope Indian band, near Yale, B.C. The three of us would go to our friends, taking orders for salmon. I sold my motorbike, bought a Ford pick-up, and put a box in the back inlaid with a tarp.

It was mighty illegal to run salmon off the reserve. We risked being fined, jailed, truck impounded and stuck in a hard situation if caught. But there was the thrill of running fresh fish.

Inside the box, we would place 20-30 bags of ice. We'd clean about 100 salmon, pack them in the box, and drive from Hope to Vancouver. Once back, it was sometimes mayhem. People would flock to us for fish, and we were making money hand over fist.

Cat and I were inseparable. I had the best sex ever with a woman, that is to say, *true* sex with love. I loved her very much.

Deb and Cat worked at the same restaurant, called "Bert's Café" on Main Street in east Vancouver. We did all kinds of things together, and did not once fight.

The salmon season was short, so I had to find work. I found a job doing drywall, which paid me well. Cat and I were having a great time.

After work, we would go to a bar called The Biltmore Hotel. In our immediate group, there was every walk of life-Hell's Angels, lawyers, actors, drug dealers, you name it. Cat and I hung out partying with them all.

I was still riding the wave, in a way, from all that had happened in Penticton. I was into drugs, mostly cocaine and pot. There was lots of pot, and booze every night.

Deb found a guy, and eventually the four of us were living in a two bedroom basement suite, on St. George Street and 25th Avenue in east Vancouver. With all the drugs, booze, bar hoping, pot and bullshit, my relationship was not going to last long. The first time I saw this guy hit Deb, I put him through the kitchen table. She broke up with the asshole and hooked up with Pete the plumber. He would drink beer with me at Bert's Café while I waited for Cat to get off work.

One day we were out walking towards the Biltmore, when we saw a house for rent. We knew the family, as the woman would come to Bert's Café once in awhile.

Cat and I moved in, and finally had our own home.

I soon realized I had lost my total perspective as to why I moved to Vancouver in the first place. Money, drugs and the fast lane overtook me, to the point where I was working two jobs, selling drugs. I was living with the woman I loved, and had not been thinking about what I had planned.

I had to go to Calgary at one point, and Cat came with me. She was only the third woman I had ever brought home to meet Mom. It was great! We all enjoyed ourselves, and I felt complete.

One time, my brother came to visit us in Vancouver. He ended up staying for some time, even through the worst critical periods.

One night, my brother and his girlfriend were at the Biltmore Hotel barroom, with Cat and I and a bunch of friends. Altogether, about 16 -20 people. We sat at the end of the room, near the dance floor. Cat and I loved to dance.

While I sat there talking with Cat and a few friends, some guy walked up to me, on my left side, and asked me if I was calling his old lady a liar. I said I don't know you or your old lady, so you better take a hike. Cat told him to leave our little party area.

CHAPTER SIXTEEN

BROKEN BONES AND SHATTERED DREAMS

A ll I really remember is the commotion. People where screaming. Then it hit me-I was the one every one was freaking out about. My brother was holding me on the ground, tables, chairs, glass, blood and screaming. Cat was screaming, and off to my left was a big fight. Then the paramedics, the cops and the whole bar were in a frenzy.

All I felt was an incredible pain, such as I never thought possible. My girl, Cat, was telling me I'd be okay. Then I passed out!

I was stabbed with an 8" buck knife in the right leg. The knife hit my thigh bone, which bent the blade sideways. My bone broke in what is called a spiral compound fracture about 6 inches in length. My bone splintered. I don't know how this happened so fast. I never saw it coming, yet people at the table say they watched it unfold, as if in slow motion.

I don't know who she was, but every fifteen minutes this woman put a needle in me full of morphine. I was told by the doctors my leg wound was very serious and would require multiple leg operations. I would walk in about a year, if it healed well. I spent a month in the Vancouver General Hospital. They put an 18 inch pin through my thigh bone from the hip to my knee. The doctors set my leg wrong *three times,* so in total I had six operations for what should have been three, but who's counting. This happened on February 3, 1986, and to this day I am suffering in more ways than one.

During my stay at the Vancouver General, my friends, including the

Hells Angels, came and put me in a wheel chair with my IV pole. Ten or so people would wheel me out of the hospital and down the street to the Ramada Hotel, and right into the bar. I was pissed in no time, as I had not had a beer in three weeks. With the help of the morphine, I wasn't feeling any pain.

My doctor was a young, GQ type. He told me I would be going home soon, but I would need lots of physio. My leg was not able to bend for over a year.

I found out the guy who stabbed me was named Franciso, so I called him Fran whenever the topic came up. He was charged with the stabbing, and I was told he got four years. Still, he was out on bail, pending appeal. Many people, myself included, thought that was wrong, but you know the way it works.

One day Cat and I were on our way to the Biltmore bar. This was good exercise for me. Cat would walk there with me. We got to the intersection of Kingsway and 12 Avenue in east Van, a major thoroughfare. We both heard it at the same time. Thunder was coming towards us. The louder it got, the more people would stop. It was about fifty bikers.

They stopped the traffic for Cat and I to cross the street. This was their sole purpose. I was accepted into the East End Biker Clan. They got off their bikes, and acted like traffic cops. They stopped every car, every truck. They let us walk right through the middle. Once in the bar, that party was on! It was my first trip to the bar since I got stabbed, so it was a big party.

Things got back to normal quickly after that big night. I wanted to work, and also sell drugs, since I was good at both. So I worked during the day and then partied at night. This worked well for Cat and I. She stood by me. But my life was in for a sudden and drastic change. I was about to lose all I loved, all I worked hard to get. When I got paid, usually I would hit the bar, watch a couple of strippers, go home, and give all my money to Cat.

The bills got paid and the dope was there for the party. However, the effects of all the partying started to take its toll on me. I started to get hang-overs that would last a week instead of 24 hours. I was losing all my energy, feeling awful, and I had no idea why.

This lasted for almost four years. It took its toll on my relationship with Cat. I started to want out, as I could not take all the stress that was starting.

My relationship was a wreck. Then Cat slept over at my dealer's place one night, and I lost it! We started to fight all the time, never doing the things we liked. I saw Di and old friend from Calgary at Expo 86. We partied at our house for three days. Cat would not let this go for years, the fact that I let them party at our house, running around naked or semi-clad on hot days. To me she was a friend, but to Cat, she was the enemy. She also hated all the girls that started to phone for drugs. Then there was Wreck Beach. But that is a whole book in its self. Still, it only added to the problems.

I got over $5000.00 in victim's compensation for the stabbing, but I thought I would get more. I used the money to start a company called Beach Brakerz. It was an import/export beach accessories company. My friend Tac and I came up with some products for a beach line, and in no time we got it up and running. Our friend Perry was a graphic artist and did promotional art work. Soon we were doing business in the states with a company named Lazercraft International. We negotiated the contract for rights to Canada and overseas. By now, Cat and I had separated. I had a nice place in Kitsalano, near Kit's beach.

I was coming home from Wreck Beach one day when I met this woman named Vanessa. We started to see one another. She lived in Richmond, B.C., just south of Vancouver. She is beautiful and always will be in my heart, even though we have differences today.

I made one contact with Mothers Against Drunk Drivers and had to take our art down to Santa Ros, California to the head office of Lazercraft. This is when I realized I could be a very rich man with my company in Vancouver. The tour of the plant was shocking, as the machine alone cost 3 million. I had the rights to Canada, and my first contract was to provide a graduation day card for every student in the province of British Columbia. It would be somewhere in the neighborhood of 25,000. I thought of all the applications for this form of printing or carving paper with a beam of light, to within 1-100 of an inch. It would maintain its structural integrity. This blew me away. I had finally hit it big. It had taken me a very long time to finally feel good about what I was doing.

The hit in the big leagues didn't last long. I was not adept in the legal world of business, and lost my whole company.

Vanessa and I started to see each other all the time. I wanted to work, to get away from the drugs. The chance came when I applied for a job as a deck hand at a sports fishing resort. I would be gone for six months, which would have helped get me started again. I saw Cat every now and then.

One night Vanessa was at my place when Cat showed up. All hell broke loose, as Cat and Vanessa started to fight. I got mad and punched the kitchen cabinet. The sound I made got the girl's attention, and I was rushed to the hospital. I hit the cabinet so hard the bones in my hand were showing.

My new job did not start for another two or three months, so I was lucky. I told Cat this was the last step. Here I was, telling the love of my life to stop. It was baffling. But, there was Vanessa, and she was my light at the end of the tunnel. Our love making was the best in the world to me. I must tell you, I've bedded well over 1,000 people in my life and she was it. I was never gay, just a male hooker/prostitute.

It was nearing time for me to go to work for the fishing resort. Life could not have been any better. I was going to work on the ocean as a deck hand, working my way to guide. I was in love with a beautiful woman who was pregnant! I was walking in the clouds. I was so happy, I was at a loss to put the feeling into words!!!

There was only one thing bothering me, and that was when I would get drunk and party till 5 or 6 in the morning, I would be sick for four or five days. I started to worry. Not wanting to raise any alarms, I went to my doctor and had a complete physical.

Vanessa was due in August. I thought 1990 was going to be the best year of my life. The resort people were understanding about the pregnancy. I got two weeks leave. While I was back in Vancouver, I went to my doctor to check the results of my physical.

I got to visit with Vanessa, although she seemed to have a new found partiality to her. I do not know how to describe it.

We were not together, and that was bad. She was six months when I left, and the timing was right. Vanessa was not at all welcoming to me. I was told it's a "woman" thing in the last stages of pregnancy, so I left it alone, and stayed with friends. They say you only have three true loves in your life. I guess for me, first, the daughter of the mayor of Didsbury, Cat the wild and willing and (Vanessa) the mother of my only true child, conceived out of true love and respect. But it was not returned.

My birthday was August 21st. I saw Vanessa and she was due any day. I could not celebrate till after my doctor's appointment. My doctor was in a strange mood. When I sat in the chair, after examining me, we talked

170

of Vanessa, my work at the resort, and how I felt overall. I told him I was feeling good, despite cancer sores in my mouth every time I drank a beer. I told him about my nasty hangovers. He said my leg healed well, but I was sick!!!!

My doctor told me to sit down and listen to what he had to say. He said, "I've got some good news, and I've got some bad news." I said tell me the good news, I can always get over the bad. He said my leg tests where great. I would only need to worry about a hip replacement later in life. The tone he used made me feel uneasy. He said I would only have to have one last operation, for the removal of the 18" nail, with the pins in my hip and knee. I said okay, now cut to the bad shit. What he said next cost me my whole life's dreams. Broken bone's and shattered dreams." You're sick with the AIDS VIRUS. You also have Hepatitits C. You only have 5-8 years to live, so you had best get your affairs in order." I was shut down inside. I was still on morphine, but would sell it for blow and cash. I thought, he better give me some extra pain pills now.

My prescription was for 50 pills. I marked it up to 150 pills. I took them straight to the bar. I did not really think about having Aids, or Hep C, or that I was dying, and I was about to a Dad. I only thought of getting more pills, selling them, getting some blow, a woman, a hotel room, and piss drunk.

There went all my dreams of helping people. The life I loved. The life I was coming into and the life that was in Vanessa's body. What the fuck was I going to do? This all started in the year *1986* with a stabbing and six operations with four pints of blood. 1990 was my official diagnosis. Now, in the year 2005, I just finished doing another lecture.

I still have a lot to tell you, the reader, about life. Remember: "It's not what you do in life. It's how and by what methods you do it."

So, now who do I tell? I thought. This person, then that person, then these people, then... Why tell anyone? I kept it to myself. As a result, I went slightly nuts. I thought, first I'll finish the year out at the resort and then I'll come back here to Vancouver.

I was at the hospital the night my daughter was born. She is a perfectly normal, healthy girl, 16 years old now, and no virus.

I can only tell you my heart exploded when I was told my news. It exploded again when my daughter was born. From August to October, I worked up in Rivers Inlet as a deck hand.

One time, I was flying back into the resort from Vancouver after a break. I often got to sit near the pilot, and he would let me fly. I was sitting behind the pilot in a four seater. The window in the door behind the pilot was a bubble window. I was looking right down at the water, as we flew straight over the ocean.

We had to bank the plane to the left, the side I was sitting on. There was one passenger, the pilot and me, with one empty seat. As I looked out the window, (the bubble window) behind the pilot, (banking to the left), I thought if anything was to drop, it would go straight to the ocean. The more we banked, the louder the noise in the plane. All of a sudden, the door with the bubble window, that I was looking out of popped open. I was screaming at the pilot, he kept saying "hold the fucking door shut and hang on". Well what the fuck do you think I did? A cat stuck to the ceiling with all four claws-that was me with the door of the plane. The pilot leveled out, and then we landed without any further problems. But the decompression of the cabin of the plane had it's effect no less. I ruptured an ear drum, and my equilibrium was fucked. I was told I was dying anyway. I was scared, but not scared. I had looked death in the eye already, and we have not stopped staring at each other since then.

All ended well at the resort. I was now a guide, and deck hand, and was salt water safety approved.

The first thing I did was rent an apartment with an old buddy who worked at the resort. I had known him for years. It was Big Al, who went with Di. He lived with Cat and I for some time, and had his brother live below Cat and I on 18th Ave. and St. George St. in Vancouver. In other words, another fishing hard-on, a term we often used when we wanted to go fishing (whether in a bar, river or ocean).

I got lucky and rented KD Lang's old place in east Vancouver with Big Al. During our time at Big Springs Fishing Resort, there was a rather interesting thing that happened to me.

A bear would come to the edge of the bay, where the resort was moored. It was a floating resort, tied to land via a boom interlocking system. The grizzly did not ever try to come on the float itself, but would call for me. Everyday, at a certain time, this grizzly would come to the edge of the bay and beg for fish. I would catch him one a day, and the guests saw this. I would take them with me when I went to feed the bear. During my bear feeding trip, this bear would copy every movement I made in this little boat, within leaping distance, if the grizzly had been so inclined.

One day, some elders from the Haida Nation came to the resort. They had heard of this guy, a Mohawk, dancing with bears. It was me, and I was given the name "Dancing Bear" by the Haida Elders. This name has stuck with me to this day, and is now my company name. My middle name represents "a wandering soul that will roam the world forever."

My bud, Big Al and I shared an apartment. Al still had his car. There was an old 18 foot, deep V Mastercraft boat on a trailer, with a 75 Evenrude motor. We watched this boat for about a month. Finally, I said to Al, "let's take the boat out, jimmy the motor, paint the trailer, and the boat and re-pin stripe it, register it for the ocean so we can get a 13K number," which is an ocean license. We did this, and no one in the building was the wiser. For three weeks, we kept the boat elsewhere while we worked and fished. That's all we wanted to do, fish.

It got to the point where we would park the boat in our stall underground, right from where it came, only painted, pin striped, new plates and painted trailer. We were never asked one single question about it.

One day it was beautiful out, nice sea breeze coming in the balcony window. We thought we would go to the south side of White Rock, which is just before the U.S. border. We loaded up beer, bait, sandwiches, smokes, pot, short tank tops, and a full tank of gas. We registered at the point registry office and off we went, out on the water by 11 A.M.

We drove all over the place, about two miles out in the Juan de Fuca Strait. We did not catch a fucking thing, and around 4 P.M. we saw a gale storm coming from the south. We floored the motor, full throttle, and headed for shore. This gale storm came on with blistering speed. We lost sight of land, but kept it at full throttle. Soon enough, we ran out of gas. Our little boat lay idle in the water. We had 3 beer left and it was cold as fuck, raining, no life jackets, lots of pot, and smokes. Food all gone, lost in the storm, floating in the dark. Some time around 11 P.M., I started to yell and scream. I even ripped open a beer can, flicking my lighter in it like a beacon. Nothing was working.

Around 2 A.M., I heard a loud noise. I told Al "something is coming, and we best hold on." We felt the waves first. Both of us saw this black wall go by our little boat. In the fog, at night, this was a fucking scary situation. Al and I started to yell as we realized a freight ship about 360 feet long just about hit us. I was flicking my lighter so much, my thumb started to bleed. Then the noise stopped, and we saw spot lights pointing in our direction. Thank God!!! We were rescued by a huge 360 foot long ship. The coast guard came and took us off the ship. I guess we floated right out into the freight lanes of the fastest moving waterways in the world, the Juan de Fuca Strait. This is a dangerous place at any time, let alone during a gale fog storm.

Soon after, all the shit settled down. Al wanted to do other things, and I didn't really care-so we kind of went our separate ways. But I heard he went for my ex, Cat. That was the last I heard of either of them.

Now everything I wanted to do had to be done soon. The doctor gave me 3-5 years. I was only 30 years old. I know how AIDS works, and I've known 100s of people that have passed on, as well as those still alive today. My dreams had to be fulfilled.

I got a job on a fishing ship, 52' long and 22 ' wide called the "Resolution 2". My captain was named Lee. He was a Newfie, and drank a hell of a lot. There were 5 of us on this ship, and we went all over the west coast of Canada. I was happy I lived through this. The ship set out. We were heading 100 miles west of Vancouver Island, fishing in about 300 feet of water. We all were in communication with each other, as you could see nothing but water. Every time we went out, we were at sea for at least two weeks at a time.

Have you ever watched the movie "The Perfect Storm" or seen the beginning to Gillian's Island, where the tiny ship was tossed? The storm that hit the five ships out here was a monster. We had 15 meter waves and water coming in the hull from the huge waves. It was enough to make you piss your pants or scare the shit out of you. The storm lasted a good two hours, when it was over, there were only 3 ships left. I only remember the name of one, as a friend worked on it. It was "The Fiddler".

When the last of the three ships got back to port, there was a big ceremony for our lost friends. I thought it was ironic: I'm the one dying, and no one knows. I'm on this fucking ship, being tossed around the ocean like dice in a crap game! What else could I get myself in to?

My last stint with these guys was when we were 100 miles west of Vancouver Island.

Our codding (the net) was about 100 feet long. Suddenly, it pulled like there was a big tug on the lines. I thought, oh shit, first the storm, now

A LIFE NOT WORTH TAKING

what? Lee, our captain, stopped all engines and we sat there for a few moments. Then it happened. Our codding, 100 feet long with 350 pound weights (one on each corner) came bursting up out of the water-the most amazing sight of my life! The codding hit a school of cannery fish and in one swift passing filled the net with over 50,000 pounds of fish. When the codding burst to the surface, we all got on it and danced a jig. It had never happened before. Thousands of fish!!! We were heading back to Victoria to sell our cargo, singing and drinking all the way.

I soon moved on, back to the downtown scene.

I thought, no way am I going to let this bug called HIV/AIDS kill me, nor its companion, Hep C. My dreams will always be. One by one, I've achieved them.

Once back in the downtown world, it was that fast pace and the high speed women I liked.

I started to sell drugs, not thinking about the fact I was sick. I was living day to day. With the help of the biker world, I started selling in 5 big bars in east Vancouver.

In no time, I was selling more that I had. This caused me some problems at certain times. It was a buyer's market.

For one year, I did what ever I felt like doing, no matter what the risks. Whether it be falling out of a plane (which would have sucked), or drowning in 15 meter waves, The Perfect Storm, before it ever happened on film. (But I survived.)

Being able to fly, but nothing really, 20 minutes at the wheel, but I did it.

I was drug dealing in downtown Vancouver, where people got stabbed, shot, OD, or took a good shit kicking. I was always safe. I never once thought of getting busted. I just did not let it phase me.

I've had guns pulled on me, and was stabbed again, by this guy hyped out on coke, with a letter opener. Good thing he didn't get to plunge it all the way-like the other guy did 4 -5 years ago. I was starting to think about my sickness, and did not know how I was going to tell the family. Even though I felt shame, it was because of the virus, not the way I got it. From a BLOOD TRANSFUSION!!!!

CHAPTER SEVENTEEN

GOING HOME TO DIE

In 1992, I jumped on a Greyhound bus. I didn't tell my mother I was coming, or that I was a drug addict. I got off the Greyhound in Calgary, Alberta. I've called it home since 1992.

When I first arrived in Calgary, I did not know what I was going to do. At first, I found odd jobs, making pocket change. It was during this period I came to accept the fact I was terminally ill, with two killer diseases. Two things ran through my head: 1) I don't have much time left. 2) I better do something right.

In 1992, I was still talking to Vanessa. Sadly, she would not let me speak to my daughter Brittany. It was heartbreaking, because Brittany continued to be a part of my life, even though a distant one. I want her to be so much!

I had been sick for 5 years. I did not know how to fight it, or where to go. My doctor had given me 5-8 years to live, so the thought I had only three years left bothered me.

One day, my mother was reading the paper and noticed an ad looking for HIV positive clients for drug studies. I thought what the hell, it can't hurt. I definitely was sick.

I went to the Foothills Hospital and walked to the front desk. I told them I have HIV and Hep C and want to do any possible drug trials that are ready for testing on humans. It was a major turning point.

I was asked to use a new drug. For a time, the drug worked, according to the doctors. However, I was still sick, apparently a winning situation. I kept wondering when I would feel better.

Twice a week, I went to the hospital, finally securing a place in the AISH program (Assured Income for Severally Handicapped). I was given $850.00 monthly.

It was rough going at first. I longed for my former life, and started looking for it, though in a slower form.

We lived in south Calgary, where my brother was showing me all kinds of things in the heritage line, like hunting, tracking and skinning. George explained that he and Mom were working on our family tree, tracing our native heritage back to the early 1700s. Also, they were doing bead work, and I soon developed my own interest..It awoke in me an old love of all things artistic. George gave me these plexiglass circles, asking me if I wanted to use them for art. I did. It was the spring of 1992.

When not seeing doctors, I was making things, taking them across the street to the bar and selling them. Eventually I met my friend Harold, who introduced me to Buba. Before long Harold was out of the picture and Buba became my partner in the art world. He worked with a candle making (or dipping) machine, and we started making carved candles. By May, 1993, we had worked making molds for dipping candles, painted cow skulls (decorating them with fine things) and all kinds of other western art. We set up shop at Eau Claire Market in Calgary, where Buba and I met Ryan. Ryan owned Soft Tub West and needed men to sell for him. So, Buba and I would rotate days, since Ryan's soft tub show was in Southcenter Mall, a long way from Eau Claire Market. When Ryan's show moved to Chinook Mall, we happened to be off that week, so we both worked it, becoming good friends with Ryan.

By the time the 1993 Calgary Stampede had arrived, Buba and I set our minds on big money. Somehow, we worked the selling of soft tubs into our routine, and it proved to be lucrative. It was deeply satisfying on another level- it was real, *honest* money I was making, not drug money.

I was put on a different, more successful drug study. Every month, I received a shot, and blood work. Business was great for Buba and I, and our relationship with Ryan just blossomed. He bought a ton of wax for us to use for our candle company, and we managed to sell approximately 30 hot tubs at different malls throughout Calgary. We met a young guy named Neb, who worked in the tub business with Buba and who also sold us good pot. Buba and I liked to smoke, even at work.

The chance came for the soft tub enterprise to expand and Buba and I asked Ryan if we could run soft tubs to the Okanagan, and, if successful, eventually to the lower mainland. It seemed like a golden opportunity. Once back in Vancouver, I did not seek out any old friends, except Den, the best street brother a guy could ask for. We set up a store in Surrey Place Mall, and found a nice house in Surrey, away from all the drug shit. I would still come to Calgary once a month, staying 2-3 days to see Ryan at head office, as well as the endless doctors probing and prying at my well being. I held out hope that results from all this research would eventually help others. It simply did not matter what I had to go through. I met some great people selling tubs. At the same time, I even ended up showing work in art galleries around the world. I also shot a video for Quantas Airlines, during the stampede of '93. We had two locations where our work was selling. I was very happy to be doing something positive, something good.

One day Neb asked me if I wanted to open a grow house, I agreed, ensuring it would be an even split. The plan was set. I moved back to Calgary. Baba turned out to be a hard businessman to work with, so we separated. I was back in cow town, living in a grow house, selling to people I had known for some time. I was soon moving 20 pounds of pot a week. When Neb moved to B. C., I assumed control of his grow-op.

Our first grow show was busted when we went to Vancouver to see Neb's father. Still, it worked out just fine. I moved into Neb's dad's place. Around the same time I met a guy we called Smag. His sister was sick, and it took almost a year for him to tell me she had contracted AIDS from her boyfriend. She was scared. Since I had already told Smag about my condition, he put us in touch.

Her name was Tina and she lived in Toronto. It soon got to the point where we were more than friends. Despite the constant fear the fucking doctor put in me head, I wanted and needed a companion. If you only have five to eight years to live, it's like the ticker tape in your brain goes off, and desperation can set in.

Meanwhile, Neb and I had it going on. We always had thousands in our pockets. I moved back to my family's place, and they were in the process of moving to a new house, with the option of rent-to-own. It worked out well for some time.

I co-signed with my mother for our house. It was going to be my hospice, when the time came. Being on AISH was a bonus, since it meant I could not lose the house.

My mother owned her first house. George and I lived there as well; a good situation. Unfortunately, as with all dysfunctional families, soon the shit hit the fan. I moved out, and found a nice house which I rented for $700.00 per month. I picked up three cats; a mother, father and son. I called them Kyler, Caylie and Salem. They have cost me thousands in medical bills, but they are a family that gives unconditional love.

I set up a good house for a few years. I did all kinds of drugs, parties and bars. I hung out with people from different organizations, whether it was the Hell's Angel's, or the Triads-Lebanese or independents. I was working with well over 200 people, with drugs alone. I was a dealer again, and alone. With dealing came the fast life, the fast women and the big name bands. I was well known.

One time, I got real sick, and had to be put in the hospital. Much to my delight, Ryan (the owner of Soft tubs) was there as well, and we renewed our friendship. I met his son Walter.

Walter owns one of the largest photography studios in Alberta. Since I kind of hit it off with him, we became friends. At this time, I was going to the local strip clubs. I got to know a couple of the girls working as dancers. Soon the introduction came (again) to the Hells Angels Biker Club.

I met a woman named Lynn. She was, and is, a complex beauty. I will hold a spot in my heart for her forever. She did more with me than a lot of people would have. She knew I was sick, but it did not seem to bother her. We were always extremely safe with sex, but soon the drugs took over. Lynn was a free spirit, and I could not stop what she wanted to do. I was learning I might never find the soul mate I needed, my virus being the biggest prohibiting factor.

Lynn and I lasted six months. When we split, I started spacing, and went into a bit of debt. It's not that I could have not recovered, I just went too far. I was at my mom's, and had just finished smoking a joint. There was a knock at the front door. No one knew where I was, as I always kept my family life away from my drug life. As I opened the door a cloud of pot smoke billowed out. To my utter and total shock, there stood two cops, looking for me. They gave me their card, which read: Ontario Provincial Police, Sexual Crimes Unit. I thought, holy fuck, what did I do that I don't remember?!! Instinctively, I panicked, telling them I was George, and that

Jeremiah was out. I really was unprepared for this! They told me about an investigation into White Oaks Village for Boys in Hagersville. I was stunned. Not after all these years! I had totally buried this, but the arrival of these cops messed my head up once again. The abuse I suffered as a child was back to haunt me. I sat down after the cops left. They had told me that Jeremiah was to get in touch with them, while they were in town. They were staying at the Delta Bow Valley Hotel downtown.

For hours, I sat there, by myself, going through a tremendous assortment of feelings. Eventually, I came to terms with this new reality. I phoned the cops at the hotel, and told them that it was in fact me who had answered the door. I explained that their appearance had shocked me, so I pretended to be my brother at the time. I went to the hotel and was interviewed by the two detectives from Ontario. The meeting lasted for over an hour. I left feeling like I had not felt in over 20 years. During the interview, I would be in mid-sentence, when suddenly I would start crying. The emotions were intense. The influence on my personality of what Rob (the staff member at White Oaks Village For Boys) did to me is impossible to measure. Had this never been acted out on me, I'm certain I would have become a different type of person. Not one who killed, nor harmed anyone. I doubt I would have become a prostitute. I know now that I am successful at whatever I do. It just took me 30 years to find myself, 30 years of dealing with painful memories of stolen innocence.

During the interview, the police asked me if I would testify against Rob. I agreed to do it, also relating that I had written a book about my life. The police said it would be subpoenaed as evidence. I would have to fly back to Toronto to attend court. The trial lasted for 6 years. The cops had to interview (or at least get in touch with) over 350 kids that went through White Oaks Village between the years 1969-1970. They traveled all over the world, looking for past residents of the Village. I was going through hell with this trial. It brought back so many painful memories that I wanted to leave behind. Still, it brought with it some answers. I hired a lawyer to represent me. The trial was going full tilt, and I met with some of the people I knew when I was between the ages of 9-13.

As the trial entered its 3rd year, it went to the Supreme Court of Canada. In the Hamilton Court House, Justice N. Borkovich issued a warrant for my manuscript, in order to use it in the proceedings of the trial. Over the course of the trial, I flew back 6 or 7 times. I was put up in hotels, and given a food allowance. I saw family I hadn't seen in years, so some good came of it all. But the trial was awful. First of all, the person I so much admired and trusted as a kid, Les Horn, showed up supporting my attacker Rob. It was crushing to see my mentor sitting in support of Roy. The trial was long, hard and emotionally draining. I was forced to talk about dark events that took place 30 years ago. I must mention that at the time the cops were interviewing me in Calgary, they were in the process of getting Rob extradited from the U.S. He had become a minister in a youth detention center in Nashville, Tennessee.

As the trial dragged on, witness testimony was brought to question. There were only 15 witnesses to testify, and, during the last two years, 8 of them had testimony rejected by the Supreme Court Justice (N. Borkovich).

In the end, seven former residents of White Oaks remained. Tragically, one victim, a young man who I will not name, was so traumatized by the trial that he killed himself. Only six witnesses remained.

Justice N. Borkovich told me during the proceedings that upon reading my life story, "I found it to be one of the most concise documented pieces of one's life I have ever read". He wished me well. The courts knew I was terminally ill, and that my story had to be told. At the final trial, only three victims remained. My testimony was decisive in Rob's conviction. In the end, I was just grateful it was over.

I still call myself and the others "kids." Out trust and innocence was stolen when we were children. Rob was found guilty on many counts. I was deeply affected by the trial. Not only did I not get to talk about all events, I felt we really did not get to tell our side of the story. It was disappointing. It made me very angry that all Rob got was an 18 month conditional sentence, under house arrest. He lost his job, but was allowed to go back to the states and serve his time. Time is supposed to heal all wounds. This is what I'm living on right now, and I don't know how much is left.

I had a heavy reputation in Calgary as a top drug dealer. For a long time, I passed myself off as an artist. Ironically, that is what I truly am, an artist. I was involved with bikers, Asian drug lords, and Columbian drug kings. I was living well, doing photo work for a local company who I much respect. But my life went awry after the trial. I could not deny feelings of vengeance. I decided to sue, for 5 million. My lawyer was a complete ass, and I lost. I was awarded victim compensation; how much, I did not know.

I got deeply involved with the subculture once again. I was dating strippers, having sex (protected). I had almost 300 people working for me selling coke. People in one bar I used to frequent would walk up to me and say, "Jeremiah, I want to be one of your soldiers". Soldiers in my little drug army. I had some very powerful friends in this city, and still do. I would go hard for weeks, and then I would shut it down, and rest. At one point, I was selling 17 ounces of cooked coke (what is called crack), here in Calgary, at 3 points a gram for 40 dollars. Per day, I averaged $63,000. And the people! I was partying with stars, people like Snoop Doggy Dog, Joan Jett, Molly Hatchet, the Commitments, Allana Myles, Nazareth and the Tragically Hip. At the same time, I was financing 2 to 3 local bands, and drinking with local celebrities like Red Dog, Jerry Forbes and the other C- Jay-92 D-J's. I drove a nice jeep. I never had to wait in line for local bars. I bought a small company in town that took pictures in bars and put them on little key tags. Thus, I was able to go to all the hot bars and not pay or wait.

Things were going well, but I started to smoke coke again. This put me in the "my shit don't stink" kind of head space. No good. This story will show what I'm talking about. I was coming home from doing a pick up, going through a school zone in the left lane. A car started to pass me in the curb lane, and when it got beside me, I could tell it was driven by an under cover cop. I gave him a dirty look, because he was speeding through a school zone. He did not like the look. My friend Pistal Pete was with me. The cop and I kind of played tag, all the way down Center Street. We drove up to 16 Avenue and Center Street. By this time, there was enough room for 3 vehicles going south. I was in the center lane, and the cop was on my left. By the time we came to a stop at the lights, I had a cop in front, on my side, and behind. There was no one on my right side. When the light turned green, I floored it to the right. The cop behind was cut off by the traffic, and I was in the clear. It was a good thing, since I was holding half an ounce of cooked coke with me.

After about two blocks, I went south, then east, then south, then east, and then south, and then west, and I was home. I was sitting in my living-room, having a big blast, with my friend Pistal Pete going on and on about how I lost the cops.

I smoked all afternoon, then I sent Pistal Pete for more, as I was getting low. He jumped in the jeep. As I sat back down on the couch with a big rock of crack cocaine, I thought I was hearing things. It was Pistal, screeching the tires around the block, and I mean *screeching*. I sat there. Pistal Pete came up the street and braked in front of my house. He ran up the stairs, in the house, and yelled, "Jeremiah, the cops are here for you!" I thought, "it took you long enough." They did not come to my door; instead, they blocked both ends of my street. It was the same cop that I gave the dirty look to in the school zone. He parked his car on an angle in front of my house. I was standing in the window, with my crack pipe in one hand and a cup of tea in the other hand, looking out at the cop as he looked at me. I took one big toke then walked out my front door to the cop. As I approached him, he said he wanted to know why the dirty look back up on Center Street. I told him, he's a cop, and in a school zone during school hours he was speeding. I told him he had better be a better driver. Then he asked why I took off like I did, and that he could charge me with dangerous driving. I said, "Nice try, when you weren't even around, and I beat you to my house, and you just showed up now." Obviously, there was no reason other than harassment. Next, he said I had an outstanding fine, and that I should pay it or he would take me downtown. I said let's go. The cop said he did not have the time to process me for a fine, and that he would be watching me to fuck up. He jumped in his car, called off the S.W.A.T. team and left.

I walked back into my house. Pistal Pete was just shaking in his pants. I told him to sit down. We did a blast, and he said I was just too damn blantant, doing what I did. I was so into coke, I did not give a shit about anything, certainly not the cops.

I moved twice before I moved home. At the last place, I had to take a baseball bat to one guy. He was going to hit a girl, and I freaked out. I took the bat to him, hitting him about 10 times then lining his head up for the last swing. I would have killed him if I had not stopped in mid swing. I told him you're dead. The next day I moved home. I had to dry out. I was smoking about 1 ounce of coke a day, with the help of 2 other people most of the time. I went cold turkey, which has never been a problem for me. I just shut down, and say NO.

I kicked around the house, getting back into my art work. My mother really inspires me when I am honest with her. She treats me with respect, and I get lost in my art. I am very lucky to have an open line of communication with her. I tell her everything, and never feel judged, only understood. I only wish I had a companion with whom I could have that same level of openness. I guess time will tell.

CHAPTER EIGHTEEN

THE TRIALS AND THE SENTENCES

During a time of relative calm, I was sitting around the house, doing good. Mom and I had an art show, with good response. This was an inspiration-my mother did the best she could with certain art projects, and to see her sell it made me feel proud.

On the other hand, I was at total war with my family. I had fallen behind in my bill payments, and asked my mother if she would co-sign on the mortgage of our house. I had not lived there in the longest time, and was unaware that my mother and my brother, George, had already done that! At the last minute, I found out that if I had obtained this mortgage on our house, I would have been charged with bank fraud. My brother had signed my name, when he and my mother did this, and did not tell me. I lost everything and did not recover.

I lost my job as a photographer. My brother is friends with my friend, who owned the company. He was there one night, and I did not want to be. He propositioned me, and I flipped. I walked home from Priddis, a distance of about 30 km. Before I left, I took $20.00 from the cash box. To this day, they say I took more. They will not accept what they did, so we don't talk... just say "Hi" and that's it.

Because I was using too much, I got way behind, and lost all the people that worked for me in the drug business. I was living at home and was flat broke. I received AISH (Assured Income For The Severely Handicapped), because I'm diagnosed with HIV and Hep C. I was classified as unemployable, due to my illness. So, $850.00 per month was my ticket. A far cry from $63,000.00 per day! Fuck. I was sliding downhill fast, and kind of needed this to happen, in order to ground myself for a while. I was way too high in the clouds...

I tried making plans to go back to school. It seemed every time I thought about it, I got distracted by cocaine and women.

Eventually I met with an old friend I used to do crimes with in Vancouver. He was buying coke from me when I was on my little run ways. We hooked up, and started to pull jobs again.

Back in the old days, we would flip locks from doors of businesses, go in, and rob them. We did hundreds of crimes, and the biggest thrill was finding a safe, and having to crack it. You see, I finally went over the edge.

Living at home is awkward. We are a totally dysfunctional family when it comes to expressing feelings to one another. This sucks, because we used to be good friends, and now we don't trust one another.

We live on like this.

At one point, I got word I would be receiving a cheque from Ontario Victims of Crime Compensation Board. How much I did not know, although I was really not ready for it. I was still doing drugs, and paying no attention to any of my responsibilities. I would leave home for weeks at a time, doing drugs and partying.

One day, the cheque came in. I got $21,000.00 from Victims Comp. I bought all kinds of shit. I took my uncle Ben and my brother to Mexico for 7 days, and we had a blast. I took my brother George because we never really went anywhere before. My uncle had never been on a plane, let alone outside Canada. So, I wanted to take them and just kind of bond (or try to). But, after the trip, we remained distant.

I went back to dealing drugs and smoking coke. I used my money on the trip, and once I got home I blew $7,000 on coke. I really did not care. For some reason, it did not matter to me how much I spent, or where I spent it, or on whom. I started to really not give a shit. I felt let down by my lawyer in Toronto over a 5 million dollar law suit. She fucked up. I was suffering from severe depression, as a result of the trial I went through. I felt I never really had my say in court. Plus, my family situation was building. I did not know when it would blow, but it was coming.

I felt the trial was set up for no real reason, after seeing this child molester punished so lightly. All the years I put up with child molesters, some of them thinking they were using a 17-18 year old for sex. In fact, they were with a 12-15 year old male prostitute. To me, once again it was the old adage: "it's not what you do in life, it's by how and what methods you do it."

I was royally fucking up. I was smoking coke too much, not caring about anything. I tried quitting a couple of times, but I was very weak, with a circle of bad friends. I would get high with them, and stay away for weeks at a time. I lost all concern for my well being and could not figure out why. I just kept doing what I was doing.

For well over three years, 2001 - 2003, I did nothing worthy of anything, other than deal drugs and commit crimes with my buddy from Vancouver. Things started to get really crazy, to the point where I don't know how we got away with some of the crimes. How much we would make was boggling to the mind. We kept nothing to show for what we did. My buddy was into IV drugs, mostly downs like morphine. I was a smoker. I would smoke 100-700 dollars worth of coke a day. When Larry and I (my buddy from Vancouver) really hooked up and started this little team, we were going through about 700-1500 dollars worth of coke per day. I was, at one time, a big name here in Calgary.

Times had changed, and now I was at the lower end of the totem pole. Fuck, I've been there lots, so no biggy.

I'm slowing down, and it takes time to climb back up on top of things when you get older. Now, I find I take longer to get where I have to go. Before, I would just get there, using whatever means possible to get what I wanted. I seem to have lost the edge, somewhat, due to age, health, stress and trials.

One time, I was on a seventeen day stone, smoking at least a quarter ounce (or 7 grams) of coke a day, with my partner from Vancouver. I had money, dope and women. What more could a man ask for? *That* answer is eluding me at this particular time. For years, I had thought: work, drugs, sex and money. Almost in that order!

For 30 years, all I did was sell myself (or other people) and drugs. Looking back, I thought I knew myself, but I was wrong. My life style allowed me to do what I wanted, when I wanted. The people around me stayed as long as I was up to something.

My mother is one of the strongest people I know. She kept telling me, everyone was using me, and I did not really care. But I would close my eyes to this, knowing she was 100% right. Having withdrawn into myself, I was so lonely. As result of having HIV and HEP C, I found it impossible to play the field, and possibly find the relationship I dreamt of. I was so scared of infecting someone, I just acted like nothing was wrong, that it would all go away, but it didn't. I was making money hand over fist, with and endless supply of dope. I wanted to start over, when suddenly, I hit the wall!!! I got busted in Edmonton for crimes I did while on my 17 day binge.

I had not been in jail for 26 years, other than for short 1-2 nights, plus my time in the states. This was a whole new deal.

This whole ordeal had started with a girl. I was with one I thought I loved, but it was nothing more that a drug induced infatuation. Her name was Trinity. Larry, myself, Trinity and Nole (from Trinidad) became fast friends. Nole wanted me to be his mentor in the crime world. He admired me for what I had done, and wanted in. I told him he had to do exactly what I said, and the team was off.

Edmonton was our home base. We arrived with cash registers in the trunk of our stolen car. We would steal a car or 4 per day, just to keep on the move. We rented a hotel room. I contacted a friend who hooked us up with some more coke. After staying awake for 17 days, coke was the only thing that kept me going.

Our first night in Edmonton consisted of 7 grams of coke (cooked), a bunch of beer, and about 10 robberies. We stole 4 cars and by 7:30 in the morning we had accomplished what we had set out to do. Suddenly, on our way back to Calgary, a cop appeared out of nowhere and pulled us over. Larry and his girl friend Sue were in one car, while Nole, Trinity and I were in the other. Naturally, the cop chose to go after my car. I think I was driving a Mazda Cressida. When the cop made his move, I freaked out and took off. The chase was on.

I was driving like a pro racer, blasting down the streets of Edmonton with the cop in hot pursuit. Eventually, there 28 cops chasing me. Somehow, I lost them! I pulled into a convenience store, changed my appearance, and bought smokes and a drink. Trinity and Nole were freaking out. I sat on the curb smoking.

Just then, Trinity saw a cop car. The cop heard her scream, and he came over. Within 10 minutes I had 28 guns pointing at me. The cops were yelling all kinds of directions, but I was so tired and stoned I really did not care what was happening, let alone what was going to happen.

187

I know for sure if I had not stopped what I was doing, I would have become very sick, and died—I was not ready for that.

I found myself sitting in a 6 by 8 cell, outside of Edmonton, with no visitation rights. In any case, my family believed I was a lost cause.

When my court appearance came, I did all that I could to stay out of jail, and it worked.

I was let out on bail. My co-accused and I met up with Trinity. We were far from finished. We went to Edmonton for court, and on the way home decided we would do a job. Trintiy, Sue and I were on our way to see what Larry's bail status was.

On our way home, we did the stupidest thing I have ever done. Trinity wanted some more dope, so we did this job in Red Deer, and got popped. Now, not only did I have Edmonton court appearances, I was expected to appear in Red Deer and Calgary. I had accumulated close to 30 charges over a 1 ½ year period. I had fallen over the edge. I was devoid of respect for myself, with little or no respect for the people I was involved with. Even though I was out on bail, I was still being used, and I had enough of it.

I applied for admission at art college, specifically, Alberta College of Art and Design, one of the hardest in Canada. I put together a resume, dropped it off at ACAD, and was told I would be contacted in a couple of weeks.

CHAPTER NINETEEN

SETTING MYSELF STRAIGHT

With the help of the police, my 1 ½ year self destruction trip was finally over. It was for the best that I did end up this way. I had too much on my plate. Now that my plate was empty, where were all the people that hung around when it was full? Gone, which shows that the more you give, you end up giving more. People, who use any and all kinds of drugs, treat people like dirt. If you accept this, you won't feel lonely. I was tired of that life.

Despite having many people around me all the time, I was, and still am, a very lonely person. I've come to terms with this, because the reality is, it would take an awful lot for someone to fall in love with me. As my mother says, I am "damaged goods." This loaded term has connotations, and it is difficult to accept it's the bitter truth. On the street, you never really have friends, just drug dependants.

I was accepted by ACAD much to my surprise. It was a two semester course in black and white photography. I used this acceptance letter and schedule to show the courts I was cleaning up my act. It worked, much to my relief, as well as to my mother's (who was active during my court trials in three cities in Alberta). I spent 2 ½ months locked up before trial, and 6 months out on bail. The judge in Edmonton gave me a 2 year conditional sentence. The judge in Red Deer gave me six months probation. In Calgary I was handed well over $5000 in fines. My license was taken away for 1 year (for out running Edmonton's finest), and I was given 50 hours of community work.

Considering everything I had done, I'm one very lucky person to have avoided jail over the last 3 years of my life. I was still going to go through a lot, before settling down and behaving like a responsible person again.

Things started to look good, but in a different light. I was staying away from dope, an incredibly difficult thing for me to do, as everyone I know uses dope in one way or another. I was sentenced to house arrest for 6 months, followed by 6 months with a curfew and 12 month probation. In the spring of 2005 I finished all my trials and tribulations. Once again, I look forward to any other adventure that comes my way.

At home, with my mother and brother, there is much animosity floating in the air. It's so thick at times you could cut it with a knife.

I called my P.O., telling him I was going to move, because my family situation was poor, and I need my space. I was granted permission to move, so I did just that. In August of 2003 I found my own place. I found a roommate, someone I knew from working on the mall in downtown Calgary (with my mother, selling our artwork). I was once again back on track selling art with my mother and I was attending ACAD, studying for a degree in photography and jewelry making.

Prior to moving out of the house I shared with my mother and brother, I did an interview with the University of Alberta. I spoke about HIV, and my first year of living with being terminally ill. The U of A was impressed with my interview. They asked me if I would consider doing some public speaking on this subject. I felt the change coming over me. I was sure moving out would be a good thing. I needed my space, since I've been on my own since the age of 9. I had a hard time living with family, and do not expect this to change. We have grown so different. Despite everything, there remains a strange closeness between us, although at the same time, no strong foundation to cement our relationships. But, we are working to get along as best we can.

Things started out well with this new house and roommate. I was going to school, and achieving a B+ level. This made my mother happy, but I was still feeling lost. All my life, I have been very active in the bar scene, as well as fucking around with all kinds of famous bands. I met hundreds of women. This was (and is) the key. I'm lonely. Throughout my life, I could have sex (or a relationship) if I wanted, but I find I won't allow myself the opportunity. The fact that I have this killing virus is ripping me apart with loneliness. I have one friend I trust. I must stress it: *One Friend*. Looking back over the years, it seems the people I associated with looked to me for one of two things: drugs or my ability to get rid of huge amounts of drugs. When you put yourself in this world, all you get is a membership in Sargent Pepper's Lonely Heart's Club. I am the C.E.O.

My friend is named Nappy. We have done all kinds of nutty things with women and drugs, but now he has quit drugs, to the point where he is no longer a heavy user. He is more of a recreational user, much like me.

My college endeavors were going fine, until I caught double black lung pneumonia, and had to be hospitalized for two weeks. I thought to myself "Shit, I'm just starting to begin again, and now this shit, is this the onset of AIDS or what?" I was so scared. For the first week in the hospital, all I did was cry and cry. My family visited me, along with one lady friend. I love her in a special way: I've known her for over twenty years. Sadly, right now she is fighting her own demons, and there is no way we could ever be together. Her name is Ange.

After being released from the hospital, I let things start to slip again. This time, I could not stop it – well, I could have, but I didn't.

My doctor would not let me go to school, so I used it as an excuse to start using again. I have to keep busy or I lose it. I can't do anything. It's like turning off a dim band of hope.

CHAPTER TWENTY

I'M STILL ALIVE

As the spring of 2004 approached, my health had improved. I had cut down my drug use significantly, and began to ponder moving. I had unfortunately attracted a whole circle of undesirables; meaning I was back in the underworld. I was spending $10,000.00 every week, on cocaine and deadbeat people. What was worse, I wasn't making any money doing it. The people were more violent this time around. I even got into a couple of brawls, which did me no good. I won't put any names on paper. I want these people to stay in my past-and that is the best thing for me. It lessens the chance of me falling back into that world, which is unfortunately the only one I know.

I now have a few goals I feel I must achieve before I die. The first is to publish this book, in order to hopefully help others, instead of hinder. I got a call in March of 2003, from the University of Alberta. I was asked to participate in a public seminar, concerning first year diagnoses. Of particular interest to them was the fact that I had achieved what most people don't – staying alive.

This seminar was schedules for Banff, Alberta. Little did I know, I was to be the keynote speaker. I would address an international audience, including doctors, nurses and medical students, as well as care-givers in the health industry. The conference was called The International Institute For Qualitative Methodology. I. I. Q. M. It one of the biggest conferences in Canada, and I was more than a little nervous. The only place I've ever addressed a listening audience was in a court room. Now, I was to stand at a podium, talking to an international group of health professionals. I was so high, not on drugs, but the adrenalin high! It was great!!

I left my house in the care of a person I trusted, and much to my chagrin, when I got back from the conference, my living room was packed with people, sitting around smoking cocaine. I had been clean for awhile, but the temptation was so overwhelming that I gave in and had a few tokes. The same shit began all over again.

I told everyone to leave, eventually, and I moved home to my mother's. At the conference, I felt better, talking about who I was, and am today. I'm tired of running away, getting lost in the underworld life of sex, drugs and rock and roll. Since May of 2003, I have attended over a dozen seminars. I'm a member of the board of directors of and Aid's Foundation, here in Alberta. It is deeply satisfying to hear how my story has affected others. I've had some of the leading authorities on health issues say they would rather hug me, than shake my hand. That tells me that I'm doing something right for mankind, by giving what I can.

I've taken almost every drug trial concerning the proof needed for AIDS research. At present, I live a very quiet life. I go to my seminars (regarding AIDS and AIDS research) all over the country. I recently attended an event in Halifax, for the C. A. A. N. (Canadian Aboriginal Aids Network). I was nominated to sit on that board as well, but only time will tell.

I guess I'm still walking down the middle of the road - reveling in the safety of one side, tasting the danger of the other. It seems no one ever really picks a side. I choose the middle. Remember: it's not what you do in life, it's how and by what methods you do it. That's what counts. There is always a life not worth taking.

My name is attached to journals from the University Of Alberta and I've written articles for AID'S magazines and I am opening up World Aid's Day in Lethbridge, speaking in front of hundreds of people.

But there is so much more to life than committing crimes and dealing drugs.

CHAPTER TWENTY-ONE

AREN'T YOU DEAD YET

I keep thinking to myself: If I had done all the things the medical world wanted me to do, I would have to give up and die, just to try and live. I know that seems to make no sense. Just think about it: I was fighting two of the world's biggest killers. Without the conditioning my lifestyle gave me, these diseases would certainly have finished me before now.

If I did play along, and did all that was asked of me, undoubtedly I would get sick and die, so I go about life as if nothing is wrong. There is far too much for one person to attempt controlling, let alone live with. My battle with HIV has been going on for twenty years now. To give up my lifestyle seems absurd. Of course, there is the other specter looming over me: Hepatitis-C. I'll say this-this gruesome twosome put one hell of a damper on your social life.

I don't do half the things I used to, which has probably bought me a lot of extra life. Having good people like my friends Nappy, and the old shyster Bill, brings a sense of normality to my once very drug and alcohol riddled reality. It feels good to have two good friends left after the passing of all these years. Knowing this, I value these friendships more than anything.

The year is now 2005. I made it this far by living life to the fullest, by not allowing these viruses to exert too much control. For more than thirty years I've lived life *my* way, with no basic rules established in my formative years. I did not have any parents or any other figure of authority for the longest time. I learned doing it my way was the *only* way, much to the chagrin of those populating the legal and medical worlds.

I've taken as much as twenty pills a day, and then needles. Fuck, I'm tired of being a pin cushion. However, if the research I've been a part of through my involvement in countless drug studies, proves to find any relief at all for the millions of others that suffer as I do, it was all worth it.

I have been speaking on the conference circuit, for the past two years, to thousands of people about the AID'S/HEP C catastrophe. I will soon address another international conference on people living with AIDS and HIV. The International World Conference on Aids with over 15,000 delegates. I'm to be a guest panel speaker in Toronto in August of 2006. It's amazing, but when I'm at these conferences, for some reason, I never feel sick. There, I really *see* the sickness, and it is heartbreaking. I don't care if you are the toughest fucking guy in the world, these meetings will break you down. They are testament of a true global tragedy.

I have been going to the same family doctor for twenty five years, and he does not know how to break the system, so I might be compensated. We will be at odds forever, I fear. He knows every last detail of my life. He agrees if it was not this way, I would be a lot sicker. When you learn about your sickness, and start self-medicating, the "legitimate" medical world does not take it lightly.

Let's face it. This is a trillion dollar deal for drug companies. Some leaders keep their people sick, while different, wealthy nations keep supplies of treatment drugs in abundance. It's absolute insanity. Since contracting HIV, I have been inundated with all kinds of illness. Some potentially fatal and some not. Now, I face the biggest challenge yet" degenerative bone disease. It will immobilize me within five years, I've been told by qualified medical professionals.

In 1990, on my birthday, a doctor told me I had five to eight years left, I had best get my affairs in order. Time has proven him wrong, by a long shot. No matter where I go, people say, you should do this, you should do that, you should take this, you should take that, this will help you. Aren't you dead yet???!! Just fucking wait. This adventure is not even close to being over. I have lots of goals, and I'll achieve them. The only way I know how is to keep fighting.

All my court cases have been resolved. I'm on probation till sometime in 2006 or 2007, I'm not sure. I just show up for my monthly visit with my P.O. The beat goes on. The parole officer I have is quite nice, even though on her bad days she takes it out on her clients. I have had to put her in check more than once. Still, if she were to find out where I've been, I'd be locked up. No one is allowed to leave the province, while on probation or parole. I feel in my case, if the government refuses to compensate me for receiving bad blood, then I'm going to prevent others from getting this virus from any product, person, needle, or sex. So I've been to Halifax, Ottawa, Nunavit, Toronto, Regina, and beyond, educating people of all kinds. Obviously, the law does not look to closely at criminals to ensure they are doing what they are told to do. I will travel again, and to hell with going to jail if they catch me. The work I do will go on. I'm not afraid of going to jail, and I refuse to be intimidated or deterred by that threat or possibility. I go to all kinds of places, and make positive changes. I get a high that is hard to explain, but it is better than drugs.

I have three cats. They take about all the love I have left (after being jilted, dropped and forgotten). It sounds crazy, but my cats give me 100% unconditional love and comfort me when I'm not feeling well. But their health bill is as large as mine.

I am told I must take a needle called pegacus, an interfuron drug for me HEP C. I should have been treated years ago, but never got around to it. I'm told I will be very sick for 48 weeks, will lose all my hair and be confined to the couch. Give me something I can't handle.

I found one thing I have a hard time with, and that is working (or trying to work) in an AIDS Service Organization. There is so much to do, it's overwhelming sometimes and just coming out of being a recluse for years makes it all that much clearer as to why I was there in the first place. Stigma! Discrimination! Mental/physical abuse, emotional stress. Shit, this is a disease in itself. Oops, no pills for this. I now sit as a member of the Board of Directors for one of the largest aboriginal foundations in Alberta called the Kimamow Astokinow Foundation. This role means extensive traveling to some very remote places, just to educate the general public regarding AIDS/HIV. I also sit on the Alberta Community Counsel For HIV/AID, and the Canadian Aboriginal Aids Network as a committee member. I go to all the necessary functions, which is slowly becoming tiresome. There is only so much one can do before burning out. I have done well over 40 public speaking engagements in the last one and a half years and loved every minute of it. When I tell someone I have HIV, and they hear me speak in front of trained professionals, opening their eyes, the out poring of emotion can be quite intense.

This year alone, I have traveled more 18,000 miles, to talk to doctors, nurses, support workers, students, mothers, fathers, children and elders. I feel compelled to open up the lines of communication between all ages, genders, and cultures. In the last ten years I have seen and done enough to fill 10 lifetimes. I have so many extraordinary memories. There is a CFL player named Tony Johnston, who now plays with Ottawa Renegades. At one point he played with the Calgary Stampeders, and I got to know him. He was going through a very hard time with crack cocaine, and I happened to be a drug dealer, and, well, you get the picture.

It all came in to focus when he asked for help. Tony Johnston is one very big boy, and how he got so lost is beyond me. I guess it was the sex, drugs and stature that went to his head. I was making numerous trips to his hotel, where he was cracked up with a bunch of parasitic losers. I got pissed off, even though I was going there every four to five hours with hundreds of dollars worth of crack. I told Tony he should think of getting away from these people, as they would bleed him dry. Already, it was starting to look that way. I talked to a buddy of mine. He and I are connected with the Hell's Angels. I told him about this pro football player caught up with some of our regulars, and he told me to drag him away. And that's just what I did.

I took him to another hotel. The first thing he did was buy more cocaine, cooking it to rock form. He then ordered in some women. After about two weeks of this, Tony said he wanted to quit. I agreed that would be a very smart thing to do: his career was at stake, and he wanted out so bad he would do anything. It just so happened I was dealing with some very powerful people from Colombia, Venezuela, Mexico, U.S.A and Canada. Two of my many contacts from Columbia were adherents of a religion that practiced voodoo, essentially they were voodoo priests. It seemed my sense of adventure had no limits. I thought the cocaine from my friend was so good, there had to be something special going on, and this was it.

One night, over dinner, I told them about Tony, that he wanted to trade something for crack, as he was now having money problems. My voodoo priests wanted what Tony was selling, and as soon as I put them in touch, they found out he was under control. They saw the potential of stardom in this kid, and told me they talked to him about performing a voodoo ceremony to get rid of those who caused him the sickness over crack cocaine. Even though my friends were bringing in kilos of coke, and I was selling it, they did not wish to aid in the downfall of a pro athlete. As it happened, street people had used him, stole his bank card, and eventually robbed him.

The voodoo ceremony was planned, and I did the foot work to set it up. It was one of the most shocking experiences I have had in recent years, though I'm sure it will not be the last. The tricky part of all this was finding a black rooster to sacrifice. It took me three days to find one. There were two other kinds of birds to be offered. The priest was with me when I went to get it. One minute, this rooster was running around his pen; the next, he was under the priest's arm. Even the owner of the farm could not believe this. When he tried to say something, he could not. It was unsettling, to say the least. Without going into much detail it was a very bloody affair. Three birds were placed in different parts of the city, after the ceremony was over, Tony and I washed off the blood. Finally, he said he wanted to go home.

The people who robbed him were dealt a very bad hand in the life game of poker. Now, Tony is doing well for himself, even though it took a couple of years to fully see results. Still it happened, and I will attest to the fact that it was because of a voodoo ceremony.

Recently, I learned I do not have to take the Hep-C treatment that was going to make me so very ill. Miraculously, I beat the virus on my own. The doctors at the University of Calgary's hospital said that I fell into the 10-15% of people world wide who somehow cure themselves naturally. I'm tired of the games we play, some serious, some not. After awhile, they are boring, and when you sit back and watch them being acted out you have to wonder. If you don't, you're playing one of those games.

I do not want to be around people solely for what they need from me. I'm capable of anything, as my abilities are limitless. Most of all, I'm tired of trying to find that special love. It seems like the more I look, the harder it becomes. So I drown myself in HIV/AID work. I don't go to bars anymore. I don't use coke. The more it's around me, the less I want it. I meet all kinds of people. You know the old saying: :Too many drugs, not enough space". So it's like 50 first dates with some people, and others I sometimes wish not to meet again. I'm weak with drugs, so I stay away.

The women I know are so close to drugs, I would never find happiness being with them.

I have a daughter I have not seen for over thirteen years. I would very much one day like to know her. My life is simple. I don't look for anything. I stay home, smoke my pot, and make art. Recently, a problem arose with the art thing. I was charged for trafficking in animals parts. (Some of the jewelry I make is out of deer antler or leg bone). As a native artist, I've created many works now in government hands. Unfortunately, my mother has been charged with the same offence. My mother and I just looked at each other in disbelief when this happened. The irony of it made me laugh so hard I almost pissed my pants. After thirty five years of crime, I finally retire and become an artist, only to be charged with trafficking in animal parts. Fifty-six counts to be exact. Each count carries a $100, 000.00 fine, for a total of 5.6 million dollars. It also includes a possible 2 to 10 year jail sentence. I have sold art that is all over the world and everyday for 3 months out of the year my mother and I display our work for sale in front of 10,000 people, in the heart of Calgary, where the west was won and the aboriginals were told not to make art!!!! I don't think I've ever been bitter. I can tolerate being overlooked for compensation for HIV/HEP-C and not having a chance at a normal life with a woman. I became an artist after studying at one of Canada's foremost art schools, "Alberta College Of Art and Design." Now, it seems I'm being made a criminal. It's anything but fair.

As I look back on my life, I recognize I was very undisciplined until about 10 years ago. I am no longer working with the Hell's Angels. I was starting to feel like I was being controlled by them. As I've said before, once you start it is hard to stop. Stealing, selling drugs and dodging the law only led me to end up in trouble. I am now in demand as a public speaker. It is hard sometimes to keep up with the travel and hectic scheduling, but I know it's the right thing to do.

I realize now I am a highly sensitive person. The simplest things can make me break down crying. It is not self pity; rather, loneliness that causes the emotional floodgates to open. You see, if you're not a part of this world of crime, drugs and sickness, hearing about it doesn't really make an impact. ('That's terrible," someone might say, then change channels). I've changed worlds, and what I see is truly terrible. There is far more accomplished with crime, drugs, and sickness than is possible with a 9-5 job, no recreational drug use, or perfect health. Fuck, is there a happy medium!!!! Don't get me wrong. I'm not advocating a life of crime or drug use. It just seems more is done about that than anything else. (Compared to child abuse, used for sex trade, etc). The fast pace of our world dictates people grow up fast (in my case, too fast). In a way, I found that medium. If you want it, I want you to have it as well.

When in trouble, face it. Do not run, because running is like lying. Again, "once you start it is hard to stop". If you have to judge anyone, judge yourself, before you judge others.

Anything you do to others, shit yes, it comes back to you! At the most inopportune time!! You can turn your life into a shit show. I've seen people die for things they tried to pull on others.

Help someone you don't know, and the reward you receive is priceless. Crime pays, when you do it short term. But it is bad money (conscious less money.) Crime pays in the long run for those who make it their life's work, but it can take your life in return. I will never be happy unless I'm helping some one. (Fuck! Where did that come from?) I have arrived at a good place, after walking a long hard road to get here. I find now if I want something bad enough, I will get it one day. There are still some on going issues I have to work out, but that's what keeps me going.

The charges against my art work are still pending. I am still single, sleepless in Calgary. The days of rolling joints in $100 bills are over, but you know, I'm just as well off broke as I was rich. What's the difference, you ask?

Being broke slows me down, to the snail's pace of the 9-5er. I like it, because things are done when they need to be done, and cost is the only object and a true challenge. Now, I work for what I want, instead of having it delivered. People put value on material things, but I could care less. I would give you the shirt off my back, knowing I will get another. Some people are not so lucky. One thing though - I will not let you into my house. After 40 years of bullshit, When I close my door and lock it at night the adventure stops, till I open my eyes the next day. Today is the first day of the rest of my life. Hell, today is the first day of a new adventure! I was working hard to prove I have a terminal illness due to government negligence. I was hoping to receive compensation, but I fear it will never happen. It is some consolation that the government gave me the right to grow marijuana for medicinal purposes (25 plants at any time, for life). I was also given authorization to have 150 grams on me, at any time. I guess in a small way, I was compensated. I can't help but look back over my life and think, "Damn, will it ever end?!" I'll tell you something: "I'm not dead yet." because "it's not what you do in life, it is how and by what methods you do it". It could be a "Life Not Worth Taking."

"Bye for now! Open your eyes, and let the adventure begin. I do, every day. Stay young at heart, don't hurt others, and live a good life. I'm trying, so can you!!!!"

Comment by Dr. Fred J. Moriarty:

Doug Gauld
May 2006

A family physician has an opportunity to involved in an individuals life by inquiring into their past history, defining their present state of health and anticipating their future. I have known Doug Gauld for over 25 years. He has experienced many challenges to his physical and mental health during this period of time. Despair, frustration, anger, denial, blame could have been his reaction. Instead Doug showed true grit. He took control with courage and vision.

Doug realized he could not make a difference by being a pessimist because no one will follow you. He decided to use his **TIME** and **TALENT** to define a future for others less fortunate. He became a communicator through his art. He worked hard to forge an educational program for youth to avoid ill health.

Doug's **STEWARDSHIP** of his life is an inspirational story for each of us to try and emulate. His leadership is to be admired. It continues to be my privilege to know Doug.

Fred Moriarty

ISBN 141209243-4

9 781412 092432